丛书主编　彭新良

The Mid-Autumn Festival

汉英对照

中秋节

田阡　栾为　编著

汪世蓉　潘洁　等　译

全国百佳图书出版单位

APTIME　时代出版传媒股份有限公司

安徽人民出版社

图书在版编目（CIP）数据

中秋节：汉英对照 / 田阡，栾为编著；汪世蓉，潘洁等译 . -- 合肥 : 安徽人民出版社，2018.8
（多彩中国节丛书 / 彭新良主编）

ISBN 978-7-212-10027-8

Ⅰ . ①中… Ⅱ . ①田… ②栾… ③汪…④潘… Ⅲ . ①节日－风俗习惯－中国－汉、英 Ⅳ . ① K892.1

中国版本图书馆 CIP 数据核字 (2018) 第 005207 号

《多彩中国节》丛书

中秋节：汉英对照
ZHONGQIU JIE

彭新良　丛书主编
田阡 栾为　编著　　汪世蓉 潘洁 等　译

出 版 人：徐　敏　　　　　选题策划：刘　哲　陈　娟
出版统筹：张　旻　袁小燕　　责任编辑：胡小薇
责任印制：董　亮　　　　　装帧设计：陈　爽　宋文岚

出版发行：时代出版传媒股份有限公司 http://www.press-mart.com
　　　　　安徽人民出版社 http://www.ahpeople.com
地　　址：合肥市政务文化新区翡翠路 1118 号出版传媒广场八楼
邮　　编：230071
电　　话：0551-63533258　0551-63533259（传真）
印　　刷：安徽联众印刷有限公司

开本：880mm×1230mm　1/32　印张：8.625　字数：250 千
版次：2018 年 8 月第 1 版　　　2018 年 9 月第 1 次印刷

ISBN　978-7-212-10027-8　　　　　　定价：38.00 元

代 序

我们共同的日子

个人一年一度最重要的日子是生日,大家一年一度最重要的日子是节日。节日是大家共同的日子。

节日是一种纪念日,内涵多种多样。有民族的、国家的、宗教的,比如国庆节、圣诞节等。有某一类人的,如妇女、儿童、劳动者的,这便是妇女节、儿童节、劳动节等。也有与人们的生活生产密切相关的,这类节日历史悠久,很早就形成了一整套人们约定俗成、代代相传的节日习俗,这是一种传统的节日。传统节日也多种多样。中国是一个多民族国家,有 56 个民族,统称中华民族。传统节日有全民族共有的,也有某个民族特有的。比如春节、中秋节、元宵节、端午节、清明节、重阳节等,就为中华民族所共用和共享;世界文化遗产羌年就为羌族独有和独享。各民族这样的节日很多。

传统节日是在漫长的农耕时代形成的。农耕时代生产与生活、人与自然的关系十分密切。人们或为了感恩于大自然的恩赐,或为了庆祝辛勤劳作换来的收获,或为了激发生命的活力,或为了加强人际的亲情,经过长期相互认同,最终约定俗成,渐渐把一年中某一天确定为节日,并创造了十分完整又严格的节俗,如仪式、庆典、规制、禁忌,乃至特定的游艺、装饰与食品,来把节日这天演化成一个独具内涵、迷人的日子。更重要的是,人们在每一个传统的节日里,还把共同的生活理想、人间愿望与审美追求融入节日的内涵与种种仪式中。因此，它是中华民族世间理想与生活愿望极致的表现。可以说，我们的传统——精神文化传统，往往就是依靠这代代相传的一年一度的节日继承下来的。

然而，自从 20 世纪整个人类进入由农耕文明向工业文明的过渡，农耕时代形成的文化传统开始瓦解。尤其是中国，在近百年由封闭走向开放的过程中，节日文化——特别是城市的节日文化受到现代文明与外来文化的冲击。当下人们已经鲜明地感受到传统节日渐行渐远，并为此产生忧虑。传统节日的淡化必然使其中蕴含的传统精神随之涣散。然而，人们并没有坐等传统的消失，主动和积极地与之应对。这充分显示了当代中国人在文化上的自觉。

近 10 年，随着中国民间文化遗产抢救工程的全面展开，国家非物质文化遗产名录申报工作的有力推动，传统节日受到关注，一些重要的传统节日被列入了国家文化遗产名录。继而，2006 年国家将每年 6 月的第二个周六确定为"文化遗产日"，2007 年国务院决定将 3 个中华民族的重要节日——清明节、端午节和中秋节列为法定放假日。这一重大决定，表现了国家对公众的传统文化生活及其传承的重视与尊重，同时也是保护节日文化遗产十分必要的措施。

节日不放假必然直接消解了节日文化，放假则是恢复节日传统的首要条件。但放假不等于远去的节日立即就会回到身边。节日与假日的不同是因为节日有特定的文化内容与文化形式。那么，重温与恢复已经变得陌生的传统节日习俗则是必不可少的了。

千百年来，我们的祖先从生活的愿望出发，为每一个节日都创造出许许多多美丽又动人的习俗。这种愿望是理想主义的，所以节日习俗是理想的；愿望是情感化的，所以节日习俗也是情感化的；愿望是美好的，所以节日习俗是美的。人们用合家团聚的年夜饭迎接新年；把天上的明月化为手中甜甜的月饼，来象征人间的团圆；在严寒刚刚消退、万物复苏的早春，赶到野外去打扫墓地，告慰亡灵，表达心中的缅怀，同时戴花插柳，踏青春游，亲切地拥抱大地山川……这些诗意化的节日习俗，使我们一代代人的心灵获得了美好的安慰与宁静。

对于少数民族来说，他们特有的节日的意义则更加重要。节日还是他们民族集体记忆的载体、共同精神的依托、个性的表现、民族身份之所在。

谁说传统的习俗过时了？如果我们淡忘了这些习俗，就一定要去重温一下传统。重温不是表象地模仿古人的形式，而是用心去体验传统中的精神与情感。

在历史进程中，习俗是在不断变化的，但民族传统的精神实质不应变。这传统就是对美好生活的不懈追求，对大自然的感恩与敬畏，对家庭团圆与世间和谐永恒的企望。

这便是我们节日的主题，也是这套《多彩中国节》丛书编写的根由与目的。

中国56个民族是一个大家庭，各民族的节日文化异彩纷呈，既有春节、元宵节、中秋节这样多民族共庆的节日，也有泼水节、火把节、那达慕等少数民族特有的节日。这套丛书选取了中国最有代表性的10个传统节日，一节一册，图文并茂，汉英对照，旨在为海内外读者通俗、全面地呈现中国绚丽多彩的节庆文化和民俗文化；放在一起则是中华民族传统节日的一部全书，既有知识性、资料性、工具性，又有可读性和趣味性。10本精致的小册子，以翔实的文献和生动的传说，将每个节日的源起、流布与习俗，图文并茂、有滋有味地娓娓道来，从这些节日的传统中，可以看出中国人的精神追求和文化脉络。这样一套丛书不仅是对我国传统节日的一次总结，也是对传统节日文化富于创意的弘扬。

我读了书稿，心生欣喜，因序之。

冯骥才

（全国政协常委、中国文联原执行副主席）

Preface

Our Common Days

The most important day for a person is his or her birthday while the most important days for all are festivals, which are our common days.

Festivals are embedded with rich connotations for remembering. There're ethnic, national, and religious ones, such as National Day and Christmas Day; festivals for a certain group of people, such as Women's Day, Children's Day, and Laborers' Day; and those closely related to people's life and production, which enjoy a long history and feature a complete set of well-established festive traditions passed on from one generation to another. These are so-called traditional festivals, which vary greatly, too.

China, consisting of 56 nationalities, is a multi-ethnic country. People in China are collectively called the Chinese nation. So it's no wonder that some of the traditional festivals are celebrated by all nationalities while others only by certain nationalities, with the representatives of the former ones being the Spring Festival, the Lantern Festival, the Dragon Boat Festival, the Tomb-Sweeping Festival, and the Double Ninth Festival, etc. and that of the latter being the Qiang New Year, a unique festival for Qiang ethnic group. Each of ethnic groups in China has quite a number of their unique traditional festivals.

The traditional festivals have taken shape in the long agrarian times when people were greatly dependent on nature and when life was closely related to production. People gradually saw eye to eye with each other in the long-term practicing sets of rituals, celebrations, taboos as well as games, embellishments, and foods in a strict way and decided to select some days of one year as festivals with a view to expressing their gratitude to nature, celebrating harvesting, stimulating vitality of life, or strengthening bonds between family members and relatives. In this way, festivals have evolved into charming days with unique connotations. More importantly, people have instilled their common aspirations and aesthetic pursuits into festive connotations and rituals. To put it simply, festivals are consummate demonstrations of Chinese people's worldly aspirations and ideals, and Chinese people's spiritual cultures are inherited for generations by them.

Nevertheless, the cultural traditions formed in the agrarian times began to collapse with human beings being in transition from agrarian civilization to industrial one, esp., in China, whose festive cultures were severely hammered by modern civilization and foreign cultures in nearly one hundred years from being closed to opening up to the world. Nowadays, people strongly feel that traditional festivals are drifting away from their lives and are deeply concerned about it owing to the fact that dilution of traditional festivals means the fall of the traditional spirit of Chinese people. Of course, we don't wait and see; instead, we cope with it in a positive way. This fully displays the contemporary Chinese people's cultural consciousness.

In recent ten years, the traditional festivals have been earning more and more attention and some significant ones are included to the list of the National Heritages with the vigorous promotion of China's Folk Heritage Rescue Program and China's intangible cultural heritage application; for example, China set the second Saturday of June as "Cultural Heritage Day" in 2006; the State Council decided to list three significant traditional festivals as legal holidays—the Tomb-Sweeping Festival, the Dragon Boat Festival, and the Mid-Autumn Festival in 2007. These measures show the state gives priority to and pay tribute to the inheritance of public traditional cultures.

Holidays are necessary for spending festivals which will be diluted otherwise; however, holidays don't necessarily bring back traditional festivals. Since festivals, different from holidays, are equipped with special cultural forms and contents, it's essential to recover those traditional festive customs which have become stranger and stranger to contemporary Chinese people.

In the past thousands of years, our ancestors, starting from their aspirations, created many fine and engaging traditions. These aspirations are ideal, emotional, and beautiful, so are the festival traditions. People usher in the New Year by having the meal together on the New Year's Eve, make moon cakes by imitating the moon in the sky, standing for family reunion, or go to sweep the tombs of ancestors or family members for commemorating or comforting in the early spring when the winter just recedes and everything wakes up while taking spring hiking and enjoying spring scenes by the way. These poetic festive customs greatly comfort souls of people for generations.

As for ethnic minority people, their special festivals mean more to them. The festivals carry the collective memory, common spirit, character of their ethnic groups as well as mark their ethnic identities.

Are the traditional festive customs really out-dated? We're compelled to review them if we really forget them. What matters for review is not imitating the forms of the ancient Chinese people's celebrations but experiencing essence and emotions embedded in them with heart and soul.

Traditions have evolved with history's evolving, but the traditional national spirit has never changed. The spirit lies in people's never-ending pursuit for beautiful life, consistent gratitude and awe for nature, constant aspiration for family reunion and world harmony.

This is also the theme of our festivals and the root-cause of compiling the series.

The Chinese nation, featuring its colorful and varieties of festive cultures, boasts the common festivals celebrated by all nationalities, such as the Spring Festival, the Lantern Festival, the Mid-Autumn Festival, and the ethnic festivals, such as the Water Splashing Festival (Thai people), the Torch Festival (Yi people), Naadam (Mongolian nationality). This series, selecting the most typical ten festivals of China, with each festival being in one volume with figures and in both English and Chinese, unfolds the colorful festive and folk cultures in an engaging and all-round way for appealing to foreign readers. If put together, they constitute a complete set of books on Chinese traditional festivals, being instructive and intriguing. The ten brochures elaborate on the origins, distribution, and customs of each festival in an engaging way with figures, tales, and rich literature. Chinese people's spiritual pursuit and cultural veining can be tracked in this series, serving as a summary of Chinese traditional festivals and innovative promotion of them.

I went over the series with delight, and with delight, wrote the preface, too.

Feng Jicai

CPPCC National Committee member

Former Vice-president of the China Federation of Literary and Art Circles

目 录

第四章 中秋节的特色节庆地

多彩中国节

中秋节

Contents

第一章
中秋节的起源与传承

　　"床前明月光，疑是地上霜。举头望明月，低头思故乡。"唐代著名大诗人李白的这首《静夜思》，在中国家喻户晓、妇孺皆知。这首诗歌唱的是中国秋季里的一个重要传统大节——中秋节。中秋节是仲秋之节，在农历八月十五日这一天。与春节、清明、端午并列为中国四大著名传统节日。作为中华民族最重要的传统节日之一，中秋节蕴含的意义和象征最丰富，融合了多种传统文化意义，在时间的累积当中，最终确立为以赏月拜月为中心的重要中华传统节日。

一、
月亮崇拜

　　八月，是进入秋季的第二个月；十五日，是一个月之中的满月时分。八月十五日这一天，月亮最大最圆，月色明亮，月光皎洁，如银盆似的月亮给人以圆润丰满的美感，中秋之夜是一年中最迷人的月夜，因此，中秋节又名"月亮节""月节"。

　　月亮与太阳是原始先民重要的崇拜对象，它们都能够照亮黑暗带来光明，能够让人们战胜恐惧和害怕。而与太阳相比，月亮的光芒不那么刺眼灼热，在人没能控制火的时代，皎洁的月光能够在漆黑的夜里带来温柔的光亮。为此，中国人特别的喜爱月亮，热衷于歌唱月亮。

　　中国人认为太阳和月亮代表着宇宙中的"阳"和"阴"两极：太阳升起，月亮落下，意味着白天的开始；太阳落下，月亮升起，标志着夜晚的来临。太阳和月亮的正常运行是生存世界的保证。人们对月亮的崇拜同世界上其他地方的文化一样古老而悠久，从殷商时代开始已经有文字记录下对月亮所进行的祭祀。中国先民根据月亮的阴晴圆缺来计算时间，制定律历，叫作"阴历"，又名"农历"。这种历法最早可以追溯到夏代，所以又称为"夏历"。经过日常的观测经验检验，先民发现月亮具有神秘的力量，它能够控制影响大地上江河的潮汐：当月亮是最大最圆的满月时，涌起的潮水最大最盛；当月亮是最细最小的弦月时，潮水波动就最小最弱。于是，先民们认为月亮是一种神灵，是水之精魂，随之产生了很多与月亮有关的神话。

神话传说月亮的母亲叫作常羲，她是天神帝俊的妻子，她的姐姐也是帝俊的妻子，叫羲和。羲和生了十个太阳，常羲则生了十二个月亮。十个太阳每天一个轮流在天上值班，十二个月亮则每月一个也轮流在天上值班。"常羲"的名字在神话流传过程中，随着语言的音变，逐渐变为"常仪"，"常仪"又变为"尚仪"，"仪"字又转变为"何"，最后，常羲生十二月的故事逐渐演变为"嫦娥奔月"的神话传说。

嫦娥是羿的妻子，夫妻二人生活在大地上。羿是有名的神射手，以打猎为生。起初每天由一个太阳在空中值班，从东边的扶桑树上出发，乘坐着六条龙驾驭的太阳车由东边行驶到西边，最后在西边的羽渊结束一天的工作。每次值班都是一个太阳，太阳感到很寂寞。有一天，十个太阳相互商量决定一起去值班，这样就不会寂寞了。于是这一天，天上出现了十个太阳。它们把江河晒干了，把大地晒得冒烟了，植物、动物都被晒死了，人们被晒得活不下去了。羿看到人们可怜的生活，就用足力气张弓搭箭，一口气射下了九个太阳，只留下一个继续每天东升西落的留在天上。为了奖励羿拯救人类的功绩，西王母将不死之药赏赐给了羿。吃了不死药，就能够飞升到天界，成为不死之神。羿将不死药带回了家，告诉嫦娥："你好好保管这包药。我们找一个好日子一起吃了它，就能够长生不老，永不分离。"羿依旧每天出去打猎，有时好久也不回来。终于有一天，嫦娥忍不住，偷偷打开了药包，将不死药吃了下去。突然，她的身体变得像羽毛一样轻，不由自主地飘了起来，向天空飞去。天空辽阔无边，嫦娥不知道应该往何处去。明亮的月亮挂在天上，在月亮上也许能看到自己的亲人吧。于是嫦娥就来到了月亮上的广寒宫，并住在了那里。等羿回到家，发现嫦娥不见了，不死药的药包被打开了，赶紧追出门去，可是已经太晚了。而嫦娥，她在登上月亮的一刹那，变成了丑陋的蟾蜍。

这个神话传说还有另一个版本。嫦娥是天神帝喾的女儿，也称姮娥，她美貌非凡，是羿的妻子。羿因为射杀了天帝的九个太阳儿子，获了罪，被天帝贬到了人间，嫦娥也跟着丈夫一起来到了凡间。夫妻俩成了凡人，渐渐有了凡人的生老病死，嫦娥美丽的容颜也在时间的流逝中慢慢变得衰老憔悴。为此，嫦娥常常埋怨羿。羿觉得特别对不起妻子，想找到一个长生不死的方法。他外出云游，奔走了数年，终于得知昆仑山上的西王母有不死的神药。羿凭借着超人的意志和盖世的神力，越过炙热的炎山，渡过羽毛也会沉没的弱水，攀上一万三千一百一十三步二尺六寸高的悬崖峭壁，最后在昆仑山巅的宫殿里见到了西王母。西王母钦佩羿的勇敢，同情羿的遭遇，于是将不死之药赠给了羿。嫦娥等不及和丈夫一起吃，迫切地想要美丽永驻，于是背着丈夫，自己偷偷吃了不死之药，身体逐渐变轻，飞升上天。在空中飘荡的嫦娥心想：到哪去呢？现在背弃了丈夫，天庭的诸神会责备我，嘲笑我，看来只能在月宫中安身了。嫦娥到了月宫，发现这里出奇的冷清，空无一人。在凄清冷漠的广寒宫里，嫦娥在漫漫长夜中咀嚼着孤独和悔恨……

"嫦娥奔月"神话，是中国流传最广影响最大的四大神话之一。随着神话的传播，后代的人们逐渐在其中添加了更为丰富的情节和其他生动的人物故事。

首先有"天狗吞月"的故事。善射的羿有一条忠心耿耿的黑色猎狗，名叫黑耳。当嫦娥偷吃了不死药，抛下丈夫飞上天去的时候，门外的猎狗黑耳看见了，叫唤着扑进屋里，舔食了剩下的灵药，朝天上追去。嫦娥听到黑耳的叫声，又惊又怕，慌慌张张地闯进月宫，躲了起来。黑耳抖动身上的毛，身子越长越大，一下子扑了上去，连嫦娥带月亮一起吞了下去。明亮的夜晚一下子变得漆黑一片。天帝与王母忙派夜游神前去查看。夜游神发现一只大黑狗吞吃了月亮。天兵天将擂动战鼓，手持兵器，前来捉拿黑耳。天帝看到是羿的猎狗，发慈悲饶恕了黑耳，封它为天狗，命令它看守南天门。于是天狗黑耳吐出了肚中的月亮。

"玉兔入月"。很久以前，在山塘乡的云峰岭上，有一对修行千年的兔子，得道成了仙。他们有四个可爱的女儿，一个个生得聪明伶俐。一天，天帝宣召雄兔上天述职。当兔仙来到南天门时，正好看到嫦娥被天兵天将押着从身边走过。兔仙不知道发生了什么事，忙问守门的天兵。天兵告诉他：嫦娥偷偷嫁给了羿，而羿射死了天帝的九个太阳儿子，现在将嫦娥贬到月宫去，把她永远禁闭在那里。兔仙听了，觉得嫦娥无辜受到牵连，很同情她。但自己力量单薄，能帮她什么忙呢？兔仙想到嫦娥一个人关在月宫里寂寞死了，要是能有个人陪伴她多好！兔仙忽然想到自己有四个女儿，于是，顾不得朝见天帝，返身回到了自己家。四个女儿听了嫦娥的遭遇都争着要去。最后决定让最小的女儿兔玉去陪伴嫦娥。兔玉虽然年纪小，但比起姐姐们都稳重，又最会唱歌。于是，兔玉告别了父母和姐姐们，动身到了月宫里陪伴嫦娥。兔仙因为无视天帝的旨意命令，没能按时朝见天帝，又擅自将女儿送进了月宫，获了罪，被关进了天牢。妻儿被罚变作了石头，永远静静地伫立在云峰岭上。

"吴刚伐桂"。吴刚，也叫吴权，是汉朝河西人。吴刚本是个无所事事的游手好闲之徒，每天吃喝玩乐。有一天从外面回来，忽然茶饭不思，呆呆地坐了半天。他的妻子缘妇来叫他吃饭，他却一拍大腿，

005

第一章 中秋节的起源与传承

说要去学仙求道。说干就干，第二天吴刚就收拾了简单的行李，带了不多的钱，离开了家，到处拜师学艺。然而几年过去了，吴刚依然一事无成。他心灰意懒，衣衫破旧，蓬头垢面，经过很多天的跋涉，形容憔悴地回到了家。妻子缘妇在吴刚离开家之后，苦苦守候了很多年，渐渐失去了希望，便改嫁给了一个名叫伯陵的男子，生下了三个孩子，重新组建了美满的家庭。当吴刚推开家门，看到三个孩子在院子里嬉戏玩耍，缘妇在织布机前织布，而一个陌生男子正在劈柴。吴刚异常震惊，并感到羞辱与愤怒。他夺过伯陵手中的斧头，一脚将伯陵踢倒，用斧子砍断了伯陵的脖子。然而，吴刚不知道的是，他所杀死的伯陵是天神炎帝的孙子。获了罪的吴刚，被流放到月宫里。奉命监管吴刚的是神仙辛，他给了吴刚一把斧子，命令他砍伐月桂树，什么时候月桂树被砍倒了，什么时候吴刚的惩罚才能结束。月桂树有五百丈高，每砍一下，树干的伤口会随着斧子的抽出而愈合。吴刚日夜不停地砍树，月桂树不停地愈合。千万年过去了，神奇的月桂树依然生机勃勃，每到月圆之夜，馨香四溢。而吴刚的妻子由于内心负疚，给三个孩子分别取名叫作"鼓""延"和"殳"。他们也飞往月宫，陪伴吴刚。他们中的"殳"开始制作箭靶；而"鼓"和"延"开始制作钟、磬，制定做乐曲的方法。从此，寂寞的广寒宫里时常飘扬出动听的仙乐。

到了唐代，传说唐玄宗李隆基曾梦游月宫，将这些动听的仙乐记录了下来，回到人间，创作了著名的《霓裳羽衣曲》。

广东潮州"拜月娘"

潮州，广东省下辖地级市，位于韩江中下游，是广东省东部沿海的港口城市。潮汕地区在中秋节这天依然保留有隆重的"拜月娘"活动，传统礼仪习俗浓厚。潮州的古城文化具有独特的魅力。

潮人称拜月为拜月娘。月属阴，叫太阴娘，潮人简称她为月娘。在"男不祭月，女不祭灶"的例俗之下，祭月的主角是妇女孩童。村里祠堂灯火通明，吃过晚饭，妇女们便换上新衣，带领孩子们在祠堂安好香案，摆上供品，等候月亮升起。中秋时节，柚、柿、阳桃、石榴、油甘、菠萝、林檎、芋头等果蔬，一齐登场，还有潮汕月饼、黑芝麻糕等奉献给月娘。当夜晚天空中月亮升起的时候，人们在祠堂的庭院中向高挂天空的一轮明月顶礼叩拜。

在潮汕流行有歌谣这样唱道："中秋夜，月娘娘。深深拜，团团圆。好夫婿，结良缘。"待出嫁姑娘拜月的重要心愿是寻求一个好夫婿，点燃长长的龙香，跪在地上对着月亮祈祷。孩童们则将新买的书本和文具摆在供案的最前面，因为听老人说用这些祭拜之后，月娘能保佑学童读书刻苦，成绩优秀。你想要什么就祈祷什么，祈福保平安，心想事成。

拜月后，家人们闲笑庭前，吃潮汕月饼，喝工夫茶，边赏月边谈天论地，享受一份闲情逸致。

二、
神仙信仰

　　与太阳相比，月亮在中国古人看来是"阴柔"的代表，月亮与女性紧密相连。在中国人的神话传说和民间信仰当中，月亮是由女神司职掌管的，司职月亮的女神被称为"月姑"。于是，八月十五这一天又被称为"女儿节"。

　　从原始时期至今，中国人始终相信所生活的世界里具有一种神圣存在与人们同在。随着道教在汉代的兴起，普通有血肉的必死凡人，能够通过炼丹服食养生等一整套可操作的方式获得长生，达到一种仅次于神灵的不朽存在——仙人。关于月亮的神话传说，逐渐在后代又产生演化出很多与月亮有关的神仙故事。这些故事将中秋节的含义从单纯的月亮崇拜发展为更为丰富的神仙祭祀。

　　由于"嫦娥奔月"的神话广泛流传，人们相信月亮上居住着美丽的女神。那么，同作为女性，女神自然就会倾听和满足凡间女子的祈求，于是，人们将月亮神称之为"月姑"或"月婆"。对于中国传统女性来说，最关心的莫过于婚姻子嗣问题，因此，"月姑"或"月婆"主要掌管的是人间女子的婚嫁子嗣。"月神"在职能上成为"媒神"。到了唐代，出现了关于"月老"的传说。"月婆"演化成为一名老年的男性，即"月下老人"。"月老"成为婚姻之神的信仰对象。

　　"月下老人"的故事开始于唐代。相传有一个名叫韦固的孤儿，有一次在城中的客栈住店。一天晚上，韦固晚饭后到店外散步，看见一个老人背靠着桂树，身子下坐着一个布口袋，在月光下翻看一本书。韦固感到很奇怪，就上前询问："请问老人家，您看的是什么书啊？"老人笑着回答："天下人的婚书。"韦固觉得不可思议，从没有听说过有这样的书。接着，韦固又问："您口袋里装的是什么啊？"老人低头看了看袋子，微笑着回答："里面装的是红绳，用来绑住男女双方的脚。两个人被我的红绳一系，哪怕是百年的仇敌之家，哪怕是贫富差距极大，哪怕是相隔天涯海角，都注定会成为夫妻的。此绳一系，婚姻就定了。如果没这红绳，哪怕两人再恩爱，也不能成为夫妻呀。"韦固听了十分惊讶，连忙打听自己的婚事："老人家，您说我的妻子现在在什么地方呢？"老人翻书查看，笑着对他说："你的妻子今年三岁，就是店北头卖菜的瞎眼婆婆的孙女。"韦固听了勃然大怒，心想："我抱负远大，怎么会娶一个卖菜人家的女子，更何况今年才三岁！"韦固心中愤愤不平，返回客店，立刻叫来随行的仆人，命他暗中去杀死那个三岁的小孩。仆人心里害怕，慌乱中刺杀不成，只刺伤了小女孩的眉心。主仆二人连夜逃跑了。十几年之后，韦固成了一名战功显赫的大将军。刺史王泰见他仪表堂堂，就将女儿嫁给了他。妻子容貌美丽，知书达理，就只是眉心总爱粘贴着花钿。一天，韦固好奇地问妻子是怎么回事。妻子回答说："我其实是一个卖菜人家的女儿。家里虽然贫穷但还是幸福和美的。可是不知道为什么，有一天晚上，家里突然闯进一个人要杀死我。幸运的是他没有成功，只是刺中了我的眉心，留下了难看的伤疤。父母将这件事报告了官府。刺史王泰大人负责审理这件案子，可是始终没有弄清楚前因后果，见我可怜，便收养为女儿，对我如同亲生一般。这个疤痕醒目又难看，我就贴上花钿遮挡一下。"韦固这才知道眼前的妻子正是当年他派人行刺的女孩。故事传扬开去，那家客店被人们叫作"订婚店"，牵红绳的"月下老人"逐渐成了"媒人"的代名词。

到了元代，王实甫创作了戏剧《崔莺莺待月西厢记》，剧中塑造了一个活泼可爱的婢女名字叫红娘。红娘在剧中是"牵红绳"的媒人，在她的帮助下，丞相小姐崔莺莺和书生张君瑞结成了一段美满婚姻。随着戏剧作品的广泛演出，"红娘"逐渐被神化成为"月老"的又一个变体，慢慢和"月姑"相融合，成为人们在中秋之夜祈求婚姻子嗣的祭拜对象。

旅游小贴士

杭州月老庙

月老庙，在中国各地都有，不过最有名的是杭州的月下老人祠。在杭州有两个月老祠，一个在白云庵，另一个在黄龙洞。

白云庵在夕照下雪峰塔遗址西侧、原为宋朝名园"翠芳园"。光绪年间，由杭州著名藏书家丁松生重建。园中绿树叠影，山石林立，幽静闲雅，别成风景。虽称为"庵"，却不是尼姑庵，里面都是清修的僧人、道人。白云庵在杭州的西湖旁边，距离雷峰塔也很近，周围著名景点众多。

地址：浙江省杭州市西湖区南山路 15 号

另一月老祠，在杭州栖霞岭北麓，是黄龙洞的主景。祠内正中有月老塑像一尊，手执"婚书"，神色和蔼，似在祈求天下有情人

多彩中国节

中秋节

终成眷属。两旁有两幅壁画：左为明代才子唐伯虎点秋香的三笑姻缘故事，右为唐代状元郭元振牵红线选宰相之女为妻的故事。

　　地址：浙江省杭州市西湖区曙光路 16 号（近黄龙体育中心）

三、
秋报祭祀

　　秋季是收获的季节，粮食、蔬菜、瓜果在这个季节里大部分都成熟了。以农耕经济为主的中国社会，需要汇集全部的家庭生产劳动力来完成食物的收集。中秋这一天是各种瓜果收获之后，亲朋好友团聚的日子，所以又被称为"八月半""团圆节""果子节"。

　　其实，每个月都会有一次满月出现。阴历八月十五日满月的这一天之所以会成为一个重要的节日，是因为它还与历史悠久的"秋报祭祀"密切相关。

　　对于进入农耕社会的中国先民来说，没有什么比春种秋收更重要的事情了。一年的辛苦劳作能不能获得丰厚的回报，需要依赖肥沃的土地和及时的雨水。农业生产的好坏与神灵的赐福降灾密切相关。自然神灵崇拜在中国起源很早，人们很早就懂得，一年的风调雨顺主要依靠的是日月稳定运行，如果获得了丰收就应该以更丰盛的祭品来报答神灵的福佑。因而，早在先秦时期，中国人的生活中就已经确立了春季祭日、秋季祭月的礼仪制度。而土地则是更重要的祭祀对象。

土地神最早被称为"社神"。传说最早的社神名字叫句龙，他是共工氏的儿子，是神农氏的第十一代世孙。颛顼打败了共工氏，任命句龙为官，管理土地，负责平整土地疏导河流。到了帝尧统治时期，句龙被封为"后土"，即土地之神，人们修建祠堂纪念他。到了周代，人们认为周族的始祖后稷出生很神异，对于庄稼的种植有很大的贡献，于是将后稷奉为社神，又称为"田祖"。土地神和始祖神开始合二为一。祭祀土地，也包括祭祀祖先。

从西周开始，人们在八月祭祀土地神。《诗经》《周礼》等文献记载，人们在秋高气爽的仲秋之季，敲击着土鼓，唱着歌跳着舞，欢送夏季炎热的暑气，迎接即将到来的冬日寒气，感谢土地之神的赐予。人们用刚刚收获的蔬果来供奉神灵，祈祷明年还能得到神灵

○土地神

的赐福保佑，希望还能继续获得丰收。

在汉代祭祀土地神已经有了等级之分，皇帝祭祀的是总司土地的最高神灵，各地祭祀本地的土地神。随着道教的兴起，很多对百姓生活做出贡献的人，都被尊奉为掌管一方土地之神。在中国的故事传说中，担任土地神的人数最多。最早被称为土地神的是汉代的蒋子文。

传说蒋子文是汉代末年秣陵地方的卫尉，负责当地的治安。一次，蒋子文追逐一个贼人，一直追到钟山脚下。贼人拒捕，打伤了蒋子文的头，没过多久蒋子文就死掉了。过了几年以后，到了三国孙权统治时期，有一个从前和蒋子文共事的官员在路上竟然又一次遇见了他。只见蒋子文骑着白马，拿着白羽，仆从跟随着他，就跟生前一样。这个人非常害怕，慌忙逃走。蒋子文在后面追上去说："我已经做了这个地方的土地神，一定会保护当地的百姓。你回去告诉人们，应该为我建一个祠堂。否则的话，就会有灾祸了。"于是蒋子文被人们称为中都侯，人们为他修建了祠堂，从此钟山又被叫作蒋山。

中国人对于土地神的信仰十分普遍，人们认为"有土即有财"，所以土地神也就是财神、福神。北方将土地神称为"土地爷"，南方叫"土地公公"，在福建、台湾一带，人们则将土地神称为"福德正神"。

传说福德正神，本名叫做张福德。从小就非常聪明而且十分孝顺。36岁时，他被任命为朝廷的总税官。张福德为官清廉，做了许多对百姓有益的好事。102岁的时候，张福德去世了。死后三天，张福德的容貌还是像有生命一样，没有任何改变。葬礼过后没多久，有一户贫穷的人家用四块大石头搭建了一个石屋奉祀张福德。没想到，这家人很快就变得有钱了。人们相信这是张福德的保佑，于是大家出钱为张福德建立了祠庙来供奉他，并尊称他为"福德正神"。特别是做生意的商人至今仍常常祭祀他。

作为地方保护神，土地神是中国民间供奉最普遍的神灵。为土地神建立的土地庙已几乎遍布每个城市村庄。在南宋以前，土地庙里只供奉着土地公公；南宋之后，土地庙中增加了土地婆婆。自明代开始，对土地神的崇拜越来越兴盛，土地庙又被称为城隍庙。春、秋两季是祭祀土地神的重要时刻，特别是秋季，获得丰收的人们会在土地庙前举行盛大的聚会，唱歌跳舞娱神。于是，农历八月十五日这一天，也是人们举家团圆，共同祭祀土地神、纪念家庭先祖们的重要日子。

盂县藏山

坐落在太行山西麓的藏山，是中国著名的祭祀文化汇聚地，被誉为晋东第一名山。藏山祠规模宏大，走进藏山茫茫山间，在每个景点都发现一座小型的土地庙，这里的土地庙又称福德庙、伯公庙，十分有特色。

藏山古名盂山，东临石家庄，西接太原市，南望娘子关，北倚五台山和西柏坡，造化神奇，独钟灵秀。相传，春秋时晋国大夫赵朔被晋侯杀害，赵朔死前将遗腹孤儿托付给门客程婴，程婴舍去己子，携赵朔的孤儿赵武潜入盂山藏匿 15 年之久，后人就把盂山改名为藏山，并立祠祭祀，距今已有 2600 多年的历史。境内峰峦叠嶂，古刹栉比。山间神祠祀赵家遗孤之位，中华忠义苑弘扬忠孝爱国之情，志士仁人视为圣洁忠义之地，千百年来留名篇佳作无数。山以史传，史以文传，中华儒家文化汇于此山。藏山中祠庙规模宏大，由文子祠、寝宫、藏孤洞、梳洗楼、八义祠、报恩祠、启忠祠等组成，是一个气势壮观的建筑群体，遍布其间的土地庙也非常有特色。

地址：山西省阳泉市盂县藏山

经过漫长的历史时间累积，秋季农历八月满月的这一天，人们在明亮的月光照耀下，负载着原始月亮崇拜的记忆，祭祀月神，全家团聚向神灵祖先献上丰盛的果蔬贡品，祈求婚姻和美，家庭和睦，子嗣繁盛。虽然在中国传统节日中，中秋节是确立时间最晚的一个，直到宋代才被政府确立为法定的节日，但是中秋节是所有中国节日中蕴含意义最丰富，最受中国人重视和欢迎的一个节日，其重要程度仅次于春节。

Chapter One
The Origin and Inheritance of the Mid-Autumn Festival

"A silver moon hangs by the balustrade, I fancy moonlight as frost on the ground. Gazing up of the bright moon I'm looking, lowering my head of my native land I'm missing." The Homesick at a Still Night written by Li Bai (the great poet in the Tang Dynasty) is a household poem in China. This poem describes an important Chinese traditional festival in autumn —the Mid-Autumn Festival which is listed as one of the four famous traditional festivals as well as the Spring Festival, the Tomb-Sweeping day, and the Dragon-Boat festival. The Mid-Autumn Festival is on August 15th of the lunar calendar, in the second month of autumn. As one of the most important traditional festivals of the Chinese nation, the Mid-Autumn Festival with rich symbolic significance is combined with a variety of traditional cultural significance. And as time goes by, it is finally established as an important Chinese traditional festival represented by the activities of moon-viewing and moon-worshiping.

1. Moon Worship

The 8th month is the 2nd month in autumn, while the full moon comes on the 15th day of every month. The moon is at its biggest and roundest, shining as brightly and clearly as a silver plate on the 15th day of the 8th lunar month. The beautiful full moon makes the night of Mid-Autumn Festival become the most charming one in a year. Therefore, the festival is also called the Moon Festival.

Chinese people especially love the moon, and they are keen to sing for it. The moon and the sun are important objects of worship for primitive people, both of which can bring lights to banish the darkness, helping people overcome fear and terror. Compared with the sunlight, the bright and clear moonlight is less dazzling and scorching. It brings gentle lights on the pitch-dark nights in the era without fire.

The sun and the moon, named "yang" and "yin" in Chinese, are regarded as two poles and the normal movement of them is a guarantee of living in the world. The rising of the sun and the setting of the moon mean the beginning of a day, while the converse marks the coming of a night. The history of moon-worshiping is as ancient as that of cultures in other regions around the world, because the fetes of the moon have been recorded since Yin and Shang periods. The calendar is made by observing phases of the moon in ancient time, which is also called lunar calendar or Xia calendar for it dates back to the Xia Dynasty. They found that the moon had the mystical power to control and influence the tide of rivers on the ground due to the daily empirical test. When the moon is at its biggest and roundest, the rising tide will be the largest and the most forceful, while when the moon is at its smallest and thinnest, the tide will be the lowest and weakest. Therefore, early Chinese people thought that the moon came with divinity and the spirit of water.

There is a myth saying that Chang Xi, the moon's mother and Xi He, Chang Xi's sister are the deity Emperor Jun's wives. Xi He gave birth to ten suns who needed to be on duty in the sky every day in turn and Chang Xi bore twelve moons who take turns monthly to be on duty in the sky. "Chang Xi", and with the phonetic change in the language, gradually turned into "Chang Yi", and then "Shang Yi", "Shang He" during the spread of this legend. Lastly, the story about the twelve moons has evolved into a legend of "Chang'e Flying to the Moon".

The famous archer Yi hunting for a livelihood lived in the human world with his beautiful wife Chang'e. At first, a sun was on duty in the sky every day starting from the east of the hibiscus tree (Solar Holy Tree in Chinese myths), ending a day's work in Yu yuan (Chinese name of a pool) and rode the sun carriage pulled by six dragons from the east side to the west side of the sun. Every time there was only one sun on duty so that the sun felt very lonely. One day, all ten suns decided to go on duty together in case of loneliness. Ten suns appeared in the sky in the same day, scorching the earth, drying the river, killing plants, animals and human beings. Yi was sympathetic with people's torture and then he decided to save them. He bowed his bow with enough strength and shot down nine of the ten suns one by one, leaving a sun in the sky rising from the east and setting in the west every day. In order to reward Yi's merits of saving mankind, the Heavenly Queen Mother of the west gave Yi the elixir of immortality that was said to be very powerful and people who took it can fly to the heaven and became an immortal immediately. He brought the drug home and told

Chang'e, "You take good care of this drug package. We'll find a good day to eat it together and then we can live forever and never be separated." He went hunting every day, and sometimes he was out for a long time. Finally one day, Chang'e couldn't help herself opening the drug package and then swallowed the elixir slinkingly. As soon as she took it, her body became as light as the feather and she flew from her house toward the heaven. The sky was boundless, and Chang'e didn't know where to go. But when she saw the bright moon hanging in the sky, she thought she might be able to see her relatives in the moon. Therefore she came to the Moon Palace (the mythical palace in the moon) and lived there. When Yi returned home, he found that the drug package was opened and Chang'e was gone. He chased out of the door immediately, but it was too late. When Chang'e landed on the moon, she turned into an ugly toad at that moment.

There's another version of this legend. Since Chang'e was the daughter of the god Emperor Ku, she was also named Ku E and known as Yi's beautiful wife. Yi was demoted to secular world companied by Chang'e for he was convicted of arrowing down nine sons (suns) of the Emperor of heaven and the couple became mortals with illness and death, and Chang'e became older over time. Therefore, Chang'e complained about Yi who felt particularly sorry for his wife, and wanted to find a way of immortality. So he traveled far and wide for several years, and finally learned that the Heavenly Queen Mother of the West on Kunlun Mountains had the medicine for immortal life. Yi crossed the hot Yan Mountain and Ruoshui River, and climbed about 13113 *cun* (1/3 decimetre) to visit the Heavenly Queen Mother of the West in the palace on Kunlun Mountains With strong will and extraordinary power. The Heavenly

Queen Mother of the West admired the courage of Yi, and felt sympathy for Yi, so she gave the medicine to Yi. One day, when Houyi was out, Chang'e swallowed the medicine secretly hoping that she would become immortal and beautiful forever. The result was quite unexpected: she felt herself becoming lighter and lighter and started to fly to the heaven, drifting and floating in the air, and then she thought:" Where to go? I betrayed my husband, so the gods in the heaven will blame me and laugh at me. It seems I can only stay in the Moon Palace." When she arrived at the Moon Palace, she found it quite chilly there and felt lonely and regret.

The legend of "Chang'e (the goddess of the moon) Flying to the Moon" is one of the Four Great Chinese myths, which are most widespread and affected. With the spread of the myth, generations of people gradually added more abundant plots and vivid character stories to it.

First, there is a story of the "heavenly dog swallowing the moon". Yi, a skilled archer having a loyal black hound, named Black Ear. One day, Black Ear shouted into the house after finding Chang'e (Yi's wife) stole the elixir, leaving her husband behind to fly to the heaven and he wanted to stop her by licking the residues of the elixir, chasing after her to the heaven. Chang'e broke into the moon palace in a panic and hid after hearing the barking. Black Ear shook his hair and darted up to swallow her and the moon with his growing body. The bright night suddenly became dark. The king and the queen of the heaven quickly sent the night owl(the legendary god on patrol at night) to check on it. The night owl found a big black dog had devoured the moon. The divine troops descending from heaven armed with weapons rolled drums and came to arrest Black Ear. However, the king released him for mercy's sake after knowing Black Ear was owned by Yi, and sealed him as "heavenly dog", ordering him to guard the South Gate of the Heaven. So Black Ear spit the moon out.

Long time ago, a pair of rabbits, living at Yunfeng Ling in Shantang country became immortal after thousands of years of discipline, and they had four lovely daughters who were all skin white and clever. One day, the father rabbit was announced to report to the Emperor of Heaven on his work and he saw celestial soldiers and generals sending Chang'e under guard when he arrived at the Heavenly Southern Gate. The father rabbit asked a soldier as he didn't know what had happened with Chang'e. The soldier told him that she secretly got married to Yi who killed nine sons (nine suns) of God by bow and arrow, so she should be banished to the Moon Palace where she was confined permanently. The rabbit wanted to help Chang'e for he believed she was innocent. However, he worried that he was too weak to offer a help. Suddenly it occurred to the rabbit that it would be much better if someone accompanied Chang'e since she must be very lonely in the Moon Palace. Then he hurriedly came back home and didn't visit the God. Each of his daughters scrambled to live with Chang'e after they knew what she had suffered. One of them, Tu Yu, the youngest was chosen in the end as she was more prudent than her sister and sang the best. So Tu Yu left her parents and sisters for the Moon to stay with Chang'e. This is a legend of "Yu Tu entering the Moon". Unfortunately, the father rabbit was put into prison as he didn't visit the God on time, ignoring the God's command, and sent his daughter into the Moon. As for his wife and daughters, they were punished with becoming stones silently standing on the top of Yun Feng Ling forever.

The legend of "Wu Gang Chopping the Cassia Tree". Wu

Gang (Woodcutter), also named as Wu Quan, was an idle loafer who lived in Hexi in Han Dynasty. One day, he came back from outside and sat for a long time, having no appitite for food or drink. His wife, Yuan, told him to eat, but he said he wanted to cultivate himself to become an immortal, slapping the thigh. Wu Gang left home with a simple baggage and a small amount of money the next day, and learned magic arts from masters everywhere. However, Wu Gang achieved nothing after a few years and returned home frustrated with disheveled hair and a dirty face in rags after a long and rough journey. His wife who waited for him for many years gradually lost hope and married another man named Bo Ling, and then gave birth to three children, living a happy life. Wu Gang saw three children playing in the yard, his wife weaving in front of the loom, and a strange man chopping up sticks when he opened the door. Wu Gang was shocked, and felt humiliated and angry, so he took the ax in the hands of Bo Ling, and kicked him down, cutting off his neck with the ax. Wu Gang was convicted and banished to the Moon Palace, because he didn't know that Bo Ling was the grandson of the God of Yan. The immortal Xin who supervised Wu Gang gave him an ax, and ordered him to cut down a huge cassia tree of five hundred zhang (a unit of length, 10/3 meters) before he could return to the earth. Though Wu Gang chopped day and night, the magical tree restored itself ceaselessly, and thus he couldn't stop chopping. The magical tree was still vibrant for eons and it was fragrant on every full moon night. His wife named three children Gu (The drum), Yan and Shu (An ancient weapon made of bamboo) because of her guilt. They also flew to the palace of the moon, accompanying Wu Gang. The "Shu" started to make arrow targets, "Gu" and "Yan" started to make bells, chime stones to develop ways of making music. Since then, the fair-sounding music could be heard from the palace of the moon.

It was said that Li Longji, the Emperor Xuanzong of Tang, had roamed the palace of the moon, and recorded these beautiful music in the Tang Dynasty. He created *the Melody of White Feathers Garment* when he returned to the world.

Extension of Knowledge

Worshiping the Moon in Chaozhou, Guangdong Province

Chaozhou, the eastern coastal port city and a prefecture-level city in Guangdong Province, is located in the middle and lower reaches of Hanjiang River, showing its unique charm in the ancient city culture. People in Chaoshan area of Guangdong Province still retain the big event of worshiping the moon, which is the traditional ritual on the Mid-Autumn Festival.

Worshiping the moon is called worshiping Moon Mother for the moon belongs to Yin (the feminine or negative principle in Chinese philosophy). Tai Yin Mother is called Moon Mother for short among people in Chaoshan area. Women and children offer sacrifices to the Moon Mother under the custom "Men don't offer sacrifices to the moon, while women don't offer sacrifices to the stove." The village ancestral hall is brightly lit after dinner. Women wear their new clothes and lead children to set incense burner table on which offerings are placed to the moon including grapefruit, persimmon, carambola, pomegranate, Indian gooseberry, pineapple, crabapple, taro and other fruits and vegetables as well as Chaoshan moon cakes, black sesame cakes, waiting for the moon to rise in the Mid-Autumn Festival. People bow in salute in the yard of the ancestral hall to worship the moon when the moon appears to rise in the sky in the night.

A popular song in Chaoshan sings "The Mid-Autumn night, the

Moon Mother. Deeply worship, happy reunion. Good husband, good marriage." The unmarried girls will light long ambergris and kneel on the ground praying to the moon for meeting a good husband. And children will place new books and stationery in forefront of the incense burner ta—ble, because they hear from the elderly that the moon can bless them get excellent grades after worshiping the moon with these offerings. You can pray for whatever you want, such as safety.

The family will talk about anything with Chaoshan moon cakes and tea in the yard, appreciating the moon and enjoying the leisure time after worshiping the moon.

2. Immortal Beliefs

The moon, compared with the sun, represents feminine beauty in ancient China, and is closely connected to women. It is ruled by the goddess called "Yue Gu" in Chinese myths and folk beliefs. All of these mark the 15th day of the 8th lunar month as "Girl's Day".

Chinese people have always believed that there was a deity in the human world we live, since the original period. With the rise of the Taoist religion in the Han Dynasty, the mortal man of flesh and blood can get immortality, becoming the celestial being second only to the deity, through a set of way which is able to handle, like making pills of immortality, keeping nourishing life by the diet. The myths of the moon gradually evolved into many fairy tales by posterity, in which the meaning of the Mid-Autumn Festival has been changed into rich immortal sacrifices from the simple Moon-worshipping.

The legend of "Chang'e flying to the moon" is so popular that people believe that the moon is inhabited by the beautiful goddess who will naturally listen to and satisfy the desires of mortal woman as a female, for which people call it "Yue Gu" or "Yue Po". Traditional Chinese women concern the marriage and offspring issues the most that are in the charge of "Yue Gu" or "Yue Po", for the "Goddess of the Moon" becomes the "Goddess of Matchmaking" on the function. "Yue Laou", replacing the role of "Yue Po" later, being the God of marriage, initially appeared in the Tang Dynasty.

It is said that the story of "The old Man under the Moon" can date back to the Tang Dynasty. An orphan named Wei Gu once put up at an inn. When he took a walk after the dinner outside the inn at the night, he saw an old man leaning against a cassia tree and paging through a book, with a cloth bag under his body. Feeling strange, Wei Gu stepped forward and asked "Excuse me, could you tell me what book you are reading?" the old man answered, "The book of marriage for people all over the world." Not having heard such book, Gu Wei asked again with surprise, "What is it in your bag?" The old man looked down at the bag and smiled, "There are red cords which are used to bind the feet of couples. After that, no matter how strong the hostility is, how great the gap between the rich and the poor is, and how far it is, they are bound to be together as a couple. After red cords are fastened, the marital relationship is established. Even they love each other deeply without the red cord, they will not have the husband-and-wife relations." Wei Gu inquired about his marriage promptly, after hearing what the old man said in amazement, "Could you tell me who my wife is?" Looking through the book, the old man smiled, "Your wife, the granddaughter of the blind old lady who sells vegetables on the north side of the street. She is 3 years old this year." Wei Gu exploded with rage after hearing that and thought, "How can I, with big ambitions, marry a woman whose family makes the living by selling vegetables. Moreover, she is only 3 years old this year! " Wei Gu went back to the inn resentfully, calling his servant, ordering him to kill the 3-year-old girl. But the servant bungled the task with panic, hurting the girl's area between the eyebrows. After that, the master and the servant fled overnight. After a dozen years, the prefectural governor realized the imposing appearance of Wei Gu who was a remarkable general due to the military exploits, married his daughter to Wei Gu. The wife was pretty, well-educated and sensible as well, but there was always a Hua Dian stick (a kind of make up in ancient) between the eyebrows. One day, Wei Gu could not help asking his wife why she did so. His wife answered, "Actually, I am a daughter of a family whose members earn their living by selling vegetables. Poor as we were, we felt happy and nice. I did not know yet why someone breaking into my house wanted to kill me until one night. Fortunately, he failed. But he hurt the area between my eyebrows, leaving an ugly scar there. Wang Tai, the prefectural governor, took charge of this case after my parents reported the event to the government. Not having known the cause and effect of it, he took pity on me and then he adopted me as if I were their own child. I use the Hua Dian (a kind of ornament of head or face for ancient women) to cover the striking and ugly scar." Wei Gu did not know that the wife in front of him was the girl who was stabbed by the servant until that time. With the spreading of the story, the inn became "the inn of engagement", while "Old Man under Moon" evolved into the synonym for "matchmaker".

Wang Shifu created the drama called *Cui Yingying Waiting the Moon at the West Chamber* to the time of Yuan, in which the image of a cheerful and lively maidservant named Hong Niang was shaped. Hong Niang in the drama was a matchmaker who had a duty to "fasten the red cord". Cui Yingying, the daughter of the prime minister, married the scholar, Zhang Junrui happily with Hong Niang's help. With the wide performance of the drama, "Hong Niang" has been deified as another variant of "Yue Laou" little by little, and became the object of the worship for marriage and offspring issues at the Mid-Autumn night, gradually blending with "Yue Gu".

Tips for Tourism

Matchmaker's Temples in Hangzhou

The Matchmaker's Temples can be found everywhere in China, while two of the most famous temples are in Hangzhou. One is in the Baiyun Temple, and the other is in the Yellow Dragon Cave.

Standing at the west of the Xuefeng Tower on the foot of the Xi Zhao Mountain, the Baiyun Temple is a celebrated garden called "Cuifang Garden" in the Song Dynasty, which is rebuilt by Ding Songsheng, the well-known bibliophile in Hangzhou under the reign of Guang Xu in the Qing Dynasty. The garden is quiet and elegant with a lot of towering mountains and green trees, being a unique landscape. Although it is called the "temple", it does not mean the nunnery. Monks and Taoists cultivate themselves according to the religious doctrine of abstinence there. The Baiyun Temple, surrounded by many scenic spots, is beside the West Lake in Hangzhou near the Leifeng Pagoda.

Address: No.15 Nanshan Road, Xihu District, Hangzhou, Zhejiang Province

The other old temple, located at the north of Qixia Mountain, is the main feature of the Yellow Dragon Cave. A statue of Yue Laou stands in the middle of the temple, with the papers of marriage in hand. He seems to be praying that the couples can finally get together, appearing amiable. There are 2 frescoes on the wall, the left one of which shows the story of

Flirting Scholar in the Ming Dynasty, while the right one expresses the story of the Number One Scholar Guo Yuanzhen marrying the daughter of the prime minister through the red cord in the Tang Dynasty.

Address: No.16 Shuguang Road, Xihu District, Hangzhou, Zhejiang Province (Near the Yellow Dragon Sports Center)

3. Thanking Offerings Ritual

Autumn is the harvest season when most of the fruits, vegetables and food crops are mature, which requires the whole family members in the Chinese society dominated by agricultural economy to complete the food gathering. The Mid-Autumn Festival is the day when a variety of melons and fruits are harvested and friends and families are reunited, which is also known as "the 15th day of August", "Reunion Festival" and "Fruit Festival."

In fact, there will be a full moon every month while the day of the full moon on the 15th day of the 8th lunar month will be an important festival because it is also closely related to the long history of "Thanking Offerings Ritual".

As early as the pre-Qin period, the Chinese people had established the rites of offering sacrifices to the sun in spring and the moon in autumn, while the land is more important to worship. Nothing is more important than the spring sowing and autumn-harvesting for the Chinese ancestors in the agricultural society. Whether they can get rich returns or not through arduous work counts on fertile land and suitable growing climate for the crops. People believe the quality of agricultural production is closely related to the blessing or the calamity from the gods. The worship of natural gods originated in China early. People have already understood that a year of favorable weather mainly depends on the sun and the moon's stable operation. If they had a good harvest, they should repay the gods with more abundant sacrificial offerings.

From the earliest times the Earth God was called "the god of She". People recorded the oldest name of She is Ju Long, who was the son of Gong Gong clan and the 11th-generation descendant of Shen Nong clan. Zhuanxu defeated Gong Gong clan, and then he appointed Ju long as the official to manage the land and take charge of leveling the land to divert the river. In the reign of Yao, Ju long was conferred the title of "Houtu"—— the god of land, for which people built an ancestral temple to commemorate him. In the Zhou Dynasty, it was believed that the ancestor Houji of the Zhou clan was born miraculously and dedicated to the cultivation of crops. So Houji was treated as the god of She (the god of land), and also known as "Tian Zu, the original land." Therefore, the god of the land and the god of ancestor began to integrate into one. Thus, offering sacrifices to the land god also comes with the worship of ancestors.

From the Western Zhou Dynasty, people worship the land god in August. Beating the drums, singing and dancing, people send the hot summer off and welcome the upcoming cold winter to thank the Land God for the good harvests in the crisp midautumn season, according to records in *The Book of Songs*, *Zhou Li (The Rites)* and other literatures. People serve the gods with harvested fruits and vegetables, praying for another blessing from the gods the next year, and hoping good harvests in succession.

Hierarchies had already appeared for offering sacrifices to the Earth God in the Han Dynasty. The emperor was to worship the Supreme God of the land, while others was to worship the local Earth God. Many people who made contributions to people's lives were respected as the gods in charge of the land with the rise of Taoism. There is the largest number of land gods in Chinese stories and legends. The earliest known as the land of God was Jiang Ziwen in the Han Dynasty.

It is said that Jiang Ziwen was the chamberlain in charge of the local public security in Shu Ling at the end of the Eastern Han Dynasty (25—220).He chased a thief to the foot of Zhong Mountain once, while the thief resisted being arrested and struck him on the head. It was not long before Jiang Ziwen died. After a few years, under the reign of Sun Quan in the Three Kingdoms period, an official worked with Jiang Ziwen before, actually met him again on the way and saw him riding a white horse, holding a white feather with the servants following him, just like before. The official ran away in a hurry with fear. Jiang Ziwen chased after him and said: "I am the Land God in this place to protect the local people. When you go back, you can tell people they should build an ancestral hall for me; otherwise, there will be a disaster." So people regarded Jiang Ziwen as the Zhong Du Hou, and built an ancestral temple for him. From then on, Zhong Mountain was also known as Jiang Mountain.

It's very common for Chinese people to believe in the Earth God. They think that "Where there is the land, there is money."for the land of god is also the God of Wealth or the God of Good Fortune. The northerners in China call the Land God "Tu Di Ye"while the southerners call him"Tu Di Gong Gong"(the God of Earth). People call the land of god "Fu De Zheng Shen" in Fujian and Tai wan areas.

It's said that,"Fu De Zheng Shen"(commonly known as the Earth God) whose real name was Zhang Fude, was very smart and filial when he was very young. He was appointed as the general tax official of the court at the age of 36 and died at the age of 102. He was an honest and incorruptible official who had done a lot of benefits to common people. Three days after his death, Zhang Fude's appearance was the same as before, as if he was alive. A poor family built a stone house with four large stones to worship Zhang Fude shortly after the funeral. Unexpectedly, the family soon became very rich. It was believed that this was the blessing of Zhang Fude, so people spent money on establishing an ancestral temple to worship him, and respectfully called him "Fu De Zheng Shen". Especially, businessmen often offered sacrifices to him.

As the local patron saint, the Land God is the most common god for Chinese people to worship. The Earth Temple (The tiny temple housing the village god) can be found all over the country. The land temple also known as the town god's temple only worshiped the "Tu Di Gong Gong" (the God of land) before the Southern Song Dynasty; since then, the temple also has the "Tu Di Po Po" (the Goddess of the land). The worship to the Land God has become more and more popular since the Ming Dynasty. It is important to sacrifice the Land God in the spring and the autumn. Especially in autumn, people who get a good harvest will hold a big party in front of the temple, singing, dancing and entertaining the god. Therefore, it is also an important day for reunion to worship the Land God and commemorate the family ancestors on the 15th day of the 8th lunar month.

Tips for Tourism

The Cang Mountain of Yu County

Located in the west of the Taihang Mountains, the Cang Mountain is a famous sacrificial cultural gathering place in China, known as the first mountain in Jindong. The Cang Mountain's temple is so large that small land temple can be found in every attraction when someone enters into the mountain.And the land of the temple is very distinctive, also known as Fude Temple or Bo Gong Temple.

Cang Mountain, called Yu Mountain in ancient times, Shijiazhuang to the east, Taiyuan City to the west, Niangziguan to the south, and Wutai Mountain and Xibaipo to the North, is the magic of the nature with lovely scenery. According to legend, the spring and autumn when the doctor Zhao Shuo was killed by Jin Hou. Zhao Shuo left the child to theretainer named Cheng Ying before his death. Cheng Ying hid with Zhao Wu(the child) in Yushan for 15 years, so the descendants called it Cang Mountain later. Li Temple worship can date back to more than 2,600 years. Mountains overlap and ancient temples stand. The orphan is sacrificed; the patriotism is promoted, and Cang Mountain is regarded as the land of holy loyalty. For thousands of years, there have been numerous works. Mountain depends on its history and history relies on its literature. The Chinese Confucian culture is based on this mountain. Temples in Cang Mountain are magnificent, composed of Wenzi Temple,Bedroom, Canggu Cavity, Suxi Tower, Bayi Temple, Baoen Temple, Qizhong Temple and so on, which a splendid architectural group. Temples thereare also very unique.

Add: Cang Mountain, Yuxian, Yangquan, Shanxi Province

People offer sacrifices to the moon under the bright moonlight as a traditional custom with the memory of primitive moon worship on the 15th day of the lunar calendar. The whole family offer abundant fruit, vegetables and tribute to nature spirits and ancestors, praying for a beautiful marriage, a harmonious family, and a prosperous offspring. The Mid-Autumn Festival was the last one to be established in China among the traditional festivals, which was not until the Song Dynasty that the government marked it as a legal holiday. However, the Mid-Autumn Festival is the most meaningful and popular Chinese festival whose importance is only less than that of the spring festival.

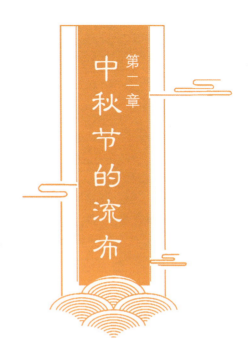

第二章

中秋节的流布

　　唐代著名大诗人白居易在诗作《八月十五日夜湓亭望月》中写道："昔年八月十五夜,曲江池畔杏园边。今年八月十五夜,湓浦沙头水馆前。西北望乡何处是,东南见月几回圆。昨夜一吹无人会,今夜清光似往年。"从西北到东南,从长安到湓浦,不同地区的人们都在明亮的月光下团聚欢度,不仅令诗人分外想念家乡亲人。中秋节是中国秋季的第一大盛会,历史悠久传统绵长,在中国的大江南北,包括我国台湾、香港、澳门等地,甚至华人聚集的东亚和东南亚都是非常重要的一个节日。

一、
在中国大陆的流布

中国古人早在夏代就创立了一种以月亮为观测对象的历法制度，叫作"阴历"，又称为"农历"，后人又称为"夏历"。在阴历中七月被定为"孟秋"，八月为"仲秋"，九月为"季秋"，三个月合起来称为"三秋"。而八月十五日在三秋的正中间，所以称为"中秋日"。

崇拜、祭祀月亮的风俗习惯早在原始先民时期就已经存在了，而"中秋节"一词，最早出现在文献中要追溯到唐代初期的贞观年间，即公元627年至649年。《渊鉴类函·卷二十》引《唐太宗记》中记载："八月十五日为中秋节，三公以下献镜及承露囊。"可见贞观年间宫廷中就已经有了中秋节的雏形，而且三公以下的大臣们要向皇帝献礼表示庆祝。而之后，盛唐时期关于唐玄宗游月宫的传说故事十分盛行。唐代的文人墨客更是喜欢在中秋之夜赏月、玩月、吟咏月亮，留下了大量的咏月诗篇。

北宋时期朝廷正式将八月十五日定为"中秋节"，但也只是一般的普通节日，还不能与端午节、七夕节以及重阳节等重要节日相等同。一直到了南宋时期，受到经济发展的推动，中秋节成为一个热闹的节日，风俗活动十分丰富，特别是娱乐程度和群体参与性有了极大的增强，不论出身阶层，从宫廷到民间，从达官显贵到平民百姓，都很热衷于此节，中秋节是举国欢庆的大日子。

明清以后，实用主义成为社会主流思潮，社会生活中的现实功利因素突出，中秋节的世俗情趣更加浓厚，以赏月为中心的抒情和吟咏减弱，而功利性的祭拜、祈求成为普通百姓中秋节俗的主要内容。中秋节逐渐发展成为融祭月、拜月和赏玩、游戏为一体的团圆节，这一观念和方式一直流传至今。

由于气候的差异，长江以北、黄河流域地区的人们在现代欢度中秋节时更重视团圆的意义。

山西民间特别注重中秋节的全家团圆。外出的人一般都要在这天回家过节，并且还习惯购买带回一些高级月饼。出嫁的姑娘则是不能在娘家过中秋节的，嫁出去的姑娘算作男方家的人，一定要回到婆家与丈夫一起赏月吃月饼。新媳妇回婆家必须由女婿来请。河北省称中秋为"小元旦"，用于祭拜的神像纸上绘有太阴星君以及关帝夜读《春秋》的图像。而山东农家在八月十五日还要祭祀土谷神，称为"青苗社"。陕西中秋夜男子会泛舟登崖，女子安排家宴，而餐桌上一定要有西瓜。中秋节还会有庙会，十分热闹。

相比之下，长江以南地区，中秋节天气舒适，人们赏月玩月的活动更为丰富。

四川省的少数民族比较多，过中秋除了吃月饼外，还会打糍粑、杀鸭子、吃麻饼和蜜饼等。有的地方还要用橘子制成橘灯，挂在大门外，用来庆祝节日。也有儿童会在大柚子上插满香，沿街舞动，叫作"流星香球"。有的地方会祭祀土地神，表演杂剧、声乐等，在民间称为"看会"。

江苏一带的中秋节最为热闹，特别是赏月、玩月等活动丰富多样，其中游"玩月桥"的人最多。人们在明月高悬时，结伴同登望月楼，

037

游玩月桥。玩月桥在南京夫子庙秦淮河的南岸，桥旁曾为明代著名妓女马湘兰的宅第，明代的士子们曾聚集桥头笙箫弹唱，对月赋诗，此桥因此而得名。直到今天，人们在玩月桥赏月玩月的兴致依然很浓，此地则成为著名的游览胜地。

在福建蒲城，女子中秋节要穿越南浦桥，以祈求健康长寿。在建宁，中秋夜已结婚但还没生育的女子会在窗口挂上明灯，向月宫的月神求子。上杭县人们过中秋的时候，儿女多在拜月时祭祀延请月姑。龙岩人吃月饼时，会在中央挖出直径两三寸的圆饼供长辈食用，意思是秘密事不能让晚辈知道，此习俗源自元末明初时朱元璋的民间起义传说，一直流传至今。金门中秋拜月则要先拜天公。

旅游小贴士

中秋节出游注意事项

现在，中秋节在中国是仅次于春节的重要节日，又是处于秋季的旅游旺季，返乡回家团圆的人很多，外出旅游者也是络绎不绝。此时出游，应适当提前计划行程安排，做好准备。

秋季气候多变，早晚温差较大，一些体弱多病者免疫力和抗病能力下降，所以应该注意气候变化，早晚添减衣服须谨慎，防止感冒，以免为旅游带来不便。外出旅行前，主动了解所去景区的地理环境、气候变化、卫生状况以及有无传染病流行等情况，并接受相应的预防接种。

秋天气候凉爽，很多人的胃口也变得好起来，在旅游景点发现特色的美味，难免要"大吃大喝"。由于卫生条件的影响和暴饮暴食，肠胃较差的人很容易发生腹泻。一旦在旅行中发生腹泻，轻者可服用止泻药，严重者要怀疑是否受到细菌感染，长时间腹泻不止且脱水及电解质紊乱者，需要到医院就医，以免发生意外。发生腹泻后人的身体容易变得虚弱，最好多卧床休息，在室内稍事活动，饮食以清淡易消化的稀粥、面条为宜，多喝白开水。

由于中秋假期时间不长，外出旅行时尽量不要选择太远的旅游地点，以免旅途奔波。也不要彻底打乱原有的生活方式，坚持自己的日常生活规律，保证睡眠，防止旅行疲劳。

二、
台湾地区的中秋节

中秋节在台湾地区也是重要的节日。台湾同胞主要沿袭了闽南地区过中秋的节日习俗，同时又经过不断的演变发展出自己的地方特色。

首先，台湾习惯称月亮为"月娘妈"，这一名称最早起源于泉州，古时泉州一带将月亮称为"月娘妈"。因为月亮像妈妈，明亮的月光像妈妈慈祥的目光，人们在月光之下可以如儿女一样向妈妈倾吐心事。有一首台湾歌曲唱道："天顶的月娘，床前的母娘……"。台湾民

○台湾日月潭

间文化中的中秋月亲切细腻，富有人情味。台湾的妈妈们都会叮嘱小孩子不可以用手指头指着中秋月，这样做一是对"月娘妈"大不敬，二是月亮会在你睡着的时候把你的手指或耳朵割掉。几乎每个台湾人在童年时代都会听到家长这样的叮嘱。中秋之夜，人们要在月光能够照耀到的阳台、庭院设置桌案，摆上各式月饼、时令水果等供奉"月娘妈"，表达对月亮造福人类的感恩，并沐浴在"月娘妈"的吉祥光辉中。

○台湾店家在中秋节推出的创意月饼

　　现在，台湾一般民众祭月用月饼、赏月吃月饼的习俗，主要是1949年以后来自中国大陆北方移民所带来的。之前，台湾民众并没有吃月饼的习惯，中秋节祭祀对象也并非月亮、嫦娥，而是土地公。中秋用于祭祀土地公的食物只要是圆的即可，象征圆满、丰收，没有统一的节日祭祀食品，例如宜兰吃"菜饼"，台湾南部则是番薯饼，甚至还有肉饼、台湾大饼、状元饼等。

现在台湾地区的农村过中秋，人们依然还是要置办牲礼、果品祭拜土地公。土地公是老百姓的守护神，祭祀土地公源于人类对土地的崇拜，主要是为了祈求农作物丰收以及生命繁衍。除了祭祀仪式外，人们还习惯将"土地公拐杖"插设在田间，即用竹子夹上土地公像，插在所耕种的田里。在人们信仰的众多神明当中，土地公的等级低位并不高，更接近人间，因此，人们大凡遇到困难，都会找土地公，祈求丰收、生意繁荣，就连治病、升职、转学等也要找他帮忙。台湾地区的土地公特别多，有"田头田尾土地公"之称。而在台南地区森林茂密，中秋之日，那里的农民们还有祭拜树王公的习惯。

除了吃月饼之外，吃柚子是台湾中秋节一个比较有特色的习俗。因为汉字"柚"与"佑"谐音，"柚子"寄托着希望月神庇护的

○中秋节拉柚子皮船，是很多中国人的童年回忆

美好意愿。台湾人吃柚子时会把柚子皮剥成花瓣的形状，可以给小朋友做帽子。中秋时节正是柚子大量上市的旺季，节日里人们吃多了山珍海味，吃柚子则可解腻助消化。台湾地区的人们习惯在中秋举办剥柚子、吃柚子比赛等活动，以增添节日的欢乐气氛。有人还会别出心裁地用柚子雕刻出供玩赏、可摆饰的艺术品。另外，游子中秋回乡，乡亲们则习惯举办"柚子宴"（与"游子宴"谐音），为他们洗尘接风。柚子宴上点柚灯、摆柚碗、喝柚茶、吃柚糖，独具情趣。

○台湾一些饭店中秋节都会为客人准备"月光野餐趴"

随着时代风尚的变迁，现在台湾中秋节流行吃"烤肉"。中秋节来临的前一个月，台湾的便利店、五金行、超市等就开始卖烤肉用具；至中秋节前一个星期，超市与市场则几乎都开始卖烤肉的食材，包括各种各样的烤肉酱，等等。而中秋节当晚，公园、景区、河边、运动场、学校操场，甚至街道两旁以及大楼公寓的楼顶都在烤肉，千家万户、大街小巷到处飘溢着炭火烤肉的馨香。

中秋节吃烤肉，据说始于 20 世纪 80 年代中期。尽管近几年政府全力推行节能减碳，但中秋节烤肉活动并没有受多大影响，还是很受欢迎。不少社区甚至封街进行烤肉。借着中秋吃烤肉的机会街坊邻居能够进行感情交流，而家人彼此间亦可借着烤肉，从准备食材、生火到烧烤，增进感情。对年轻一代人来说，光吃月饼和柚子太过单调，而且月饼的油糖含量高，台湾人觉得吃烤肉比吃月饼更健康。有专家建议民众"素烤"，即多使用素菜做原料、亲手调配酱料等。有商家引进了"红外线烤肉炉"，以减少传统木炭的油烟。还有烤肉

多彩中国节

中秋节

店将水果入菜，烤好的肉片里包上切片葡萄柚和水梨，好吃又解腻，这成为近几年台湾中秋烤肉的新吃法。

"七月半鸭，八月半芋"是台湾民间的节令食谚，意思是说中秋节期间的芋头最好吃，这时节的芋头和芋尾一样浓香酥松。"芋"与"余"谐音，吃芋头意味着"年年有余"，并借此作为丰收的好兆头。节日期间，几乎家家户户都要购买芋头，做芋饼、煮芋饭、蒸芋果、烹芋汤、捣芋泥、炸芋

○ 在台湾，中秋节除了赏月、吃月饼，吃烤肉已经成了家家户户的热门活动

枣……可以组成花样繁多的芋头全席。台湾盛产著名的"槟榔芋"，人们对芋头有着特殊感情，并且拟人化地把芋头分为芋母、芋子、芋孙，作为一种亲情的象征。对于台湾同胞来说，没有芋头，是不能过中秋节的。台湾雅美人对芋头更是喜爱有加。中秋节期间，若有新船下水，必须把自家种的芋头搬上新船压舱，因为"芋"与"鱼"发音相同，剪彩仪式后的翌日再把芋头从船舱里搬出来分赠亲友近邻，借此作为一种迎接丰收的好彩头。

台湾地区的中秋活动也很丰富多彩，其中"博饼"是很重要的一项中秋节俗游戏。相传，该游戏是350多年前郑成功屯兵厦门时，为解士兵的中秋相思之情、激励鼓舞士气而发明的。后来这一游戏传入台湾地区。

博饼，由级别、大小不一的63块月饼组成，模仿古代科举制的

四级考试，设状元饼 1 个、探花饼 2 个、榜眼饼 4 个、进士饼 8 个、举人饼 16 个、秀才饼 32 个。博饼时，取 6 个骰子在大的碗盆中投掷，谁博到规定的点数和颜色就可得到不同级别的月饼。

　　清代乾隆年间，布政使钱琦的《竹枝词》对博饼游戏有这样的描写："玉宇寒光净碧空，有人觅醉桂堂东。研朱滴露书元字，奇取呼庐一掷中。"清代《台湾府志》中也有记载："是夜，士子递为宴饮赏月，制中秋饼，朱书'元'字，掷四红夺之，取秋闱夺元之兆。"三百多年来，中秋博饼盛行不疲，为人们增添了节日的欢乐气氛。

　　此外，中秋夜还会举办社戏和猜谜等活动。台湾著名学者林再复在《闽南人》一书中写道："闽南人移居台湾（地区）后，于'中秋月'家家户户除祭月、赏月外，亦有演戏酬神。"其实，台湾地区的中秋猜谜会比演戏酬神更为盛行，节日期间气候不冷不热，尤其适宜在户外公共场所举办灯谜会。中秋节是继元宵节之后的又一个团圆节，在台湾地区的中秋灯谜会上，有不少谜作是盼团圆、怀故乡、思亲人的，如：

　　"低头思故乡"（闽南语老歌一），谜底：《月夜愁》；

　　"慈母手中线"（京剧名二），谜底：《打堂》《缝衣》；

　　"悬明月以自照兮"（台湾著名作家一），谜底：余光中；

　　"何人不起故园情"（中药名二），谜底：熟地、当归。

　　另外，台湾地区的灯谜比较通俗，如：

　　"无味之泉"（台湾地名一），谜底：淡水；

　　"饮水思源"（台湾地名一），谜底：知本。

　　台湾地区的中秋谜会多在公园、广场、寺庙举行，猜谜形式与台胞重点祖居地闽南的"击鼓悬猜"相近。

　　在宜兰、嘉义等地区，中秋节还有荡秋千的习俗。周钟瑄《诸罗县志》记载："秋千，高丈许，下容一人，绕梁旋转如纺，上下可数回。"即用竹竿搭成秋千，高达十余尺，在人坐在上面来回飘荡，如悬在半空中，相当精彩。苏澳、礁溪地区在秋千架前挂一铜铃，能踢倒的次数越多者获胜，乐趣无穷。

此外，还有一些专门与女性相关的习俗：如1.中秋夜祈求长寿：民间相传中秋夜睡得越晚越长寿，尤其是少女在中秋夜晚睡，会使自己的母亲长寿。2.祈求嫁得如意郎君：相传未婚少女如果在中秋夜偷得别家菜园中的蔬菜和葱，就表示她会觅得一位如意郎君。3.祈求子嗣：婚后尚未生育的妇女，在中秋晚上，倘能到人家菜园里偷摘一个瓜抱回家，来年就会生个胖娃娃。除此，在中秋夜深时，台湾妇女往往会在家中的神像前烧香，提出了欲问卜的事后，还要请示出门的方向，然后持香出门，一路上听到谈话和歌唱时，便占卜问神，直到得到神明的认可答案为止。

旅游小贴士

中秋游台湾

台湾有很多地方中秋节的节日气氛浓厚，不仅能够深切体验到当地的节庆风俗，还能领略台湾的美丽风光和特色美食。

鹿港，隶属台湾彰化县，西面靠台湾海峡，因输出大量鹿皮而得名。鹿港天后宫在台湾各妈祖庙中地位极高。因该庙所供奉的妈祖神像是全省唯一由湄洲而来的神像，人称为祖神。中秋节期间会举行盛大的祭祀仪式。而鹿港靠海，所以小吃以海鲜为主，主要有鸭肉羹、虾猴、蚵仔酥、蚵仔煎、虾丸、西施舌等。糕饼茶点也很有名，如凤眼糕、牛舌饼、猪油荖等。此外还有当地人经常会吃的面线糊。

　　大溪老街，位于台湾桃园县东南方，在复兴山地与桃园台地之交，大汉溪自山中流出后在此转向北行。清朝时得益于河运兴盛，发展为繁荣市镇，形成今日所谓的"老街区"。市区里古老的巷道、朴质的旧建筑，以及隐身于街衢巷弄间的传统行业，仍见证昔日繁华的市街景象，往来匆匆行旅之间，不妨在此稍停脚步，为旅途增添几许古老的知性与感性。

　　阳明山，原名草山，是台湾著名观光胜地。位于台湾北端，在台北市近郊。附近青山翠谷，原野开阔，遍植樱花、杜鹃，建有中山楼、中山公园（前山公园）、阳明山公园等，中国文化大学亦设于此，是著名的风景区。

三、
香港特区的中秋节

　　按照香港本地习俗，中秋节一般要过3天：农历八月十四先开始"迎月"，八月十五是正日子，八月十六则是"追月"。

　　舞火龙，是香港中秋节最富传统特色的习俗。从每年农历八月十四晚起，铜锣湾大坑地区就一连三晚举行盛大的舞火龙活动。火

○大坑舞火龙是香港铜锣湾大坑的传统民俗活动，相传龙能行云布雨、消灾降福，象征祥瑞，舞龙可以祈求平安和丰收

龙长近 70 米，用珍珠草扎成 32 节的龙身，插满长寿香。盛会之夜，大街小巷里蜿蜒起伏的火龙在灯光与鼓音下欢腾起舞。据说舞了火龙后可以趋吉避凶，风调雨顺。以前用稻秆扎成龙头、龙身的形状，插上燃着的香，由青壮小伙子赤膊上阵，挥舞舞动。舞毕，居民拔下火龙身上的线香分派给围观者。据说取得线香的人会交好运，于是，中秋节在巷子里等候"好运"的人很多很多。

香港大坑的中秋舞火龙已有百余年的历史。传说很早以前，大坑区在风灾后出现了一条作恶的蟒蛇，村民们四出搜捕，终于把它击毙。不料次日蟒蛇不翼而飞，数天后大坑便发生瘟疫。这时，村中父老忽获菩萨托梦，说是只要在中秋节舞动火龙，便可将瘟疫驱除。事有巧合，照办后此举竟然奏效。从此，舞火龙的习俗就流传了下来。

在八月十六日的夜晚，香港的人们还要再狂欢一次，名为"追月"。相传这个习俗是江浙一带的人们带来的，史料记载："宁波以十六日为中秋，为宋史弥远所改，至今犹然。"清人陈子厚《岭南杂事钞·序》也记载："粤中好事者，于八月十六日夜，集亲朋治酒肴赏月，谓之追月。"香港政府早年制定假日制度，规定八月十五上班，第二天公众才放假一天。八月十五过节那天，人们下班回到家都八九点了，又累又饿，无心赏月；第二天放假了，心情放松，兴致盎然，在八月十六日夜能够好好欢庆一番。

灯会在香港的中秋节是必不可少的活动。由香港旅游发展局主办的"彩灯大观园"，彩灯以"绿色"挂帅，游客可以观赏到用 7000 个废弃塑料瓶搭建的巨型半月形彩灯——"悦满中秋"，该灯直径约 20 米，设计师之一萧国健称，半月彩灯将耸立于水池上，配合特别灯光效果，与水面倒影相连，形成月圆月缺的景象。彩灯内部有"天窗"设计，参观者进入彩灯内，可同时享受天上地下两个"月亮"。

○ 香港维多利亚公园的中秋彩灯晚会，巨型箭猪彩灯有 6 层楼高

对于早前的香港市民来说，"煲蜡"也是他们喜爱的中秋月夜活动之一。中秋夜宴之后，在公园赏月吃月饼一番，月饼盒随即空出。孩子们喜欢把其当作器皿来烧蜡，待蜡融化后，再喷水，最后蜡液四溅并产生高温水蒸气。对于孩子来说，这是一个简单刺激的娱乐性节目，但却极其容易导致烫伤烧伤事故。在 20 世纪末，香港政府开始呼吁市民不要"煲蜡"。

香港的中秋节饮食也很有特色，其中"猪笼饼"最为有名。它是所有香港人都吃过的月饼，也是大多数香港人吃到的第一块月饼，味道简单，但回味悠远。

一提到"猪笼"，许多人忍不住会联想到"浸猪笼"这种诡异可怕的旧时陋习。其实，猪笼原本只是用来装运猪仔的圆筒形竹笼而已。"猪笼饼"，顾名思义就是把形似小猪的饼装在小竹笼里。它是广东人在中秋节时送给长者或小朋友的传统食品，现在除香港以外，在其他地区都已十分罕见了。

○ 猪笼饼

"小猪"做得很细致，有棱角分明的眼睛、耳朵、鼻子和尾巴，惟妙惟肖。在广东人眼里，猪笼饼肥肥圆圆的身形，憨态可掬的表情，寓意家中养着大肥猪，好意头深得人心。

猪笼饼最特别之处，是它并非用盒子盛载，而是用一个塑料笼或小竹笼装着。笼子五颜六色，有的还绑上彩带用胶花点缀，是小朋友的最爱，能吃又能玩。

"猪笼饼"由面粉制作，混合砂糖调味，除此之外没有任何馅料，口感不及现在市面上卖的任何一种月饼。然而在物质生活匮乏的过去，中秋能吃上一块"猪笼饼"，已经是件相当美好的事了。

在月饼还是奢侈品的时代，买月饼过中秋，并不是每个香港家庭都负担得起。于是，一些饼店就想出了分期付款的主意，称为"供月饼会"。做月饼时，为了测试砖炉的温度和饼皮的松软程度，饼店工人就会将做月饼剩下的月饼皮，搓成小份面团，放到砖炉测试温度。这就是猪笼饼的原型。后来，为了求个好彩头，这些不包馅的面团便被做成了多子多福的猪仔造型，放到竹编小笼子里，用作"供月饼会"的赠品福利。余下的则以廉价卖给经济拮据的家庭，使人人中秋有饼食，这便是"猪笼饼"的来历了。

049

现在，月饼已经不再是负担不起的食品了，但走进香港的传统饼店，依然还能看到猪笼饼的身影。以前买不起月饼时，"猪笼饼"吃的是一份无奈的快乐，如今再拿起它，更多的一份对过去纯真岁月的回忆和情怀。提着"猪笼饼"向月亮奶奶倾诉心声，这是每个港人童年最美好的中秋记忆。

○最新潮的冰皮月饼

此外，香港中秋节还有特色的"冰皮月饼"。20世纪80年代，"冰皮月饼"已经开始在香港的市场上出售。"冰皮月饼"得名的主要原因是它的制作方法与传统月饼截然相反。所有传统月饼都是由糖浆做皮，颜色是金黄色。而"冰皮月饼"的部分原料是糯米，做成的月饼外观呈白色，而且需要在冷冻箱里保存，售卖时也要保存在冷藏柜里。

与传统月饼相比，"冰皮月饼"油脂和糖量较低，更为健康。"冰皮月饼"的独到之处，就在于一个"冰"字，给人爽口之感，使那被传统月饼油腻住的肠胃得到解脱。好的冰皮月饼，外观如冰般亮滑，冰箱冷藏过夜后仍旧柔软，细心切开，切面馅料均如镜般光滑。

旅游小贴士

香港中秋赏月

香港中秋赏月的经典景点很多。

太平山顶，是游客必到的旅游点。在这里可以俯瞰维多利亚港的香港岛，九龙半岛两岸，日落后能够欣赏有"东方之珠"美誉的夜景。赏月的最佳地点莫过于凌霄阁的观景台。中秋月圆时带着亲朋好友来太平山顶赏月，不失为一个绝佳选择。

中环。在中环看到的夜景是五光十色的，中环是香港的政治、经济中心及高级商业购物区，有全国各地乃至世界各地的时装及餐饮品牌，建筑也富有时代特色。在中环的顶级酒店，品尝着精致的佳肴，欣赏着与明月同辉的夜景，别有一番享受。

维多利亚公园，适合所有人赏月。维多利亚公园位于香港铜锣湾高士威道和维园道之间，是香港最大的公园，也是香港最受欢迎、人气最高的赏月地点。每逢中秋节，这里都是人山人海的，至少有数万人在这里赏花灯、赏月。每年，维多利亚公园都会举办中秋节的大型灯会。当月亮升起，公园内坐满了赏月的游人，大家安静的抬头望月，身边围坐着家人朋友，一股融融暖意荡漾心间。

四、
澳门特区的中秋节

澳门在晚清已经成为华洋杂居的开埠城市，是中西文化交流的重要桥梁和枢纽之一。在澳门社会生活中，中西方多元宗教文化信仰在这里碰撞融合，但在人口上占绝对优势的华人传统文化和节日习俗仍然处于主导地位。在澳门，中秋节是人们非常重视的一个重要节日。在公园、海边、休憩区等，入夜后人流如织，全家一同猜灯谜及参与各区贺节活动，或到水边赏月，近距离欣赏烟花，其乐融融。

○澳门中秋烟花会演（张章 摄）

在 20 世纪五六十年代的澳门，每逢中秋节来临，新马路的饼铺门前一定七彩纷缤，各出奇谋，竖立起招徕的广告牌，立体布置，画上历史人物，如嫦娥奔月、吴刚砍桂树、八仙过海、太空飞船等装饰，晚上亮起霓虹灯，闪闪烁烁，整条马路观热闹的行人水泄不通，卖月饼的店号也因此其门如市。一般的饼店，每年靠一个中秋节，生意滔滔，可以赚一大笔。

澳门人的"闹中秋"，要从中秋前夜至中秋翌日热热闹闹地闹上3天。在澳门的民俗中，中秋前夜叫作"迎月夜"，中秋当日叫作"赏月夜"，中秋节翌日叫作"追月夜"。在这期间，澳门民政总署、澳门街坊会联合总会、澳门工会联合总会等纷纷在各街心公园举办文娱表演、摊位游戏及猜灯谜等活动，供民众免费参加。

中国文化传统对于亲情是格外重视的，中秋节是一年中澳门人家庭聚会的"大节日"，各项节庆准备工作从农历七月二十五就开始了。家庭富有者大多都会尽早到酒家、茶楼、店铺和饼家购买月饼、

多彩中国节

中秋节

水果、茶叶等过节食品。家境不太宽裕的人家，最晚也要赶在八月十二或十三购买应节的食物。在八月十五这一天，家家户户都会团聚"赏月"，出外工作的都趁假期赶着回来，一家大小，共叙天伦之乐。除了吃月饼以外，许多家庭都喜欢自制汤丸，只做甜的，冬节才做咸的，象征一家"团圆"的意思。还有，煮熟的芋仔、沙田柚，都是过节时一般人喜欢吃的东西。在这一天，大批澳门当地居民带着家人一起到公园和水池边赏月，孩子们则手提着纸扎或者电子灯笼，共同享受月圆人团圆的节日氛围。

○每年的"澳门国际烟花比赛会演"都吸引数以万计的民众到场

在澳门，中秋之日还有玩赏兔子灯笼的习俗，兔子机敏通达，深受人们的喜爱，而且与澳门还有不少渊源。比如澳门回归祖国的年份为兔年，古代澳门的地形与兔子相似，在澳门兔子常被作为中秋灯笼的题材。在塔石广场，还会有庆祝中秋的文艺晚会举行。此外值得一提的是，一年一度的"澳门国际烟花会演"也将在这一黄金大假期间上演压轴戏，来自世界各地的烟花制作高手，将带上自己最拿手的作品现场燃放展示。

中秋游澳门

中秋节的时候正是澳门最好的旅游时节，这个时候气温比较舒适，旅游的时候需要准备一些短袖套装和长袖套装，在白天气温较高，出门游玩的时候要穿清爽透气的短袖衣服，晚上气温会降低，则需要穿上长袖的衣服。

澳门最有名的天主教堂是圣保罗教堂，当地人称之为"大三巴"。该教堂于1637年修建，位置在距离大巴街不远的小山上，这座教堂真正见证了澳门的沧桑历史。教堂前壁雄伟壮观，上面有精美的浮雕，最上层是大大的十字架，向下的壁龛中都有铜像藏在其中，其中有鸽形的铜像，周围还雕有太阳、月亮和星星，还有一个耶稣圣婴雕像。

在澳门旅游的时候，不用事先买地图，经过澳门关时有一个旅游接待处，可以直接领到澳门一些景点的地图，上面的旅游景点都标的很清楚，以及乘坐公交车路线等信息。在澳门坐车的时候司机只收澳元和港币，需要提前兑换一些澳币带着。澳门是一个比较整洁的城市，很注重市容；如果乱扔垃圾，依照澳门法律会被罚款的。

五、
中秋节的海外流布

中秋节不仅仅是中国人重视的一个传统节日，在很多亚洲地区，它都是一个重要的节日。

在朝鲜，"中秋节"在朝鲜语中叫作"罕佳玉"或"秋夕"，是朝鲜半岛人民历来都要欢庆的民俗节日之一。在古代的朝鲜，"秋夕"是一个欢庆丰收的农家节日，也是农耕社会最重要的节日之一。在这一天，人们用新打的谷米做成各种食物，带上同样是由新米酿制

○中秋节是很多东南亚国家的共同节日

而成的清酒，跳起欢庆的农乐舞，去祭扫祖先的坟墓，全家出动到祖坟前报告秋天丰收的好消息。

朝鲜人以松饼为节日食物，家家蒸食并互相馈送。松饼形如半月，用米粉制成，内馅是豆沙、枣泥等，因蒸时垫有松毛而得名。中秋供品中还有类似"八宝粥"的"药粥"，是用糯米、红枣、栗子、糖熬成，香甜可口。这样既是为了表达丰收的喜悦，也是为了祈求来年风调雨顺、五谷丰登。据说每年的八月十五是朝鲜最热闹的一天，几乎所有的人都喝得酩酊大醉，满大街都是晃晃悠悠拿着酒瓶的人。这样的习俗如今在朝鲜农村依然可见。而除却祭扫亲人坟墓、欢庆丰收，城乡居民瞻仰烈士陵园和纪念碑，也成为今日具有"朝鲜特色"的新习俗。在首都平壤，锦绣山纪念宫和大城山烈士陵园是人们的必到之地——前者是安放朝鲜前国家领导人金日成主席遗体的地方，而后者则安葬着当年追随金日成进行抗日活动、为朝鲜革命立下丰功伟绩的重要人物。

朝鲜人自古便有在端午或中秋这样的节日里举行摔跤、跳板、秋千等民俗体育比赛的传统。之前，朝鲜最高领导人曾指示要加强发扬民族传统，于是，一些本来用于自娱的民俗体育赛事渐成气候，全国性的"大黄牛奖"民族摔跤比赛就是其中一例。之所以叫作"大黄牛奖"，是因为冠军的奖品是一头大黄牛。从朝鲜全国各地劳动者中选拔出的几十名选手参加历时三天的比赛。平壤大同江江心小岛绫罗岛上的民俗竞技场内挤满了观战的群众，时而屏息凝视，时而欢呼鼓掌。

○朝鲜：吃松饼过中秋

多彩中国节

中秋节

比赛间隙，会有由清一色头发花白的老妈妈们组成的啦啦队起劲地敲打着手里的圆鼓长鼓，而那头作为奖品的重达970公斤的大黄牛，就被拴在旁边的大树上，身披写有"冠军"字样的绶带，悠闲地甩着尾巴。

朝鲜的"秋夕"也注重家庭内部的团聚。这天，朝鲜人照例放假一天，连那些往常并不会在星期天歇业的服务设施，像餐馆、百货商场等商家，也会都挂出"今日休息"的牌子，平日热闹非凡的商业街上也看不到人影。到了晚上，朝鲜人们会一边赏月，一边进行拔河比赛、摔跤比赛，或者表演歌舞。年轻的姑娘们穿上色彩缤纷的节日盛装，欢聚在大树下做"布伦河"游戏，即荡秋千。

秋夕的清晨，韩国家家户户都会摆好新谷、水果酒、松饼、芋头汤和各式各样的水果祭拜祖先。韩国传统上是由长子继承家族的正统，因此秋夕祭拜祖先时，均是兄弟们到大哥家里祭祖。祭典开始时，男人们都要恭敬地站立在祭桌前，主祭的家族长子要先把家里的大门打开，意指请老祖宗进到家里来。然后回到祭桌前，烧香、献花与献酒，率领家庭成员行叩礼。在祖宗们享用祭品的时候，主祭者要向家人介绍祖宗的光荣事迹，然后卜问祖宗是否已享用完祭品。完毕后，主祭者再率领家族成员对祖宗行叩礼，恭送祖宗。祭祖仪式完毕后，大人们将祭酒喝掉，然后开始吃团圆早饭。

除了祭拜祖先外，秋夕还有扫墓的习俗，一般是在秋夕前一天或前两天举行，现在则多在当天举行。因为韩国人的祖坟一般都在山上，所以祭扫祖坟被称为"上山"。秋夕"上山"是一年中最重大的事情，即使有天大的事，也不能耽误了"上山"。

秋夕节在韩国有一句俗语叫"做得好松饼，嫁得好人家"，韩国女孩子从小就要学做松饼，要为"嫁得好"而努力奋斗。韩国人吃松饼就相当于中国人中秋节必吃月饼，除了品尝它们的美味，更多的是传达他们对传统文化的坚持。

　　中秋节在日本也是很重要的一个节日，日本语中"中秋节"的正式名称是"栗名月"，也叫"豆名月"或"芋名月"。"栗名月"共有七天，分别是待宵（农历八月十四）、十五夜（农历八月十五）、十六夜（农历八月十六）、立待月（农历八月十七）、居待月（农历八月十八）、寝待月（农历八月十九）和二十三夜（农历八月二十三）。

　　在"十五夜"这一天，人们将芒草、胡枝子、黄花龙芽等秋草插在瓶子里，供上水果和糯米团。日本称这一天的月亮为"豆明月"，因为此时正是大豆收获的季节，将月亮称为"豆明月"，意味着希望获得大豆的丰收。只有这一天，日本人允许外人到自己的地里偷芋薯，并认为这是一种好事。许多孩子用带钉子的竹竿明目张胆地取走邻家的供品。

　　日本人在这一天同样有赏月的习俗，在日语里称为"月见"。日本的赏月习俗来源于中国，在1000多年前传到日本后，当地开始出现边赏月边举行宴会的风俗习惯，被称为"观月宴"。与中国人在中秋节的时候吃月饼不同，日本人在赏月的时候吃江米团子，称为"月见团子"或"白玉团子"。团子用白米粉做成，内中无馅。团子确实比月饼更像月亮。祭月需要三件宝，除了白玉团子之外，还需要几枝芦草，还要摆放一只小白兔。

　　由于这个时期正值各种作物的收获季节，为了对自然的恩惠表示感谢，日本人要举行各种庆祝活动。虽然日本在明

○日本的月见团子

治维新以后废除了农历，改用阳历，但是现在日本各地仍保留着中秋赏月的习俗，一些寺院和神社在中秋节还要举办专门的赏月会。

在越南，中秋节是儿童唱主角的节日。随着农历八月十五中秋节的临近，商家之间展开的"月饼大战""玩具大战"使越南各地的节日气氛尤显浓烈。与中国的中秋节有所不同，越南的中秋节是儿童唱主角。市场上口味各异的各式月饼、千姿百态的花灯、五颜六色的儿童玩具等节日食品、玩具应有尽有，孩子们的脸上溢满了对节日的渴望。

当晚，孩子们聆听关于阿桂和鲤鱼的传说。阿桂是一个爱说谎的小伙子，一天，他从一位老人那里骗来一颗神奇的榕树。老人告诉他，这棵榕树的叶子可以使人起死回生，把这棵榕树带回家后，要常常浇水，这样才能让它长得枝繁叶茂。另外要切记，这棵榕树不能被尿水污染，如果人们把榕树种在院子左侧，人们小便时便要朝向西，绝不能朝着榕树小便，否则榕树就会飞上天去。阿桂把榕树带回家后，给妻子交代了注意事项，并要她每天给榕树浇水。有一天，阿桂上山砍柴了，妻子忘了给榕树浇水。等到阿桂回到家门口的时候，妻子才想起来还没给榕树浇水呢。她怕丈夫知道了责骂自己，但丈夫马上就要进家门了，浇水来不及了。妻子急中生智，赶忙跑到榕树下，撩起裙子撒了一泡尿。突然，榕树连根拔起，向天上飞去。阿桂正好进门，忙用手中的斧子钩住榕树，想把榕树拉下来，但是榕树飞升的力量很大，阿桂就这样连斧头一起被带到了月亮上。于是每到月圆的时候，人们就看到月宫中的榕树和树下的阿桂。

而关于鲤鱼，传说古代有条鲤鱼成精后害人，包公为救苍生，用纸扎了鲤鱼灯以镇之。于是，孩子们在中秋夜都会提鲤鱼灯出游，这还预示了长大"跳龙门"之意。

每年中秋节期间，越南各地都要举行花灯节，并对花灯的设计进行评比，优胜者将获得奖励。另外，越南的一些地方还在节日期间组织舞狮，常在农历八月十四、十五两晚进行。当地人过节时或全家围坐阳台上、院子里，或举家外出到野外，摆上月饼、水果及其他各式点心，边赏月、边品尝美味的月饼。孩子们则提着各种灯笼，成群结队地尽情嬉闹。

随着近年来越南人民的生活水平逐步提高，中秋习俗也悄然发生了变化。许多年轻人在节日里或在家聚会、唱歌跳舞，或结伴外

○越南中秋节里的儿童面具很受孩子们欢迎

出游玩赏月，增进同伴之间的了解与情谊。因此，越南的中秋节除了传统的合家团圆之意外，正随着时代变化而增添新的含义，受到越来越多年轻人的青睐。

新加坡是一个华人占人口绝大多数的国家，对于一年一度的中秋佳节向来十分重视。对新加坡的华人来说，中秋佳节是联络感情，表示谢意的好时机。亲朋好友、商业伙伴之间相互馈赠月饼，借此表示问候与祝愿。新加坡是一个旅游城市，中秋佳节无疑是一个吸

引游客的绝好机会。每年中秋临近时，当地著名的乌节路、新加坡河畔、牛车水及裕华园等地装饰一新。入夜时分，华灯初上，整个大街小巷一片红彤彤的景象，充满了节日氛围。在华人的传统聚居地牛车水，除了从尼泊尔、越南等国进口的巨型灯笼熠熠生辉之外，由 1364 盏小红灯笼组成的 44 条小龙更是令牛车水增色不少。在新

○ 新加坡中秋节主题花灯会

○ 新加坡的中秋夜灯光秀

第二章　中秋节的流布

加坡颇具中华古老园林风韵的御花园，也会举办规模宏大的梦幻彩灯会。这里既有令人们喜爱的迪士尼系列灯饰，也有巨大的北京天坛和巨龙造型的灯饰，分外引人注目。

○新加坡中秋节牛车水赏灯

新加坡中秋节的特色月饼是著名的彩色月饼。过去新加坡的月饼和中国月饼差异不大，但最近这些年，随着中秋节的商业化，月饼也不断推陈出新。市场上最流行的月饼的饼皮是彩色的，就好像热带的花一样，争奇斗艳。一般来说，颜色和口味是互相搭配的。例如粉色的月饼多是芋头馅儿的，黄色的月饼多是榴梿馅儿的。榴梿馅儿的月饼，是新加坡最有地方特色的月饼。除了榴梿月饼，冷柜里还有榴梿蛋糕、榴梿面包以及真正的榴梿。榴梿月饼在东南亚各地都会见到，但新加坡是做得最有特色的。

吃月饼、赏月、提灯笼游行是马来西亚华人世代相传的中秋习俗。在马来西亚，华人占人口的四分之一左右，中秋节是华人社会中的重要节日，并在 2003 年被政府定为旅游庆典日。中秋临近，马来西亚各地的老字号商家纷纷推出各色月饼。首都吉隆坡市内各大商场都设有月饼专柜，报纸、电视台的月饼广告铺天盖地，为喜迎中秋营造节日气氛。吉隆坡一些地方的华人社团会举行提灯笼游行庆中秋活动，除舞龙、舞狮外，一辆辆载有"嫦娥""七仙女"的花车漫游其间，服饰鲜艳的艺人和青年载歌载舞，热闹非凡。

中秋节是生活在菲律宾的华侨华人非常重视的传统佳节。菲律宾首都马尼拉的唐人街热闹非凡，当地华侨华人举行为期两天的活动，欢度中秋节。华侨华人聚居区的主要商业街道都会张灯结彩，主要路口和进入唐人

○新加坡四季酒店为中秋节准备的月饼和中国茶

街的小桥上会挂上了彩幅，许多商店出售自制的或从中国进口的各式月饼。中秋庆祝活动包括舞龙游行、民族服装游行、灯笼游行和花车游行等，活动吸引大批观众，使历史悠久的唐人街充满了欢快的节日气氛。

受中国文化影响，泰国人民也把中秋节唤做"祈月节"。八月十五日的节日之夜，各家各户的男女老少都要参拜月亮。人们在大方桌前端坐祈祷，互相祝福。大方桌上，供奉着南海观世音菩萨，面目慈祥，向祈祷者洒布"大慈大悲"；桌上还供奉着中国民间传说的"八洞神仙"，个个栩栩如生，向祈祷者传授"八仙过海"的各自神通。桌上还会摆上"寿桃""月饼"之类的美食。据泰国传说，中秋祈月，八仙会带着寿桃到月宫给观音祝寿，菩萨神仙们就会"降福生灵，寿半人间。"

缅甸人在八月的"月圆日"会举办大型灯会，以庆祝"光明节"的光临。节日之夜，万家灯火，亮若白昼，到处是"不夜城"。天上皓月，地上明灯，照耀得缅甸一片光明。缅王每年亲自主持庆祝活动。

国王在卫队和文武百官簇拥下，出宫观灯并举行盛大施舍。各地还会通宵达旦放电影、演出话剧、木偶戏、跳舞唱歌，佛塔内还有大规模的布施斋饭等活动，十分热闹。

○泰国清迈大学孔子学院的中秋节体验活动

　　柬埔寨是佛教国家，柬埔寨人在佛历十二月上弦十五日举行传统的"拜月节"。这天清晨，人们开始准备供月礼品，有的采鲜花，有的挖木薯熬汤，有的舂扁米，有的煮甘蔗水，一派欢乐繁忙的气氛。晚上，大家把供品放进托盘，将托盘放在房前一张大席子上，静待明月东升。当月上树梢头，人们虔心拜月，祈乞赐福。拜毕，老人把扁米塞进孩子嘴里，直到塞满不能咀嚼时方止。这表示"圆圆满满""和和美美"，最后，大家尽兴品尝美食而散。

　　老挝称中秋节为"月福节"。每逢月福节到来时，男女老少也有赏月的风俗。夜晚，青年男女翩翩起舞，通宵达旦。

Chapter Two
The Spread of the Mid-Autumn Festival

"I used to stand at the apricot orchards of the Qujiang at the night of August 15th. But this year, I'm in the front of Sha Tou inn, beside the Yangtze River, in Penpu street(a street of XunYang district, Jiujiang, Jiangxi province). I desired to see my hometown towards northwest, while finding the moon rounding several times. No one felt the cold brought by yesterday's autumn wind, but today's moon is still as usual." said a famous poet of the Tang Dynasty, Bai JuYi, in his poem *Seeing the Moon in Pen Pavilion on August 15th's Night*, people from different areas with a range from the northwest to the southeast, from Chang'an to Penpu get together to celebrate the festival under the bright moonlight, which makes Bai Juyi miss his family and homeplace particularly. The Mid-Autumn Festival is the biggest event in China's autumn with its long history and lasting traditions and a significant festival everywhere of China including Tai Wan, Hong Kong, Macao and so on, even in East and Southeast Asia where Chinese people gather.

1. Spread in Chinese Mainland

Chinese ancient people have set up a calendar system observing the moon in the Xia Dynasty, which was called "Yin Li", "Nong Li", "Xia Li" in later generations. July, August and September are respectively named "Meng Qiu", "Zhong Qiu" and "Ji Qiu" in lunar calendar, and on the whole these three months are thought of as "San Qiu" .While August 15th is "Zhong Qiuri" as it is in the middle of "San Qiu".

The traditional customs of moon's worship and sacrifice have already appeared in primitive society. "Zhong Qiujie" (the Mid-Autumn Festival) which was the first time to refer to in an article can be derived from Zhengguan years of the Tang Dynasty, from 627AD to 649AD.*Yuan Jian Lei Han·the 20th volume* is quoted "August 15th is the Mid-Autumn Festival when the positions of grand ministers ranked below 'San Gong' (ranks: Tai Wei, Si Tu and Si Kong) need to present a bronze mirror and others gifts from folk to the emperor for celebration." by *The Records of Tang Taizong*. It is obvious that the embryo of the Mid-Autumn Festival has begun to form in the palace during Zhengguan period. The myth of Tang Xuanzong visiting the moon palace was very prevalent in the glorious age of Tang period, which made men of letters more interested in enjoying, and chanting the moon for which a lot of poems left.

August 15th was formally nominated as "the Mid-Autumn Festival", just a normal festival, in the Northern Song Dynasty, but it was less important than other festivals such as the Dragon Boat Festival, the Magpie Festival and the Double Ninth Festival. Not until the Southern Song Dynasty did the Mid-Autumn Festival become a lively one, which was full of special activities driven by economic development, largely increasing the degree of entertainment and participation of this festival in particular. The Mid –Autumn Festival is a significant day celebrated by all the people regardless of their status.

Pragmatism became a social mainstream thought, for practical utilitarian factors are highlighted in the society and much worldly interest is added to the Mid-Autumn Festival after the Ming and Qing Dynasty. The celebration of Mid-Autumn Festival tends to be worldlier with playing a more important role than enjoying the moon purely. The Mid- Autumn Festival gradually grows to be a reunion festival, integrating the sacrifice, the admiration of the moon with enjoying and playing games, which has come down to us.

People, living in the north of the Yangtze River and the Yellow River, think highly of the meaning of rejoining with families because of climatic differences.

Much attention was paid to the reunion among people in Shanxi, thus people leaving their homes generally return on the Mid-Autumn Festival, carrying some deluxe mooncakes. Married women, belonging to their men's families, need to see the moon and eat mooncakes with husband in their husbands' families rather than in their parents' homes. Bribes must be invited by their husband if they go back to the husband's family. The Mid-Autumn Festival is called Xiao Yuandan in Hebei Province where people use paper with Tai Yin Xing Jun (the Luna in Taoism) and Guandi reading Chun Qiu at night for worshipping. Besides these habitudes, in Shandong Province, farmers should sacrifice the Earth and Grain God, named as Qingmiao Community. Men sail on the lake and climb the mountains, while women arrange a family feast that watermelons must be included at the night of the Mid- Autumn Festival in Shaanxi Province. In addition, there is a very bustling temple fair on that day.

In the south of Yangtze River, by contrast, people have more activities to admire the moon as a result of the comfortable weather.

Besides eating mooncakes, people in Sichuan Province with more minorities will make glutinous rice cakes, killing ducks, and eat sesame cakes and sweet cakes and many other things. The lanterns, painted in orange, are hang outside the gate, which are to celebrate the Mid-Autumn Festival in some regions. Some children will place incenses in big grapefruits which are named Meteor Incense Ball, waving them along the street. There is going to be a Kan Hui (called by folk) in someplace where activities include the Land God's worship, Zaju (poetic drama set to music) and vocal music performance and so on.

What is the liveliest place is Jiangshu Province as for the Mid-Autumn Festival. Especially, there are various activities of appreciating the moon, while most people visit the Bridge of Enjoying the Moon. They, with partners, ascend the Moon Watching Tower (Islam's unique architecture) and tour the Bridge of Enjoying the Moon with the bright moon hanging high in the sky. There stands a mansion for Ma Xianglan, a famous prostitute in the Ming Dynasty, by the bridge located at the south bank of Qinhuai River, Confucius Temple in Nanjing Province. Why this bridge is named the Bridge of Enjoying the Moon is that scholar-officials in the Ming Dynasty gathered to play the flutes and pipes as singing and composing poems towards the moon at the end of this bridge. People still have much interest in this bridge, watching and admiring the moon until today, all of which makes the Bridge of Enjoying the Moon become a resort.

Women need to cross the Nanpu Bridge to pray for health and longevity in the Mid-Autumn Festival in Pu Cheng, Fujian Province. A light lamp is suspended by some married women without any children at the night of the Mid-Autumn in Jian-Ning County (in Fujian Province), which is to wish for a baby from the Moon Goddess in the Moon Palace. Young men and women will treat Yue Gu to a great sacrifice when they worship the moon in Shanghang County. People will scoop out a two or three-inch-round cake in the centre of the mooncake for elders in Longyan County, which means the older can't tell the secret to the junior. This custom, originated from a folk uprising legend of Zhu Yuanzhang(the first emperor in Ming Dynasty), has lasted from the late Yuan and early Ming Dynasty through to the modern day. While in Kinmen County, people must worship the Heaven first.

Tips for Tourism

The Notes of Traveling during the Mid-Autumn Festival

Nowadays, the Mid—Autumn Festival is an important day right behind the Spring Festival and in the tourist season as well, which makes many people go home for reunion or take a trip. If you want to visit somewhere at this time, you should plan your journey and prepare well before leaving home.

Some sickly people are prone to fall ill as a result of variable weather and large temperature differences between day and night in autumn. To avoid having a cold and trouble in traveling, you need to wear comfortably to adapt to the changeable weather. Before going on a journey, you'd better have ac—quaintance with the geographical conditions, climate changes, sanitary and in—fectious disease conditions and get an appropriate vaccination.

Many people will eat and drink glnttonously when they find special food at scenic spots because they have a good appetite as it is cool in fall.

Due to the sanitary conditions and overeating to a certain extent, someone with bad intestines and stomach is likely to suffer from diarrhea. Once getting it on the journey, they can take some medicine in less case, but even worse, they need to suspect whether they have bacterial infection and go to see a doctor for safety, if suffering from diarrhea for a long time and even dehydration and electrolyte imbalance. After that, they are tend to be weak, so they should stay in bed and do some exercises indoors .As for diet, they are supposed to have light food including porridge and noodles, drinking much plain boiled water as well.

Don't choose a tourist destination far away from home so as to avoid a long and tiring journey as the holiday of Mid-Autumn Festival is not long. Nor do you upset your original lifestyle, instead, you need to insist living as usual and having a good sleep for fear of tiredness.

2. The Mid-Autumn Festival in Taiwan

The Mid-Autumn Festival is also important in Taiwan area. Taiwan compatriots mainly adhere to the Mid-Autumn Festival customs in Min'Nan area (southern region of Fujian province),

Appreciate the moon during the Mid-Autumn Festival in Taiwan

while developing their own local characteristics over the long history.

First, the moon is used to being called "Mother Moon" in Taiwan, which originated in Quanzhou, since the bright moonlight is like the look of tenderness of a mother who could care for their feelings. The Mid-Autumn Festival moon in Taiwan folk culture is so warm, exquisite, and rich in human appeal. As the Taiwanese song sings, "The moon in the sky cares for us just like our mother does beside the bed..." Almost every Taiwanese will receive mother's exhortations in childhood that no one can use their fingers to point at the Mid - Autumn Festival Moon, for this behavior means you are showing disrespect to the "Mother Moon", and if so, the moon will cut off your fingers or ears when you fall asleep. People need to set up the table in their courtyards or on the balconies where the moonlight can shine into, and put all kinds of mooncakes and fruits on it to worship the "Mother Moon", showing the gratitude to the moon for her contribution to us and being immersed in the auspicious light by the "Mother Moon" at the Mid-Autumn Festival night.

Now, the custom of sacrificing the moon with mooncakes

Crisp crust mooncakes in Taiwan

071

and appreciating the moon by eating mooncakes of Taiwanese people is mainly brought by northern Chinese immigrants after 1949. Before that, they didn't have the habit of eating mooncakes and the sacrificing objects of the Mid-Autumn Festival were not the moon or Chang'e (the goddess of the moon), but the Land God. The festival ritual foods are diverse in Taiwan, as long as the foods that are used to sacrifice the Land God are round, which stands for the perfection and good harvest. For example, the people in Yilan County usually eat "rapeseed cake", and the sweet potato pie, even the patty, pancakes, flaky pastry and many other foods, which are the favorite of the people from the southern Taiwan.

The Land God is the patron saint of people, and the sacrifices to the Land God dated from the human beings' worship of the land, which is mainly to pray for a fruitful harvest and human reproduction. So now people in the rural area of Taiwan still choose to buy offerings and fruits to worship the Land God when the Mid-Autumn Festival comes. Besides rituals, people also get used to inserting the "crutches of the Land God" in the field, that is, to clamp the Land God portraits with bamboo, inserting it in the farmland. In the belief of all kinds of gods, the level of the Land God is relatively low, leading him to closer to the human, resulting in people turning to him for praying for good harvest, prosperity, even the medical treatment, promotion and transfer to another school. It is known as "the fields filled with the Land God", because you'll find a large number of the Land Gods in the southern Taiwan. Plus, the farmers in Tainan area are habituated to worshiping the Tree Lord for the lush forests.

In addition to mooncakes, grapefruit is a kind of fruit with Mid-Autumn Festival features in Taiwan.

And in Chinese, "You (Zi)", the pronunciation of grapefruit is a homophone for the word for blessing. "You Zi" represents the good will for the shelter of Luna. The Mid-Autumn Festival is in the season for grapefruit. Eating grapefruit can help people digest after having too much greasy food during the festival. In Taiwan, the peel will be stripped into the shape of petals, which can make a hat for children after finishing the grapefruit. Taiwanese are used to hosting some activities of peeling and eating the grapefruit to add more joyful atmosphere to the festival. Furthermore, some ingenious people carve arts with grapefruit for appreciation and decoration. In addition, people who reside in a place far from home(means "You Zi" in Chinese) usually return home on that day, while the villagers will prepare a "grapefruit feast" ("You Zi" homophonic) to welcome them. During the grapefruit feast, people have so much fun by lighting up the lantern, arranging the bowl, drinking the tea, and eating some candies. All of these are made with grapefruit.

The fashion among Taiwanese right now is to eat "barbecue"

The boat made of grapefruit peel, the childhood memory of
many Chinese people

on the Mid-Autumn Festival with the changing custom of the times. The convenience stores, hardware stores and supermarkets in Taiwan start to sell barbecue utensils one month before the Mid-Autumn Festival. And almost all the supermarkets and markets were selling barbecue ingredients, including barbecue sauce, and so on one week before that day. At the Mid-Autumn Festival night, people barbecue in parks, scenic spots, school playground, by the riverside and even on both sides of the street and the roof of the building apartments, causing thousands of households and the streets filled with charcoal barbecue fragrance.

It is said that the tradition of eating barbecue on the Mid-Autumn Day is traced to the mid 1980s. Although the government has been pushing for energy saving and carbon reduction in recent years, the barbecue activity is still a very popular part of the Mid-Autumn Festival in Taiwan, and many communities even block the streets for barbecue. The Mid-Autumn Festival

"Group barbecue", a feature of the Mid-Autumn Festival in Taiwan

is an opportunity for the exchange of emotions between neighbors, and family members can deepen affections through ingredient preparation, fire making and barbecue. For the younger generation, the mooncake is a kind of food with a lot of oil and sugar, while the barbecue is even healthier than it and just eating mooncakes and grapefruit is too monotonous. Some experts suggest a "vegetarian barbecue", which requires more vegetables and hand-making sauces and so on. Some businesses introduce the "infrared barbecue grill" to reduce the traditional charcoal fumes. What's more, some roast meat shops even add fruits into the dishes, wrapping the sliced grapefruit and pear in filet, which are delicious and free of greasy. This becomes a new way to eat barbecue at the Mid-Autumn Festival in Taiwan.

"Eat duck meat in the middle of July , and eat taro in the middle of August" is a Taiwanese folk festival food saying, meaning that the taro tastes the best during the Mid-Autumn Festival since it's crisp and sweet-scented at this season. During the festival, almost every household buy taro to make deep-fried taro cake or steamed taro cake, boil rice with taro, cook taro soup, mush the taro, and fry taro balls etc, which can

Barbecue in Taiwan

make a meal with a variety of taro food. "Yu", the pronunciation of taro sounds like "surplus" in Chinese, so it is considered as "abundance" and it's a good sign of harvest. Taiwan is abounded with the famous "Pinang-taro", people have special feelings for taro, and personify taro into the mother taro, son taro, and grandson taro, as a symbol of affection. Taiwanese cannot say they are celebrating the Mid-Autumn Festival without taros. The Yami even like it more. If there is a new boat launching into the water during the Mid-Autumn Festival, it is necessary to put their homegrown taros into the new boat for "taro" has the same pronunciation with "fish" in Chinese, and then people move out the taros from the warehouse the day after the ribbon-cutting ceremony, then give away to friends and neighbors to take this as a good way to meet the harvest.

The activities of the Mid-Autumn Festival in Taiwan are rich and diverse, of which "the mooncake gambling" is a very important traditional Mid-Autumn Festival folk game. According to legend, the custom of mooncake gambling dates back to more than 350 years ago, invented by Zheng Chenggong (1624—1662), the general of the Ming Dynasty, stationing his army in Xiamen. The game can help to relieve homesickness and bolster morale among the troops. Later, the game spread to Taiwan.

The gambling game has six ranks of awards, which are named as the winners in ancient imperial examinations, and has 63 different sized mooncakes as prizes. From the lowest to the highest, the titles of six ranks are Xiucai (the one who passed the examination at the county level), Juren (a successful candidate at the provincial level), Jinshi (a successful candidate in the highest imperial examination), Bangyan, Tanhua and Zhuangyuan (respectively the number three to number one winners in the imperial examination at the presence of the emperor).The numbers of mooncakes are 32, 16, 8, 4, 2 and 1, respectively. Game players throw six dices by turns. Different points and colors they rolled decided a relevant "title" and the type of mooncakes.

Qian Qi, the commissioner in the period of Emperor Qianlong of the Qing Dynasty, has a description about the mooncake gambling in his *ZhuZhi poem*(occasional poems in the classical style devoted to local topics), "Frosty light in the clear sky at a silent night, someone seek to get drunk around the east of Guitang. Grind the ink and flourish the brush to write a 'Yuan' (a character stands for Number One Scholar), roll the dice to win the mooncake betting." This is even stated in the *Taiwan Government Records* in the Qing Dynasty, "In the evening, scholars attend the banquet to enjoy the glorious full moon, making the mooncakes together, writing a 'Yuan' with vermilion ink, rolling dices to get the mooncakes, blessing for getting the Number One Scholar in the examination(imperial examination held in autumn)." The mooncake gambling has been prevailing over the past three hundred years, adding a festive atmosphere for people.

In addition, the local operas, riddle contests and other activities also embellish the Mid-Autumn Festival night. Lin Zaifu, a well-known scholar in Taiwan wrote in his book *The Minnan People*, "After moving to Taiwan region, except for the sacrifice and appreciation of the moon, the Minnan people also thank the god by acting." Actually, the riddle contest on the Mid-Autumn Day is more popular than the acting in Taiwan. The weather is very pleasant during the time—not too cold or too hot, which is suitable to hold a riddle contest outdoors. The Mid-Autumn Festival is the second reunion festival after the Lantern Festival. There are a lot of riddles related to reunion and nostalgia in the riddle contest in Taiwan, such as:

"Lowering their heads and thinking of home." (A Southern Fujian Dialect song) Answer: *A Gloomy Moonlit Night;*

"Sewing threads in my kind mother's hand." (Two names of Beijing Opera) Answer: *Da Tang, Sewing;*

"The moon hanging in the sky shines on me."(A famous Taiwanese writer) Answer: Yu Guangzhong;

"Who wouldn't get homesick?"(Two names of traditional Chinese medicine) Answer: Shu Di (Radix rehmanniae preparata), Dang Gui(angelica sinensis)

In addition, the lantern riddles in Taiwan are relatively popular, such as:

"The odourless fountain" (A Taiwanese place name) Answer: Danshui;

"When one drinks water, one can not forget where it comes from."(A Taiwanese place name) Answer: Zhiben.

Most of riddle contests are held in parks, squares and temples in Taiwan, and the form of guessing is similar to the "Beating the drum to guess (Riddle hanging on the lamp for people to guess while people beating the drum.)" in Minnan region, the key ancestral home to Taiwan compatriots.

The custom of playing on the swings has been prevailing in Yilan and Jiayi areas, "A huge swing can hold one person to sway around the beams several times", according to *Zhuluo County Annals* written by Zhou Zhongzhi. That is, making a swing with bamboos as high as hundreds of *chi*(=1/3 metre), and keeping a person sitting on it and swinging back and forth like hanging in midair, which is really fantastic. The people in Su-ao and Jiaoxi areas usually hang a bell in front of the swing, and the person who kicks it down more times wins the game, which is also entertaining.

In addition, there are some special customs related to women:

First, praying for longevity in the Mid-Autumn night: It is said that the later the people stay up at the Mid-Autumn night, the longer they will live, and especially the parents of the young girls can live for long if their daughters stay up late.

Second, praying for finding a perfect man: Tradition has it that an unmarried girl will find a perfect man if she steals some vegetables and scallions from someone's garden at the Mid-Autumn night.

Third, praying for children: Women who have not yet given birth after getting married will get a cute baby in the next year if she steals a melon from other people's garden at the Mid-Autumn night. Besides, the women in Taiwan tend to burn incense in front of the statue of the god in their house at the dark night of the Mid-Autumn Festival. After asking about the things they want to divine, they also need to ask for the direction of door and going out with the incense in hand. When hearing talking and singing, they will start to divine and won't stop until they get the answers approved by the god.

Tips for Tourism

Traveling in Taiwan during the Mid-Autumn Festival

There are a lot of places with strong festive atmosphere of the Mid-Autumn Festival in Taiwan. Not only can you experience the local festival customs deeply, but also can appreciate the beautiful scenery and specialty foods in Taiwan.

Lugang(Dear Harbor), which is under the jurisdiction of Changhua County in Taiwan. It is bordered by Taiwan Strait to the west and named for the large amount of deerskin of output. The Tianhou Temple in Lu-gang occupies an important position among all Mazu temples in Taiwan because the Mazu statue in this temple is the only statue coming from Meizhou, which is known as "the mother of the Mazu statue". A grand ceremony will be held during the Mid-Autumn Festival. And because Lu-gang is a town near the sea, the snacks there are based on seafood. There are some major foods: duck meat soup, xiahou (Austinogebia edulis), oyster omelets, shrimp balls, Coelomactra antiquata and etc. The refreshments here are also very famous, like Fengyan cake, shortening cake, lard rice cake, and so on. There are also the pureed noodles favored by local people.

Daxi Old Street, located in the southeast of Taoyuan county in Tai-wan, is a conjunction zone of Fuxing highland and Taoyuan Tableland, from which the Dahan River flows out of the mountain and turns to the north. Today, the street has been developed to a thriving downtown and forming an "Old Block" with the benefit of river transport in the Qing Dynasty. The archaic roadway and the plain old buildings in the urban area, and the traditional industries hidden in the streets and alleys still wit-ness the prosperity of this city. You may stop your steps here for a while to add some cognitive and perceptive feelings to your journey.

Yangming Mountain (formerly known as Cao Mountain), the famous tourist attraction in Taiwan is in the suburbs of Taipei and at the north-ern tip of Taiwan. It is also a famous scenic spot with green mountains and verdurous valleys, open field, sakura and azalea all over the mountain. There also builds Zhong-Shan Building, Zhongshan Park, Yangmingshan National Park, and Chinese Culture University and so on.

3. The Mid-Autumn Festival in Hong Kong

According to the local customs in Hong Kong, the Mid-Autumn Festival usually lasts for 3 days. People begin with "welcoming the moon" on the 14th day of the 8th lunar month, then "chase the moon" on the 16th day, while the 15th day is the proper Mid-Autumn Day.

The Fire Dragon Dance is the most traditional custom on the Mid-Autumn Festival in Hong Kong. The big event lasts for 3 nights in Dakeng District in Causeway Bay since the 14th night of the 8th lunar month every year. The fire dragon is about 70 meters long with 32 sections made of Hemianthus micranthemoides and longevity joss sticks everywhere. The winding fluctuant fire dragon dances cheerfully with drums sounds under the light along the streets and lanes at the night of the event. It is said that people will pursue good fortune and avoid the disaster, while crops will be in favorable climate after the Fire Dragon Dance. The head and body of the dragon are made of rice stalks with burning joss sticks on it. The young fellows play the dragon with bare arms. After that, residents pull joss sticks out and share them with onlookers. They believe that people who get the joss stick can be lucky, for which a lot of people wait for "luck" in the alley on the Mid-Autumn Festival.

The history of the Fire Dragon Dance in Dakeng has been over a hundred years. According to the legend, there was an evil boa in Dakeng District after the windstorm disaster long time ago. It was hunted by villagers and finally died. Quite unex-

Old mooncakes in Hong Kong

pectedly, the boa disappeared without any trace the next day, after which the pestilence spread in Dakeng District a few days later. The Bodhisattva appeared in a dream of the old folk at that time, and said as long as you played the fire dragon on the Mid-Autumn Festival, the murrain would be driven away. Coincidentally, after they complied with the Bodhisattva's request, it worked unexpectedly. Since then, the Fire Dragon Dance has come down to us.

People in Hong Kong will paint the town red again at the night of the 16th day of the 8th lunar month, which is called "chasing the moon". It is said that this custom is from Zhejiang and Jiangsu Province. According to historical records, people in Ningbo regarded the 16th day as the Mid-Autumn Festival, which was changed by Shi Miyuan in the Song Dynasty and has been reserved up to now. It was also recorded in *Ling Nan Miscellaneous Affair Preface* by Chen Zihou in the Qing Dynasty that busy people in the central Guangdong Province were reunited with the family and friends, drinking, eating, appreciating the moon, which was called "chasing the moon". The Hong Kong government has made the holiday institution in the early years that people should go on duty on the 15th day, while they can have a day off on the 16th day. People come home after the work at about seven or eight o'clock in the evening, without the mood for enjoying the moon, tired and hungry. While people can celebrate the Mid-Autumn Festival on August 16th, relaxed and interested on a day off the next day.

The exhibit of lanterns is a necessary activity on the Mid-Autumn Festival in Hong Kong. The "illumination show", mainly in "green", is sponsored by the Hong Kong Tourism Board. Tourists can visit the "Happy Mid-Autumn Festival" and a huge semilunar illumination made of 7000 discarded plastic bottles, which is approximately 20 meters in diameter. Xiao Jianguo, one of the designers, said that the semilunar colored lantern will rise above the pool, connecting to the reflections on the water, which can appear the image of the wax and wane with the special lighting effects. The skylight is adopted in the inside of the colored lantern, for which visitors can go into it and enjoy the "moons" both in the sky and on the ground.

"Wax burning" was also one of the popular activities at the moonlit night on the Mid-Autumn Festival for previous Hong Kong people. People enjoyed the moon and ate mooncakes in the park, leaving the mooncake boxes empty after the banquet. Children liked burning the wax, using moomcake boxes as vessels. Water was sprinkled over it after the wax melted, which made the fluid wax spark, releasing the high temperature steam. As for children, it was a simple and exciting entertainment, but it is extremely likely to cause scalding. Therefore, Hong Kong government has urged residents to stop burning the wax late last century.

Food for the Mid-Autumn Festival in Hong Kong is quite distinctive, especially the "Piglet Cookie in a Basket". It is a kind of the mooncake that Hong Kong people have eaten and most of them also ate it firstly, with simple flavors and lingering finish.

Many people cannot help associating it with "pig cage", a weird and dreadful old custom (people are put in a "pig cage" and drowned) at the mention of "piglet". In fact, "big cage" is the cylindrical bamboo basket to load and transport piglets originally. "Piglet Cookie in a Basket", as the name suggests, means to put piglet-shaped cookies into a small bamboo basket. It is the traditional food that Cantonese usually send to elders or children on the Mid-Autumn Festival. But it has been very rare in other regions except Hong Kong now.

The "piglet" is made exquisitely and vividly with angular eyes, ears, nose and tail. In Cantonese opinion, the chubby body and naive expression of the "Piglet Cookie in a Basket" means that there is a huge big at home, and this has been popular as a good sign.

The most special point of the "Piglet Cookie in a Basket" is that it is carried by colorful plastic cage or small bamboo basket, decorated with ribbons and gum flowers instead of the box. "Piglet Cookie in a Basket" is children's favorite that they can both eat and play.

"Piglet Cookie in a Basket" is made of flour without any other filling except the sugar, which tastes less than any mooncake on the market, while it is very nice to eat the "Piglet Cookie in a Basket" on the Mid-Autumn Festival in the past on account of lack of materials.

Not all the Hong Kong families could afford it on the Mid-Autumn Festival when the mooncake was a luxury. Therefore, the installment was carried out by vendors, which was called "Mooncake Providing Fair". Workers in mooncake shops would put the small pellets made of the remaining mooncake peel into the brick oven so as to test the temperature and the degree of softness when making mooncakes. This was the prototype of the "Piglet Cookie". After that, small pellets were made into piglet-shaped, and then put into the bamboo basket which was taken as the gift on the "Mooncake Providing Fair" for good luck. The rest was sold to the families on a budget in low price, which made it available to everyone. All the above is the source of the "Piglet Cookie".

People can afford mooncakes now, while you can still see the "Piglet Cookie" when you go to the traditional mooncake shop. Eating the "Piglet Cookie" brings a sense of happiness with no choice when it was too expensive in the past, but a feeling and a memory of the past pure time now. It was a very good memory for Hong Kong people to pour their hearts out to the moon on the Mid-Autumn Festival.

In addition, the "Snowy Mooncake" was also special, which has been sold on the market in Hong Kong in the 1980s. It was named for making a method that was opposite to the traditional method.All the peels of golden traditional mooncakes are made from the syrup, while some materials of the "Snowy Mooncake" are the polished glutinous rice which makes the mooncake white. Especially, "Snowy Mooncake" should be stored in the freezer whether it will be sold or not.

The "Snowy Mooncake", compared with the traditional mooncake, has less grease and sugar, which is much better for health. "Snow" is the main feature of "Snowy Mooncake". It tastes refreshing, which can release people from greasy traditional mooncakes. "Snowy Mooncake" with good quality are shiny like ice, and even can keep soft in the freezer after one night. When you cut them apart, you can find the filling also smooth as a mirror.

Tips for Tourism

Enjoying the Moon on the Mid-Autumn Festival in Hong Kong

Many classic scenic spots for enjoying the moon prevail in Hong Kong on the Mid—Autumn Festival.

Tourists must visit the Victoria Peak where they can overlook the Hong Kong Island in Victoria Harbor and both sides of the Kowloon Peninsula. You can also enjoy the night scene which is called "Pearl of the Orient" there. The observation deck of the Peak Tower is the best choice to admire the moon. It is the perfect option to appreciate the moon on the top of Victoria Peak with family and friends.

The second place is Central, the political and economic center and the upscale commercial and shopping areas of Hong Kong, where you can en—joy the beautiful night. There are fashion and catering brands from differ—ent parts of the country and the world, and constructions with features of times. You can enjoy the life by appreciating the night with moon, tasting gourmet food in the top hotel in Central.

Victoria Park is another spot where all the people can enjoy the moon. It is the biggest park and the most popular place to appreciate the moon in Hong Kong, which is located between the Causeway Road and the Victoria Park Road in Causeway Bay. Tens of thousands of people enjoy the festive lanterns and moon there, which makes the Victoria Park a sea of people. The grand lantern show is held in the Victoria Park every year. Sitting in the park, tourists see the moon, surrounded by the family and friends, which adds warmth to people when the moon rises.

4. The Mid-Autumn Festival in Macao SAR

Macao, one of the important bridges and hubs of the cul-tural exchange between China and the West, has become a city with commercial port where Chinese people and foreign people lived together in the late Qing Dynasty. Chinese traditional culture and festival customs with the absolute superiority of population dominate the social life of Macao even if multi-religious beliefs of Chinese and the West collide and merger with each other. The Mid-Autumn Festival is a significant day in Macao. Many families are pleasant to guess riddles together and take part in celebrating activities in different areas or ad-mire the moon by the river, enjoying fireworks closely at park, seaside, rest area and other places at the night.

The cake shops at Xinma Road tried their best to lure

The firework show in Macao(photo by Zhang zhang)

customers with billboards, on which they drew some pictures about historical figures such as "Chang'e flying to the moon", "Wugang chopping the cassia tree", and "the Eight Immortals soaring over the ocean" and UFO and other decorations just a few days before each Mid-Autumn Festival in the 1950s and 1960s of Macao. The doors of cake shops must be colorful and the whole street would be crowded with people after lighting up neon lights at night, for which the shops selling mooncakes attract many customers. Ordinary cake shops can make much money just through the Mid- Autumn Festival.

The celebration of the Mid-Autumn Festival in Macao will continue for 3 days from the night before the day to the next day. The night before the Mid-Autumn Festival is called "the Night of Welcoming the Moon", the Mid-Autumn Day is called "the Night of Enjoying the Moon" and the next day is called "the Night of Chasing the Moon" according to the customs of Macao. People can freely take part in activities such as cultural and entertainment performances, games and riddle-guessing held by Civic and Municipal Affairs Bureau (IACM), UGAMM and FAOM at central parks during the Mid-Autumn Festival.

Chinese cultural tradition pays much attention to the family, while the Mid-Autumn Festival is a "big feast" for Macanese to hold home parties, and families begin to prepare from the 25th day of the 7th lunar month. The wealthy will go to wine-shops, tea houses, stores and bakeries to buy some mooncakes, fruits, tea leaves and other food for the festival, while the poor also need to purchase seasonal food by the 12th or 13th day of the 8th lunar month at the latest. Every family will get together to enjoy the moon, and people working outside will come back in the holiday on the 15th day of the 8th month. Then the elder and the young enjoy the harmony of the family. Besides mooncakes, many families usually cook sweet rice balls, and only cook salt ones in winter festival, which means reunion of the family. Also, boiled taros and Shatian pomelos are people's favorite food. A lot of local residents in Macao go to the park or the pool to appreciate the moon, while children will hold the lanterns made of paper or electronic lanterns, enjoying the full moon and reunion of the festival.

People in Macao love smart and clever rabbits deeply, and are associated with them, for which enjoying the rabbit lanterns is also a custom in Macao. For example, Macao returned in the year of rabbit, and the land form of ancient Macao was like the rabbit, so the rabbit is usually regarded as the theme of lanterns on the Mid-Autumn Festival. Variety show for the Mid-Autumn Festival also will be held on Tashi Square. What is more, annual Macao's International Fireworks Display will be the finale during the golden holiday, where talent makers of fireworks from all over the world will set off their best works on the firework display.

Tips for Tourism

Traveling in Macao during the Mid-Autumn Festival

Macao is at its best time to travel during the Mid—Autumn Festival, with the temperate weather, and some short—sleeved suits and long—sleeved suits are indispensable. You should put on light and breathable short—sleeved suit when you go out in the day for the higher temperature and put on the long—sleeved suit at night for the lower temperature.

The most famous Catholic Church in Macao is the church of St. Paul, which is also called "Da San Ba(the Ruins of St. Paul's)" by local people. The church was built in 1637, located at a hill near the Da Ba street, and truly has been witnessing the vicissitudes of history in Macao. The front wall of the church is magnificent, with some exquisite reliefs. A great cross stands on the top and some bronze statues of the pigeons, the sun, the moon, the stars and the Jesus hide in the bottom niche.

You do not need to buy a map in advance when traveling in Macao, there is a tourist reception where you can directly get some map with clear marks, bus routes and other important information of attractions in Macao. You should prepare some Macao patacas and Hong Kong dollars for taking a bus or taxi. Macao is a relatively neat city, which pays much attention to the appearance of the city. One will be fined according to the laws of Macao if littering here.

5. The Overseas Spread of the Mid-Autumn Festival

The Mid-Autumn Festival is not only an important traditional day in China, but in many areas of Asia.

In North Korea, "Zhong Qiujie" (Mid-Autumn Festival) is one of folk festivals that North Koreans celebrate all the time, called as Han Jiayu or Qiu Xi in Korean. In Korean ancient times, Qiu Xi was one of the most important festivals for celebrating harvest in agricultural society. People brought many kinds from food and sake made of new grains with happy Farmer's Music-Dance happily to sacrifice ancestors and tell them about the good news of harvest in front of their tombs.

North Koreans take the Muffin as festival food and give it away, which is half-moon-shaped, made of rice with sweetened bean paste, jujube paste and other ingredients inside of it and named for pine leaf under it while steamed. The offerings of the Mid-Autumn Festival include "Herbal gruel" boiled wth sticky rice, red jujubes, chestnut and sugar which is tasty and similar to the "Babao porridge". In this way, people can show their joy of harvest and bless propitious winds and rains for a bumper grain harvest the next year. It is said that the August 15th in the lunar calendar every year is the most bustling day when almost everyone gets staggering drunk and the street is crowded by people hanging out with the winebottle , which can still be found in the countryside of Korea. While paying a visit to Martyrs Cemetery and monument has formed a new custom with North Koreans characteristic among rural and urban residents, besides tomb-sweeping and the celebration of a rich crop. The Kumsusan Memorial Palace and Da Chengshan Martyrs' Cemetery are put on people's travel list in Pyongyang,the capital of North Korea since the former chairman Kim Il Sung's remains lay there ,while some important people who made a great contribution to anti-Japanese sentiment and revolution launched by Kim Il Sung are buried in the later tomb.

North Koreans have had folk sports competition including

wrestle, springboard, swing and so on in the Dragon Boat Festival or the Mid-Autumn Festival since ancient time. Because the country's top leader ordered to strengthen and promote the national traditions, some sports event used for self-amusement have gradually developed, for example, the Big Cattle prize (the champion's award is a big cattle.),a national wrestling game among minorities. Several dozens of players, selected from labors across the country, take part in this three-day game. The folk arena at Rungrado located in the centre of the Taedong in Pyongyang is filled with the crowd to see match who sometimes stare at players without breathing, sometimes clapping. A group of women with gray hair make up a cheerleading to beat Tambour and Tambourin heavily during the break time, while the big cattle, weighing 760 kilograms and wearing a ribbon written with champion, is tethered to a tree aside, leisurely swinging its tail.

Family reunion is also significant in "Chuseok (the Mid-Autumn Festival in Korea)". North Koreans will have a day off on Mid –Autumn Festival .Even though some service facilities such as restaurants, department stores and other merchants will not close business on Sunday as usual ,they will put up a"Closed" sign, which makes nobody appear in the business street that is bustling in the day. People will admire the moon by having tug-of-war, wrestling, or sing and dance, while young girls, dressed in colorful festival costumes, get together to play Buren river game(swing) happily.

Each South Korean family will place new grains, fruit wines, muffins, taro soup and a variety of fruits to worship ancestors in the morning of Chuseok. Traditionally, the eldest son inherits legitimacy of his family in South Korea, so brothers will come to the eldest brother's home for sacrificing the ancestor.At the beginning of this sacred ceremony, men need to stand respectfully in front of the table and the eldest son should open the door which means to invite forefathers to come in, then he returns to the desk to burn incense, present flowers and wines and lead family members to kowtow. The officiant is introducing the glory of their ancestors to families when forefathers are having sacrificial offerings. After that, he will ask ancestors whether they have done or not. If yes, families will follow their officiant to make a kowtow to ancestors and then escort them. Adults will drink libate and then have reunion breakfast after the ceremony is finished.

Muffins in South Korea

Besides offering sacrifices to them, the custom of visiting ancestors' graves prevails the one or two days before Qiuxi, while now usually on the day. Sweeping the tomb is called Shang shan since the forefathers' tomb of South Korean are usually seated on hills. Shang shan on Qiu Xi is the most significant event each year, even if huge things happen, you can't delay the activity of Shang shan.

There is a saying on Qiu Xi in South Korea that if a girl can make muffin well, she will marry a great man, which lets girls in South Korea work hard to learn how to make muffins for a happy marriage. Chinese must have mooncakes on the Mid-Autumn Festival, while Korean eat muffins, which expresses more about their persistence on traditional culture than tasting.

Yuejian Gnocchi in Japan

Mid-Autumn festival is also important in Japan, named as "LiMing Moon" in Japanese officially, also called "DouMing Moon" or "YuMing Moon". "LiMing Moon" has seven days that are respectively DaiXiao (the Lunar August 14th),the 15th night(the Lunar August 15th),the 16th night(the Lunar August 16th), LiDai Moon(the Lunar August 17th),JuDai Moon(the Lunar August 18th),QinDai Moon(the Lunar August 19th)and the 23rd night(the Lunar August 23rd).

Japanese people put Miscanthus, lespedeza, Patrinia scabiosaelia fisch and other fall grasses into a bottle and place fruits and sticky rice cake at the 15th night. The moon in this day is viewed as "DouMing Moon" in Japan, for which it is time to reap soybean and wish for good harvest. Only on this day, the owner will allow the other people to steal Yushu (a special taro in Japan) and think it is a great thing. Fearing nothing, many children take neighbors' offerings by using a bamboo stick with a nail.

Admiring the moon can also be found in Japan where it is named as "Yuejian". People hold the feast, enjoying the moon, which are called "Admiring the moon feast" after the custom spreading from China to Japan over 1000 years ago. Rice gnocchi, made of ground rice and without stuffing in it, is termed "Yuejian"or "Baiyu gnocchi" by Japanese people, which is different from the mooncakes of Chinese people in Mid–Autumn Festival while seeing the moon. To be honest, rice dumplings are more like the moon than the mooncakes. Japanese people need to prepare several reeds and a rabbit besides "Baiyu gnocchi" to sacrifice the moon.

Japanese people will hold many kinds of activities in harvest season to show their thanks to the nature. Although Japan uses solar calendar instead of lunar calendar after Meiji Restoration, Japan still reserve the custom of the moon appreciation in Mid –Autumn Festival nowadays everywhere, for example, the moon-enjoying party will be hosted in some temples or shrines.

Children play the leading role in Mid-Autumn Festival in Vietnam, which is different from that in China. "Mooncakes Fights" and "Toys Fights" run by businesses make festal atmosphere stronger in everywhere of Vietnam as the Mid-Autumn Festival comes. Children are thrilled with the coming of festival when the markets will be filled with all kinds of mooncakes, various festival lanterns and colorful toys.

Children can listen to a story about Gui and Carp at that night. Gui is a guy who often tells lies. He got a magic banyan tree from an old man by trick one day. The old man told Gui that this banyan tree needs to be watered frequently so that it can grow many branches and leaves which can resurrect someone. In addition, Gui was suggested to remember this banyan tree couldn't be polluted by urine. Don't urinate towards the banyan tree. If people place it on the left side of yard, people should urinate towards the west. Or this banyan tree is going to fly to the sky. A Gui said some notes to his wife who was asked to water the tree every day after he took it home. His wife found that she forgot to water the tree one day when Gui wooded uphill. For fear of the blame, she hurried to pee under the tree resourcefully before his husband came in. Suddenly, this banyan tree flew to the sky with its roots. He and hatchet were taken to the moon for he wanted to hook the powerful rising tree with his axe at the moment he entered the door. People can see Gui under the banyan tree in the Moon Palace at every night of full moon since this legend came into being.

Then let's talk about carps. It is said that Bao Zheng (an upright official known for his stressing the diginity of law) threatened a carp which harmed people after it grew into a person with a lantern like a carp made of paper for saving human beings .Children will have an outing with that lantern at the night of the Mid-Autumn Festival, which also means "jumping the dragon gate" (it means good winning and achieving the dreams) in the future.

A lantern festival will be hold in Vietnam, in which the winner will be awarded through comparing and assessing their design of lanterns on the Mid-Autumn Festival each year. In addition, people in some places in Vietnam often perform lion dance at the night of the 14th and 15th day of the 8th lunar month. The local families will prepare mooncakes, fruits and other kinds of desserts in the balcony, the yard of their house or in the field .They admire the moon as tasting delicious mooncakes, while children hold many types of lantern, frolicking in groups.

The custom of Mid-Autumn Festival has changed with the improving living standard of people in Vietnam. Young people

The Mid-Autumn Festival hasn't the meaning of unity, but it is one of children's festivals in Vietnam

The theme party of lanterns in the Mid-Autumn Festival in Singapore in 2016

tend to have a party with dancing and singing or hang out to see the moon with friends, which can promote understanding and friendship between partners. Thus Mid-Autumn Festival is increasingly popular among the youth since the new meaning is added besides traditional sense of reunion with the change of the time.

Singapore has the vast majority of Chinese people for which they are used to paying much attention to the annual Mid-Autumn Festival. It is the great time to socialize with friends and show thanks and wishes to them by presenting mooncakes to family, friends and business partners mutually. This festival is certainly an admirable chance to attract visitors as Singapore is a tourist city. Many renowned local spots will be decorated when Mid-Autumn Festival comes every year such as Orchard Road, Singapore River, Chinatown and the Chinese Gardens. It is fascinating that red view is filled with the streets when the streetlights come on every night. Chinatown, the traditional settlement of Chinese people, is wonderful not only because of the huge lantern from Nepal, Vietnam and other

The night scene of the Mid-Autumn Festival in Singapore

countries, but more due to the 44 little dragons made of 1364 red lanterns. The imperial garden with the charm of Chinese classical garden in Singapore will be held a dream lantern carnival in grand scale. It is compelling that the lantern festival will show the series of Disney's lanterns which people like and the huge Temple of Heaven's and dragon-shaped lanterns.

Traditionally, Singaporean mooncakes are a little different from those of Chinese while merchants contiguously develop new mooncakes from the old as the commercialization of Mid-Autumn Festival in recent years, especially, the famous colored mooncakes. The most popular mooncakes' crusts are coloured, which look like beautiful tropical flowers contending with each other. Traditionally, Mooncakes in Singapore are a little different from those in Chinese while merchants contiguously develop new types of mooncakes from the old types as the commercialization of Mid-Autumn Festival in recent years, especially, the famous colored mooncakes. The most popular mooncakes'

The light festival at Chinatown of Singapore in the Mid-Autumn Festival

crusts are coloured, which looks like beautiful tropical flowers contending with each other. Generally speaking, the mooncakes'colour would match their taste, for example, pink mooncakes mostly have taro inside while yellow mooncakes have durian inside which are the most special mooncakes in Singapore.There are durian cakes,bread and durians in freezer besides durian mooncakes. It is the most distinctive in Singapore among all over the Southeast of Asia.

Malaysian Chinese people, accounting for a quarter of the population in Malaysia, attach great importance to the Mid-Autumn Festival. And they have been sticking with the custom of eating mooncakes, enjoying the moon and parading with lanterns from generation to generation, and this festival was designated as Tourism Celebration by government in 2003. Old Malaysian merchants will launch all kinds of mooncakes when the Mid-Autumn Festival is coming. All shopping malls set shoppe for mooncakes in Kuala Lumpur (the capital of Malaysia) and advertisements of mooncakes in newspapers or on televisions are overwhelming all over the city, which makes joyous atmosphere for the Mid-Autumn Festival. Floats carried with "Chang'e" and "seven fairies" is on lively parade when there are many actors and the youth in colorful clothes singing and dancing.

The overseas Chinese in the Philippines think highly of the Mid-Autumn Festival. The two-day celebration for this festival will be held by local Chinese people in China Town of Manila, the capital of Philippine which is filled with bustling atmosphere. Major business streets in areas of ethnic Chinese will be decorated with lanterns and festoons, and streamers hang at the bridges of main intersections and China Town's entrance. A lot of shops will sell many types of mooncakes which are homemade or imported from China. Festival activities attract large audiences such as dragon dance, folk costumes and float parades, which add happy festival mood to the historic China Town.

The Mid-Autumn Festival is named as "Pray the Moon Festival" in Thailand for the influence of Chinese cultures. Each family and its members need to sacrifice the moon at the night of August 15th of the lunar calendar. Thai people say their prayers and bless each other, sitting in front of the big square table where place the statue of kind Guan Yin Bodhisattva of the South China Sea who can give infinite mercy to prayers. Each statue of "Badong Gods" (the eight immortals in Taoism of folklore) on the table is vivid and shows their ability to prayers. There are also many delicious foods such as "Longevity Peaches" (peaches offered as a birthday present) and "mooncakes". It is said that Bodhisattvas and Gods can send blessings to creatures to make the world longevity if the eight celestial beings celebrate the goddess Guanyin's birthday with those peaches when it is the time to pray the moon in Thailand.

The grand lantern show will be held on the day of full moon in August in Burma to celebrate the Hanukkah. All lamps in the earth and the bright moon in the sky light up this country, making everywhere without darkness at the festival night. Taking charge of celebration, the king of Burma will appreciate festival lanterns and give them in charity to people outside the palace, surrounded by guard and officials. There are a lot of lively activities including all-night movies, drama, puppet show, singing and dancing and vegetarian food in pagoda.

Cambodian has a festival to worship the moon on the 15th day of first quarter in December of Buddhist Era as Cambodia believes in Buddhism. It is a happy and bustling morning when Cambodian people begin to prepare offerings including flowers, cassava soup, rice and sugarcane juice. Cambodian people will put these things into tray, and then place it on a big mat in front of the house, waiting the moon to rise up. People will piously worship the moon and pray for blessings when the moon hangs in the sky. Children's mouths are stuffed with flat rice given by the elders until children can't chew, which stands for completeness and a happy and harmonious life after finishing worship. People will go back after gladly tasting delicious food in the end.

The Mid-Autumn Festival is named as "Yuefu festival" by Laotians who will also admiring the moon and young men and women will dance all night on this day.

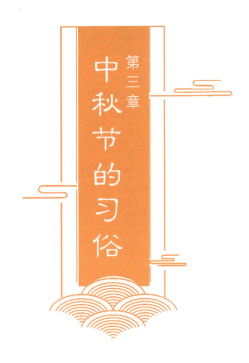

第三章

中秋节的习俗

"丙辰中秋，欢饮达旦，大醉，作此篇，兼怀子由。

明月几时有？把酒问青天。不知天上宫阙，今夕是何年。
我欲乘风归去，又恐琼楼玉宇，高处不胜寒。起舞弄清影，
何似在人间？

转朱阁，低绮户，照无眠。不应有恨，何事长向别时圆？
人有悲欢离合，月有阴晴圆缺，此事古难全。但愿人长久，
千里共婵娟。"

宋代著名词人苏轼的这首《水调歌头》创作于中秋之夜，
作品生动抒发了词人在中秋夜的欢愉中对家人略带感伤的思
念与祝福，在中国家喻户晓。中秋节的确立时间虽然最晚，
但其习俗大部分都延续下来，赏月拜月、庙会灯会、节日的
特定饮食等内容，也是现代人遵行的习俗。

一、
祭月、拜月、赏月

　　中国古代帝王有春天祭日，秋天祭月的礼仪制度。商代时人们将日月分别称为东母与西母。周代依据日月的时间属性行朝日夕月的祭礼，《礼记》记载："故作大事必顺天时，为朝夕必放（仿）日月。"这种朝日夕月的祭礼，据唐代孔颖达解释：春分这一天的早上在东门外祭日，秋分这一天的晚上在西门外祭月。因为秋分时节太阳几乎直射月亮朝向地球的那一面，所以月亮看起来又大又圆。后人有谚语说："祭日祭月不宜迟，仲春仲秋刚适合。"周人的祭祀方式是："祭日于坛，祭月于坎。"以坛和坎两种物象作为日月的象征：坛，突出在地面之上，光明；坎，凹陷与地表之下，幽静。祭祀的时候主要供奉的是猪牛羊等牺牲和玉帛之类的物品。秦汉时期，日月祭祀仍然是皇家礼制。秦雍都建有日月祠，山东有日主祠、月主祠。汉武帝时，用大牛来祭祀太阳，用猪、羊、小牛来祭祀月亮。此后，北魏、隋唐一直到明清，历代都有祭月的礼仪。北京的"月坛"就是明朝嘉靖年间为皇家举行祭月仪式专门修造的。

　　皇家的祭月礼仪，到民间则演化为带有祭祀意味的拜月仪式。民间百姓将月亮神称为"月神""月姑""月宫娘娘""太阴月光神"，或称月神为"嫦娥"，因此也有一系列的拜月活动。全国各地至今遗存有许多"拜月坛""拜月亭""望月楼"等古迹。

《燕京岁时记》记载了明代北京民间中秋拜月的景象：

"京师谓神像为神马儿，不敢斥言神也。月光马者，以纸为之，上绘太阳星君，如菩萨像，下绘月宫，及捣药之玉兔，人立而执杵，藻彩精致，金碧辉煌，市肆间多卖之者长七八尺，短者二三尺，顶有二旗，作红绿色，或黄色，向月而供之，焚香行礼祭毕，与千张、元宝等一并焚之。"

意思是说，北京人将画着神像的纸称为"神马"，在祭拜仪式的最后要焚烧掉，就如同用"马"将"神"送走，所以称之为"神马"。有专门为中秋节拜月仪式使用的神马，叫"月光马"，上面画着月亮神的样子，很像是佛教中菩萨的形象，下面画有月神居住的宫殿，旁边有一只兔子像人一样拿着杵站立着正在捣药。画面上颜色丰富，五彩斑斓的。画像纸大的有七八尺长的，小的有二三尺。画像纸的顶端插着红绿色或者黄色的旗子。在中秋节的晚上，当圆圆的月亮

○ 中秋节的晚上皓月当空，北京故宫角楼是赏月好地方

105

升上天空时，人们把画像纸对着月亮摆放在供桌上，画像纸前面供奉有新鲜的蔬菜和水果，还一定要有月饼。贡品前面摆放有香炉，人们焚香行礼。行礼完毕，将画像纸与千张纸（一种有香味可药用的叶子）、纸制作的元宝等一起焚烧掉，将月神送走。清代北京拜月有了些微变化，月光神马由道观寺庙赠送，题名"月府素曜太阴星君"。

拜月的方式很多，或供月光神马，或者向月跪拜，还有用木头雕刻出月姑形象的，但都把神像供在或挂在月出的方向，设供案摆供品。拜月后，烧掉月光神马，撤供。拜月的人们可以分食享用供品。

供品的种类有很多，各地方不尽相同，但大都是秋天当季新鲜的果蔬，北方多供梨、苹果、葡萄、毛豆、鸡冠花、西瓜。南方则多供柚子、芋头、香蕉、柿子、菱角、花生、藕等。

宋代以前，拜月活动男女都参加。宋代都城的中秋之夜，全城的居民百姓，无论贫富，从能走的孩童至十二三岁的少年都要穿上成人的服饰，登楼或者在庭院中焚香拜月，各有祈求。《新编醉翁谈录》记载人们"登楼或中庭焚香拜月，各有所期：'男则愿早步蟾宫，高攀仙桂。……女则愿貌似嫦娥，圆如皓月。'"男孩期望月神保佑能够早日科举成名，加官晋爵。女孩则祈求有美丽的容貌，获得美满的婚姻。明清以后，祭月风俗发生重大变化，男子拜月减少，月亮逐渐成为专门的女性崇拜对象，北京有谚语云："男不拜月，女不祭灶。"一般来说，男子不参与拜月活动，但是也有些地方例外，男子也可以拜月神。拜月也有一定的次序。当月亮升起来后，烧头香，妇女先拜，儿童次拜。而老年妇女在拜月时，嘴里还经常念道："八月十五月正圆，西瓜月饼敬老天，敬得老天心欢喜，一年四季保平安。"

一般说来，中秋有无月亮，甚至下雨，都是可以拜月的。凡是月光能照射的地方都是可以举行拜月仪式的地方。如遇阴天，也可以向月亮所在的方位摆放祭桌。需要使用的物品一般有：1.祭桌或祭几一张，普通的小桌即可。2.莫席若干条，普通的草席即可。用于拜月行礼，上面可以加上软垫。3.香炉一个，普通的小型香炉即可，香若干。4.盘、碟、碗、盏等盛器若干。5.红烛两根，照明、烘托气氛及点香用。6.普通的酒一瓶，酒杯三个。7.供品：月饼、野味、糯米圆饼、瓜果、毛豆、鸡冠花等当季的新鲜食物。

拜月的时间一般是夜晚月亮出现在天空时，即可以实行拜月礼仪。仪式参与人员有一名主祭、一名赞礼、若干执事，其他人均为从祭。一般来说由年长的女性长辈或家庭主妇担任主祭。集体拜月时，也从女性中选定主祭。拜月的礼仪服装要求相对宽松，不必须穿着专门的礼仪正装。穿适合秋季的日常服装就可以。

拜月前，需沐浴更衣，以示对月神的诚敬。拜月时，先要对着月亮诵读表达诚敬神灵的祝文。拜月的祝文，一般精短优美，四言、五言、七言等传统诗歌形式均可。祝文应用毛笔，工整地誊写在宣纸上。

拜月时一般使用的是汉族的礼仪行法：首先，以传统的"经坐"方式坐在席子上。所谓"经坐"是将膝盖并紧，臀部坐在脚跟上，脚背贴地，双手放在膝盖上，目视前方。对于"胡坐"（非汉族的坐姿），道理一样：端正，两腿不得叉开，双手放在膝盖上，双手可以握拳，冲前方，也可收拢抱在腹部。其次，拜月时不是站立鞠躬，也不是双手合十，而是行汉族正规的"拜礼"：直立，举手放在额头上，姿势如同揖礼，鞠躬九十度，然后直身，同时手随着再次齐眉，然后双膝同时着地，缓缓下拜，手掌着地，额头贴手掌上。这叫"拜礼"。随后直起上身，同时手随着齐眉，这个动作叫作"兴"。然后根据礼节，平身或再拜。所谓"平身"，是指两手齐眉，起身，直立后手放下。"再拜"是连续行两次拜，即"拜—兴—拜—兴—平身"。

拜月的具体仪式程序如下：

1. 沐浴，穿上干净整洁的衣服。

2. 月亮出现在空中后，向月亮的方向安放好祭桌，摆放好祭品，点燃红烛，铺设好席子。

3. 参祭者正坐于祭者席上。执事、赞礼就位。

4. 赞礼唱："祭月"。主祭出位，到奠席前，跪于席上。

5. 赞礼唱："三上香"。执事递上三支香，主祭在蜡烛上点燃，向月神鞠躬，再将香插于香炉中。如此三次。赞礼唱："三祭酒"。执事斟满酒杯，递给主祭，主祭将酒洒在席前的地上，再将酒爵放到祭桌上。如此三次。

6. 读祝文。执事递上赞美月亮的祝文，主祭借月光与烛光，朝向月亮大声诵读。

7. 焚祝文及神像纸：主祭将祝文和神像纸放到席前小盆中，焚烧。

8. 赞礼唱："拜月"。参与拜月的人们按照"拜—兴—拜—兴—平身"的次序进行拜月。主祭及参祭者一起向月神行"再拜"之礼，即拜两次。

○上海"中秋月浦江情"拜月活动

9. 赞礼唱："从献"。主祭离开奠席，参祭者按照长幼之序依次到奠席前，跪，上香（拿三支或一支），默默祈祷心中所愿，然后向月神行拜礼一次。直至所有参祭者拜完。

10. 赞礼唱："礼成"。

至此，中秋拜月仪式就完成了。

汉代已经开始有赏月的风俗，传说汉武帝曾建"俯月台"用来赏月。台下穿池，以映现登台赏月的妃嫔宫娥。每当赏月时，影入池中，似仙人泛舟，笑弄明月。自隋唐开始，随着天文知识的丰富和时代文化的进步，人们对月亮有了更多理性的认识，对月夜的赏玩成分加强。特别是唐代人精神浪漫，喜爱亲近自然，人们将月亮视为可以观赏的美丽景观。宋代中秋节正式确立，都市繁荣的世俗生活使中秋节的内容中增加了更大比重的赏月活动。拜月仪式和赏月活动紧密联系在了一起。

《开元天宝遗事》记载唐玄宗与杨贵妃中秋赏月之事：秋光溶溶，桂花香浓，佳节良宵，花好月圆，唐玄宗与杨贵妃两情缱绻，沉醉于月圆人双的幸福之中，唯恐明月西沉，于是下令在太液池西岸另建一百尺高台，名为"赏月台"。《逸史》记载，唐天宝初年，道士罗公远在中秋夜陪伴唐玄宗在宫中赏月，罗公远对皇帝说："您愿意跟随我到月宫中游玩一番吗？"说着，取出他的手杖向空中一掷，手杖在空中变成一座银白色的大桥，罗公远邀请皇帝登桥。唐玄宗与罗公远在桥上走了大约有几十里路，忽然发现来到了一座大城池下，整个城精光夺目，寒气逼人。罗公远向皇帝介绍说，这就是月宫。只见数百名月宫中的仙女，穿着白色的丝绸服装，在庭院中翩翩起舞。唐玄宗问罗公远："这是什么乐曲，如此动听？"罗公远回答说："这叫《霓裳羽衣曲》。"皇帝偷偷地将曲谱记住，同罗公远返回，回来的路上，唐玄宗回头看去，银色的大桥随着步子的移动逐渐消失了。

109

回到人间后，皇帝即找来宫廷的乐官，将曲子记录下来，命名为《霓裳羽衣曲》。唐玄宗曾游月宫的故事流传很广。

宋代宫廷中秋节赏月的风俗更盛。周密《癸辛杂识》记载，宋高宗时，德寿宫中特建一"赏月桥"，是由吴麟所进献的阶石材料筑成的，莹洁如玉，而供皇帝使用的御几、御榻、酒具等都是用水晶制成的。中秋节赏月时，宫女小童与教坊乐工分列水的南北，丝竹交响，清音悦耳，仅吹笛者就有200人之多。而宋代民间的赏月也很热闹。在北宋都城东京，中秋节前各个酒店就开始出售新酿的美酒，为人们能够在中秋节这一天畅饮欢度。孟元老《东京梦华录》记载："中秋夜，贵家结饰台榭，民间争占酒楼玩月。……弦重鼎沸，近内延居民，深夜逢闻笙竽之声，宛如云外。间里儿童，连宵婚戏；夜市骈阗，至于通晓。"描述了八月十五这一天，有钱的富贵人家会将自家的亭台楼阁装饰一新，在楼上玩赏月色。而普通的百姓则会争相抢占酒楼的高层观赏月亮。

南宋时期杭州的中秋夜更是热闹，吴自牧《梦粱录》："此际金风荐爽，玉露生凉，丹桂香飘，银蟾光满。王孙公子，富家巨室，莫不登危楼，临轩玩月，或开广榭，玳筵罗列，琴瑟铿锵，酌酒高歌，以卜竟夕之欢。至如铺席之家，亦登小小月台，安排家宴，团圆子女，以酬佳节。虽陋巷贫篓之人，解衣市酒，勉强迎欢，不肯虚度。此夜天街卖买，直至五鼓，玩月游人，婆娑于市，至晓不绝。"在月亮最明亮的时候，王孙公子、富家巨室，没有人不登上高高的楼阁，凭栏赏月，饮酒高歌，而中小商户也登上小小的月台，阖家欢聚。宋代的中秋夜是不眠之夜，主管治安的官员取消了例行的宵禁，夜市通宵营业，玩月的游人络绎不绝，直到天明。

蒙古族本无中秋节俗，入主中原建立元朝后，接受了汉族的风俗，也过中秋节。

从宋代直到明清，民间的赏月活动规模越来越盛大。特别是在江南的苏杭地区，杭州西湖的苏堤上，人们"联袂踏歌，无异白日"。

文中描绘了虎邱地区中秋节时的景象：官宦士人、大家闺秀、歌舞表演艺人、市井闲人、无业游民等各种职业身份的人，都会在八月十五这一天的夜晚出门赏月游玩。从生公台、千人石、鹤涧，到剑池、申文定祠、试剑石等到处都是赏月的游人。当月亮升上天空的时候，虎邱上百十几处会演奏音乐，鼓声擂动、锣声阵阵，人们互相之间的说话声都听不见了。从晚上八点左右开始，以鼓和铙钹为乐器的乐曲渐渐消歇，而管弦乐曲和人们的歌唱又开始了。到了深夜十点左右，人们纷纷来到游船上饮宴、听歌、嬉戏。游船上会有各种歌舞和杂耍表演。直到凌晨，还有人伴着渐渐消退的月光听着音乐，直到天明。

据记载，江苏吴中一带在中秋月夜还有"走月亮"的习俗："秋高气爽，明月高悬，市面店铺，亦多张灯烛，以助月色，借为庆赏中秋。故士女三五成群，游行街市，明月灯光之下，极一时之热闹也。店铺中咸供小财神一座，并置楼台、几案、乐器及一切杂物，以资点缀，式样精巧，颇有兴趣。故一般步月者，咸注足而视，拥挤异常也。……中秋夜，妇女盛妆出游，互相往还，或随喜尼庵，鸡声喔喔，犹婆娑月下，谓之走月亮。"

在天气凉爽舒适的秋天，明亮的月亮高高挂在天上，很多商家店铺也挂出很多灯笼，点燃许多的蜡烛，和月光相呼应。人们三三两两在街市上游逛，特别的热闹。而女人们会打扮的格外美丽动人，互相走访，有时还会到寺庙庵堂施舍，她们在月色下尽情游玩，直到天明，这就被称为"走月亮"。

而对于文人来说，中秋夜最能引发诗情与画意，唐宋以来许多诗人的名篇中都有咏月的诗句，其中最为有名的诗歌要数唐代诗人张若虚的《春江花月夜》了，这首诗被誉为"孤篇横绝"的千古绝唱，没有任何一首吟咏月色的诗词能够比得上它了：

春江潮水连海平，海上明月共潮生。滟滟随波千万里，何处春江无月明。江流宛转绕芳甸，月照花林皆似霰。空里流霜不觉飞，汀上白沙看不见。江天一色无纤尘，皎皎空中孤月轮。江畔何人初见月？江月何年初照人？人生代代无穷已，江月年年望相似。不知江月待何人，但见长江送流水。白云一片去悠悠，青枫浦上不胜愁。谁家今夜扁舟子？何处相思明月楼？可怜楼上月徘徊，应照离人妆镜台。玉户帘中卷不去，捣衣砧上拂还来。此时相望不相闻，愿逐月华流照君。鸿雁长飞光不度，鱼龙潜跃水成文。昨夜闲潭梦落花，可怜春半不还家。江水流春去欲尽，江潭落月复西斜。斜月沉沉藏海雾，碣石潇湘无限路。不知乘月几人归，落月摇情满江树。

○《春江花月夜》诗文

如今，伴着八月十五的皎洁月色，现代人们的赏月游玩活动规模更加盛大丰富了。

除了祭祀月神之外，由于秋报传统的融入，中秋节这一天在人们的信仰当中还是诸神下凡的日子，除月神之外，人们还要对其他很多神灵进行祭祀。

首先是土地神。土地神，又称土地爷、社神。《重修纬书集成·孝经元神契》中载："社者，五土地广博不可遍敖，故封土为社而祀之，以报功也。"土地神祭祀起源于对自然大地的崇拜。道教也信仰土地神，称太社神、太稷神、土翁神、土母神等。但在道教的信仰神系中，土地神的地位较低。在汉族民间信仰中对土地神的崇拜极为普遍，是汉族民间

○求签占卜

信仰中的地方保护神，流行于全国各地。旧时凡有人群居住的地方就有祀奉土地神的现象存在。在中国大地上，几乎到处可见石砌的、木建的小小土地庙用以供奉。

土地神的形象大都衣着朴实，平易近人，慈祥可亲，多为须发

全白的老者。一般土地庙中，除塑土地神外，还塑其配偶的像，称为"土地婆"或"土地奶奶"，同受香火供奉，没有特殊职司。

相传土地神出生日为农历二月初二日，而八月十五日为其得道成神之日，因此，祭"土地神"成为中秋节的活动内容之一。《诸罗县志》："中秋祀当境土神，与二月二日同；访秋报也。四境歌吹相闻。为之社戏"。

在民间信仰体系当中，土地神虽然官职不高，但管辖的内容却不少。凡婚丧喜事、天灾人祸、鸡鸣狗盗之事都需要由地方土地神经手，而且土地神一副慈祥老翁的模样，与人较为亲近，所以人们喜欢向他吐露心声，向他祈愿。如《集说诠真》中所说："今之土地祠，几遍城乡镇市，其中塑像，或如鹤发鸡皮之老叟。或如苍髯赤面之武夫……但俱称土地公公。或祈年丰，或祷时雨，供香炷，焚楮帛，纷纷膜拜，必敬必诚。"所以，小小的土地庙往往香火很旺。因为汉族民间相信"县官不如现管""土地不松口，毛狗不敢咬鸡""土产无多，生一物栽培一物；地方不大，住几家保佑几家"。

其次广州一带还有请"篮神"的习俗。"篮神"又名篮姑，民间女神之一，由女人主祭。请篮神时，在屋内选择黑暗的一个角落，置一竹筐，篮上系一椰壳饭匙，以篮为身，以壳为头，套一女人小衣，稍似人形。筐内的椰子壳，作为篮神的替身，前放一个矮凳。两个女子围坐地上，手托篮底，燃香烛于前，妇女唱"请篮歌"："请篮姑，请篮姑，你系佛山人氏女，你系省城人氏娘，家婆严令吞金死，丈夫严令早辞阳。"视该竹篮有无动摇之势：如果降神，竹筐即向矮凳叩头，这时围观的人可向篮神发问，篮神以向矮凳叩头答之，不动则不应。

南海、顺德，特别是西樵一带没成亲或未成年的缫丝女还有供"太阴案"的习俗。女孩子们在中秋节各自做出粉果（传统点心，内有肉、笋、冬菇等），摆放在中秋节的供桌上，用作祭祀祈求。同时作为比较，看谁别出心裁，做得巧妙，色香味美。

迷童子，又叫降仙童，它原与中秋节无关，只不过多在中秋夜举行，可以也算作中秋旧风俗之一。在中秋之夜及以后几天的晚上，选择一个十二三岁的男童，先令其合眼危坐，作法者用烧符一度，让数人手持一大把香火在男童前后摇拂、画圈，大约三十分钟后，男童会喃喃自语，周围的人大叫："师傅到了！"接着再问："师傅你喜欢用刀，抑或用剑？"男童选择一种，说此合意。众人即以器械授予男童，男童手拿器械飞扬起舞，一时间刀剑声铿然。还有一种与"迷童子"相似的巫术活动，叫作"埋虫"。中秋之夜，四个人分不同方向躺在地上，数人围绕他们缓行，口中念念有词，重复念至此四人瞌睡过去，便将其中一人扶起称之师傅，让他耍刀弄枪、打拳舞棒，师傅大都会打得似模似样。演毕后再扶别人，次第表演，醒后不知何因。

请桌神。这个仪式男女均可主持。取一碗，盛满水，然后把一个四脚桌反放在碗上。在桌子四角旁各站一人，他们以左手指轻按桌脚，右手持香圈其桌脚，念词曰："桌神绕绕转，四人绕绕转。"不久，桌子就转动起来，四个人也跟着跑，而且越来越快，他们坚持不住时，可由其他人代替。

在东南沿海地区，居民依靠海洋谋生，相信海潮也为神，过中秋时有观海潮、祭潮神的风俗。《中华全国风俗志·浙江》："八月间，郡人有观潮之举。自八月十一日为始，至十八日最盛。……是日士女云集，上下十余里间，地无寸隙。伺潮上海门，则有汹儿数十，执绿旗，树画伞，踏浪翻淘，腾跃百变，以夸技能。豪民富客争赏财物。其时优人百戏，击球斗扑。盖人但借看潮为名，而随意酣乐，乃其实也。"

中秋之日，还是向神灵祈求子嗣的好时机。《东京梦华录·卷八》

记载："八月秋社……人家妇女皆由外家，晚归，即外公、姨舅，皆以新葫芦儿、枣儿为遗。"因为葫芦多籽，象征多子多孕，所以葫芦是求子的吉祥物。于是在中秋节这一天，长辈们会将当季刚刚收获的葫芦、枣等物品赠送给结婚的晚辈，预示着让他们能够子嗣繁盛。

更普遍的求子方法是中秋送瓜求子，湖南就有此俗。《中华全国风俗志·卷六》记载："中秋晚，衡城有送瓜一事，凡席丰履厚之家，娶妇数年不育者，则亲友举行送瓜。先数日，于菜园中窃冬瓜一个，须令园主不知，以彩色绘成面具，衣服裹于其上若人形，举年长命好者抱之，鸣金放爆，送至其家。年长者置东瓜于床，以被覆之，口中念曰：'种瓜得瓜，种豆得豆。'受瓜者设盛宴款之，若喜事然，妇人得瓜后，即剖食之，俗传此事最验云。"那些结婚多年却没有生育的人家，其亲朋好友会在中秋节举行"送瓜"仪式。瓜，是一个冬瓜，是中秋节之前，在别人家的菜园里偷偷拿的，不能让园主人发现。偷到后，在冬瓜的表面用颜色绘制成面具，用衣服包裹着，如同一个小孩。中秋节那天，选择一个年岁大且生活顺坦的长辈抱着，敲着锣、放着鞭炮，送到该人家，放置在床上，用被子盖好，嘴里还要念叨着："种瓜得瓜，种豆得豆"。接受冬瓜的人家要准备丰盛的宴席来答谢，希望获得子嗣的女子得到冬瓜后，就将其剖开吃掉。民间也常在中秋贴"麒麟送子"等剪纸。《中华全国风俗志·安徽》记载安徽的寿春在"八月十五夜，妇人设瓜果团饼于庭院拜月，小儿执火炬，相与结队走田野，以摘取果豆等物，谓之模模。"这种风俗与各地中秋摸瓜相似，也有求子巫术的含义。

请神祭祀之外，中秋节的夜晚还是举行天气预测的重要日子。

观看八月十五这一天晚上的月亮，可以用来判断明年正月十五日夜晚的天气情况。俗谚有云："八月十五云遮月，来岁元宵雪打灯。"又云："雪打上元灯，云照中秋月。"即如果这一年八月十五日晚上的月亮周围有云，或者云层很厚将月亮遮住，完全看不见月亮，那么在明年正月十五日这一天的晚上就会有雨雪。经验证明，这种联系总是准确的。

而贩油商人常常通过观察中秋夜月亮的光亮程度来预测油价，其理由是月明亮即灯明亮，灯明亮即油充足，日后油价会降。若月暗则油不敷，油价因此会涨。

广州及四乡还有一种颇为流行的占卜，名叫"月光书"。其主要是使用木鱼书的内容进行占卜。木鱼书，是一种广东一带的地方表演曲种。清中期之后在广东十分流行，它纯用粤语弹唱，表演的内容很多，如《客途秋恨》《三娘教子》《蒙正拜灶》等。所谓"月光书"就是在中秋夜通过售卖畅销的木鱼书来占卜吉凶："中秋之夕，玉兔初升，卖木鱼书者咸集于道，大声叫喊：'月光赢、月光赢……'，皆因粤语的'书'与'输'同音，人皆怕输。妇孺多争购木鱼书以卜吉凶。买木鱼书时，只能按顺序抽取，检视其中内容，如买到的是《客途秋恨》，有落魄之兆；如买的是《蒙正拜灶》，则有先难后易之兆。"

○孔明灯

117

还有一种叫"撞口卦"的占卜，中秋月夜，住在横街窄巷的妇女，在自家门口供奉的神前点香，诉明所问之事，随即独行出门，细听街巷议论，据其所谈事实判定吉凶。

此外还有一种在中秋节用孔明灯来占卜的方法，在清朝很流行。

"孔明灯"又叫"天灯"，俗称"许愿灯"，又称"祈天灯"，是一种古老的汉族手工艺品，在古代多做军事用途。相传是由三国时的诸葛亮所发明。诸葛亮曾被围困于平阳，无法派兵出城求救。孔明算准风向，制成会飘浮的纸灯笼，系上求救的讯息，其后果然脱险，于是后世就称这种灯笼为孔明灯。还有另一种传说，相传五代时有一名叫莘七娘的女子，随丈夫在福建打仗时，她曾用竹篾扎成方架，糊上纸，做成大灯，底盘上放置燃烧着的松脂，灯就靠热空气飞上天空，用作军事联络信号。这种松脂灯，在四川被称为"孔明灯"，因为这种灯笼的外形很像诸葛亮戴的帽子，因而得名。

孔明灯一般在元宵节、中秋节等重大节日施放。放灯者视孔明灯飞翔的高度，占卜运程的好坏。

三、
聚会与赏花灯

中秋节又名"团圆节"，与天上的满月相应，地上生活的人们也要团圆。按照习惯礼俗，这一天外出的游子一定要回家团圆，回娘家的媳妇也必须回到夫家。所以，中秋节这一天，是人们聚会的大日子。特别是宋代将其确立为节日以后，中秋节变成了法定假期，人们有了更充足的时间可以举行各种聚会。这种聚会不仅仅是家庭内部的，也是地方上的盛大聚会。

《中华全国风俗志·江苏》记载，黎里县在中秋节有盛大的赛会：

"其有会也，云始于唐朝，载于里志，盖秋日祓除灾邪之意。年届中秋时，必举行赛会。当八月十二日夜阑时即有锣鼓声，盖赛会之预备也。十四、十五始盛，十六则所谓夫人会矣。

其会之仪仗，金鼓旗锣前导，神像随后。每神像之前各有仪仗，大略相似。先监察神，次安乐神，末为广祐王，即城隍也。相传姓李，唐太子也。全会之后，有善男信女凡数百人，老有男女，各手执塔香一柄，尾随于后。有穿红衣插犯条者，有手带铸练者，奇形怪状，不可思议。最可骇者，中有一人，伸其右臂，臂上挂香炉钩入皮肤，不知痛楚。其后有一对挂锣，锣重亦十余斤，不仅提锣而

119

走，且须照例击十三记。提者泰然走数十步，保护者一为烹水于挂处，惨不忍睹。此该曾因事故，许有大愿心者，其遇亦可怜矣。此十四、十五两日赛会之情况。

十六日夜间之会，为夫人会。仪仗执事，布置与前相仿佛。惟出会之主人，则神之夫人也。会过处，店肆或大家恒以纸花送夫人，喜娘即为之插戴。明日取花送大家，谓可压邪。此则夫人会之情形也。

是时市面各店，悬灯结彩，陈设一新，大有花树银花之概。又十三至十六，四日，城隍庙日夜演剧。本镇士女，莫不兴高采烈，齐往庙中观剧。剧台密布，几无立足之地。喧阗数日。"

意思是说，根据黎里县的县志记载，这样中秋节的赛会可以追溯到唐朝，源初举行的意义是为了秋天里祛除灾难和邪恶，每年快到中秋的时候必定会举行这种赛会。农历八月十二日的晚上就能够时时听到锣鼓声了，这是人们在为赛会做准备。赛会在十四日、十五日进入高潮，热闹非常。到了十六日，则是"夫人会"。

赛会由排列整齐的仪仗入场开始，仪仗队的最前面是敲击锣鼓和执打旗帜的人们，后面抬的是神像。每一尊神像之前各自都有仪仗队，形式上大同小异。神像的顺序依次是监察神、安乐神、广祐王（也即是城隍神）。民间传说广祐王姓李，是唐代的一位太子。神像之后则跟随着数百的信仰者，无论男女老少，每人手中都拿着一柄塔香。有的穿着红色的囚服头上插着标写其罪的板条，有的手上戴着铐练，形形色色的人们，让人感到惊讶异常。最吓人的是其中的一个人，他伸着右臂，手臂上挂着一个香炉钩入皮肤。然而，他似乎并不觉得疼痛。身后还带着一对挂锣，锣看起来重十多斤，但是他能够提着锣照常走路，而且边走还边按照惯例击打十三下锣。提锣的人泰然自若地每走数十步，就由旁边保护的人在挂香炉的手臂上浇一点沸水。场景惨不忍睹。估计这是一个因为重大事故而向神灵许下大

多彩中国节

中秋节

心愿的人，他的境遇让人心生怜悯。这大概就是十四、十五日两天赛会的情况。

十六日晚上的聚会被称为"夫人会"。仪仗队伍、参与人员等装扮大约与前几天的相通。只是这是抬出的神像是前几日神灵的配偶夫人。当神像从人们门前经过的时候，无论是店铺还是居户，人们都会将纸做成的美丽花朵奉献给神灵的夫人们，由喜娘为神像插戴。第二天再将纸花取下，分送给大家，以此来辟邪驱凶。这就是夫人会的大致情形。

中秋节到来的时候，各个营业场所都张灯结彩，店内陈设一新。从八月十三到十六日这四天，城隍庙全天演剧。当地的人民都特别高兴，一起到庙中看戏。城隍庙内布满了大大小小的戏台，人山人海异常拥挤，几乎没有立足的空间。人们的欢闹会一连持续多天。

中秋的月亮又大又亮，地上生活的人们也要点燃灯火与月色相呼应，因此，中秋节还是中国的三大灯节之一。

在北宋《武林旧事》中，记载中秋夜节俗，就有将"一点红"

○漂亮彩灯

灯放入江中漂流玩耍的活动。中秋玩花灯，赏花灯，多数集中在江南水乡南方一带，寓意将祝福带去。花灯也是多种多样，如芝麻灯、蛋壳灯、刨花灯、稻草灯、鱼鳞灯、谷壳灯、瓜子灯及鸟兽花树灯等，美轮美奂、精致小巧令人赞叹。

南方还广泛流传着烧瓦子灯，如《中华全国风俗志》卷五记：江西"中秋夜，一般孩子于野外拾瓦片，堆成一圆塔形，有多孔。黄昏时于明月下置木柴塔中烧之。俟瓦片烧红，再泼以煤油，火上加油，霎时四野火红，照耀如昼。直至夜深，无人观看，始行泼息，是名烧瓦子灯"。

广州则有"竖中秋"的习俗，又叫"树中秋"。相传元朝末年，明太祖朱元璋起事，先是由刘伯温卖灵符倡变，众人相约中秋夕竖旗举灯为号。自此之后广州始有了竖旗举灯之习俗。旧时广州的房子多有楼台，中秋之夕，人们会竖旗在楼台、屋顶上，旗多为七星旗，白色底，用红色狗牙镶边，以纸制或布制。七星旗之下，再横担一长方形旗，用艳色绸缎制成，上书"庆贺中秋"四字。另有灯笼，到了夜里，燃烛放内，用绳系在旗杆或竹竿上。有钱人悬灯笼多至数百个，砌成"庆贺中秋"等字，灯笼内多是蜡烛。民国初年开始有人将电灯放在灯笼里，异常光亮。竖起来的旗杆有十几米高，全家大小都聚集在楼台上，聚饮为乐。普通家庭有一条旗杆、两个灯笼，十分欢喜。但穷人既无房屋，又无灯笼。故有粤谚云："八月十五竖中秋，有人快活有人愁。有人楼上吹箫管，有人地下皱眉头。"中秋节的灯笼用竹篾扎成，各家各户可以自己制作，街上也有灯笼售卖，款式多种多样，用五色纸糊成，工艺精美，有果品灯，也有鸟兽灯、鱼虫灯等。中秋之夜，成千上万的市民手提灯笼上街游行，以示庆祝，广州花灯满街，全城灯火，繁星点点，与月同辉。

在广西南宁一带，除了以纸竹扎各式花灯让儿童玩耍外，还有

多彩中国节

中秋节

很朴素的柚子灯、南瓜灯、橘子灯。柚子灯，是将柚子掏空，刻出简单图案，穿上绳子，内点蜡烛即成，光芒淡雅。南瓜灯、橘子灯的制作方法类似。虽然朴素，但制作简易，很受欢迎，有些孩子还把柚子灯漂入池河水中做游戏。户秋灯，是以六个竹篾圆圈扎成灯，外糊白纱纸，内插蜡烛即成。挂于祭月桌旁祭月用，也可给孩子们玩。

旅游小贴士

北京龙潭湖公园灯会

中秋节晚上，中国的各电视台都会举办大型的节日晚会，现代人们习惯于一边观看晚会节目，一边和家人吃着月饼度过中秋节。同时，各省市的大中型公园都会举办隆重的花灯会。

北京的天安门、香山、欢乐谷等很多地方都会举办灯火晚会，赏花灯、猜灯谜、吃月饼，活动内容丰富多彩。此外，龙潭湖公园的灯会也是很知名。

龙潭湖公园位于北京东城区左安门内，是明朝嘉靖年间为烧制城砖挖出的大片洼地而渐次形成的水域。现在的龙潭湖公园是由三个相连的水域组成的景点，南面和东面是护城河，左安门大街穿湖而过。全园面积为120万平方米，是一处碧波荡漾、绿树成荫，以水景为主的园林，突出龙和潭的特点，湖边有龙山、龙字碑林、百龙亭、古典建筑龙吟阁、龙形石雕和龙桥等。中秋之夜，月光与湖水相应，在古香古色的建筑上布满形制新颖的花灯，赏景、玩月相映成趣。

地址：北京市东城区龙潭路8号。

四、
娱乐活动

中秋节有一项儿童的娱乐活动——玩兔爷。

传说月除蟾外，还有兔，又称玉兔、金兔、蟾兔。因此，民间在祭月时，总是与祭兔联系起来，甚至还单独祭兔。

兔爷大多以泥制成，多模型，配耳，施色，有些还描金。兔儿爷一般是用模子翻塑出来的：先把黏土和着纸浆拌匀，填入模子里，

○中秋节习俗——兔儿爷

中
秋
节

模子分成正面和背面两部分。等泥料八九分干时取出来，把前后两半泥像粘在一起，配上俩犄角。泥像全干时，给它身上刷一层胶水，然后再用彩色的颜料描画。大者一米左右，小者仅约十厘米。形象为粉白脸、金鳌，披战袍，左手抱臼，右手拿杵，背插伞或旗帜，底座为虎、鹿、狮子、骆驼或莲花。兔爷一经出现，就成为儿童喜闻乐见的玩具。在北京地区制作精美的兔爷，作为中秋节的吉祥物，也是儿童的玩偶。此外还有兔爷、兔车之戏。

这一风俗大约开始于明代末年，明人纪坤的《花王阁剩稿》："京中秋节多以泥抟兔形，衣冠踞坐如人状，儿女祀而拜之。"到了清代，兔儿爷的功能已由祭月转变为儿童的中秋节玩具。制作也日趋精致，有扮成武将头戴盔甲、身披战袍的、也有背插纸旗或纸伞、或坐或立的。坐则有麒麟虎豹，等等。也有扮成兔首人身之商贩，或是剃头师父，或是缝鞋、卖馄饨、茶汤的，不一而足。"每届中秋，市人之巧者，用黄土抟成蟾兔之像以出售，谓之兔儿爷。"旧时北京东四牌楼一带，常有兔儿爷摊子，专售中秋祭月用的兔儿爷。此外，南纸店，香烛也有出售的。

兔儿爷，经过民间艺人的大胆创造，已经人格化了。它兔首人身，手持玉杵。后来有人仿照戏曲人物，把兔儿爷雕造成金盔金甲的武士，有的骑着狮、象等猛兽，有的骑着孔雀，仙鹤等飞禽。特别是兔儿爷骑虎，虽属怪事，但却是民间艺人的大胆创造。还有一种肘关节和下颌能活动的兔儿爷，俗称"刮打刮打嘴"，更讨人喜欢。一般过了七月十五，兔儿爷摊子就摆出来了。前门五牌楼、后门鼓楼前、西单、东四等处，到处都是兔儿爷摊子，大大小小，高高低低，摆的极为热闹。

还有一种是兔儿奶奶，模仿妇女的时装、神态，梳着当时流行的发髻，跟兔儿爷配成双。还有一种呱嗒嘴的兔儿爷，上唇是活动的，中间系着线，一拽嘴就动，嘴内是空的。有的是两臂上有提线，线一牵，手臂上下移动，像是捣药的样子。另有一种是在某种生活场景中的一群兔儿爷：有一种一尺大小的玩具，是搭成葡萄架的样子，或者是天棚茶座的样子。架子下有小桌子椅子什么的，好些小小白兔子，都寸来高。兔客人进来坐在桌子边，兔小二过来给倒水，兔掌柜的在另一边拨算盘。

旅游小贴士

北京东岳庙

在老北京传统里，中秋和兔儿爷的关系，就像春节和饺子一样。每到中秋，东岳庙里都会按老北京风俗，摆上一座高高的兔儿爷山，供市民祈福。老北京人也有自家请兔儿爷、给亲友送兔儿爷的习惯。东岳庙的兔儿爷山也正成为北京中秋的一景，到东岳庙的兔儿爷山上请兔儿爷也逐渐成为一种习惯。

东岳庙，位于北京市朝阳区朝阳门外大街的北侧，原是道教"正一道"在中国华北地区的第一大丛林。东岳庙规模宏大，气势壮观，装饰精微，构思巧妙，散发出汉民族传统文化的精神、气质、神韵。现在，庙内还建立了北京民俗博物馆。庙内保存了大量各具特色的道教建筑和历代碑刻，对研究中国古代道教以及玄教的历史渊源和发展，都具有重要的参考价值。

地址：北京市朝阳区朝外大街 141 号。

中秋节所在的季节天气一般晴朗舒爽，人们在节日期间有许多游戏。

首先是夜晚赏月、赏莲，划船串月，妇女也栽花、戴花，"愿花常好""愿月常圆"。此时枣树结实，儿童多摘青枣四枚，剥成枣磨玩，俗称"猪排磨"。

其次，是斗蟋蟀。这项活动，无论老少都爱不释手，其中的"九子斗蟋蟀"具有求子之意。养蝈蝈也是秋天的重要活动。

此外还有歌舞，杂技等内容，如广东梅县在中秋节举办山歌节，纪念歌仙刘三妹；海南有一种八月会，人们聚会，唱歌，交换月饼，通宵达旦。

安徽绩溪中秋节有打"中秋炮"："十数儿童，以稻蒿扎成中秋炮、形似发辫，长约五尺，粗盈握，浸于水中数分钟，再拿起向石上打击，如放炮之声，名曰打中秋炮。"

五、
饮食习俗

中秋节的必备食品是"月饼"，没有月饼，则算不上真正的中秋节。它和端午节的粽子、腊八节的腊八粥以及元宵节的元宵灯一样，是应节的食品。

月饼是由一种祭祀供品逐步演化来，具有悠久的历史。据史料记载，早在殷、周时期，江、浙一带就有用来一种纪念太师闻仲边薄心厚的"太师饼"，这种圆饼就是月饼的"始祖"。

○ 各式月饼

汉代张骞出使西域时，引进芝麻、胡桃，为圆饼的制作增添了辅料，这时便出现了以胡桃仁为馅的圆形饼，名曰"胡饼"。

而由"胡饼"更名为"月饼"，民间传说是由于杨贵妃的才情。《开元天宝遗事》记载，唐代天宝初年的一个中秋月夜，唐玄宗和杨贵妃在大明宫的蓬莱池畔赏月，可是蓬莱池畔没有一个望月的最佳之处，皇帝不是很高兴。正巧，侍者献上"胡饼"，玄宗觉得这名字很难听，赏月没什么意思，很是乏味。杨贵妃情急之下，仰望明月，智由心生，随口说出"月饼"这个名字。

北宋皇家中秋节喜欢吃一种"宫饼"，民间俗称为"小饼""月团"。苏东坡有诗云："小饼如嚼月，中有酥和怡"。文献上正式出现"月饼"二字的是《武林旧事》，宋代的文学家周密，在记叙南宋都城临安见闻中首次提到"月饼"之名称。南宋吴自牧《梦粱录》中提到的月饼是菱花形的，和菊花饼、梅花饼等同时存在，并且是"四时皆有，任便索唤，不误主顾"。可见这时吃月饼并不是中秋节的习俗。

秋日食饼的节俗习惯始自汉代。汉代在中秋或立秋之日有敬老、养老的礼仪制度，并且宫廷会赏赐给老人"雄粗饼"。

在中秋节吃月饼，相传始于隋唐。据《洛中见闻》记载，唐僖宗在中秋节吃月饼，味极美，听说新科进士在曲江举行宴会，便命御膳房用红绫包裹月饼赏赐给这些进士们。

而中秋节吃月饼与聚会之意相联系，是源于元末明初的地方反抗。当时，中原广大人民不堪忍受元朝统治阶级的残酷统治，纷纷起义反抗。朱元璋联合各路反抗力量准备起义，但朝廷官兵搜查的十分严密，传递消息十分困难。军师刘伯温便想出一个主意，命令属下把藏有"八月十五夜起义"的纸条藏在月饼的馅心里面，再派人分头传送到各地起义军中，通知他们在八月十五日晚上起义响应。到了起义的那天，各路义军一起响应，起义军如星火燎原。很快，徐达就攻下了元大都，起义成功了。消息传来，朱元璋高兴得连忙传下口谕，在中秋节让全体将士与民同乐，并将当年起兵时以秘密传递信息的"月饼"，作为节令糕点赏赐群臣。此后，"月饼"制作越来越精细，品种更多，大者如圆盘，成为馈赠的佳品。以后中秋节吃月饼的习俗便在民间流传开来。

　　明代关于中秋吃月饼的记叙就很多了，中秋吃月饼作为一种节俗才在民间逐渐流传。当时心灵手巧的饼师，把嫦娥奔月的神话故事作为食品艺术图案印在月饼上，使月饼成为更受人民青睐的中秋佳节的必备食品。田汝成《西湖游览志余》："民间以月饼相邀，取团圆之义。"在中秋节人们制作圆圆的月饼，相互赠送邀约团聚。明代浙江《嘉兴府志》："八月望以百果为大饼，名曰月饼。"沈榜的《宛署杂记》载："士庶家具以是月造面饼相遗，大小不等，呼为月饼。"《酌中志》说："八月，宫中赏秋海棠、玉簪花。自初一日起，即有卖月饼者……至十五日，家家供奉月饼、瓜果……如有剩月饼，乃整收于干燥风凉之处，至岁暮分用之，曰团圆饼也。"月饼成为中秋拜月的必备供品，其制作由家庭自制，慢慢转变为市面出售，种类越来越繁多，工艺也越来越讲究。明末彭蕴章在《幽州土风俗》中写道："月宫饼，制就银蟾紫府影，一双瞻兔满人间。悔煞嫦娥窃药年。奔入广寒归不得，空劳至杵驻丹颜。"

经过元明两代，中秋节吃月饼、馈赠月饼风俗日盛，而且月饼有了"团圆"的象征含义。

清代，中秋吃月饼已成为一种普遍的风俗，且制作技巧越来越高。清代宫廷多在某一院内向东放一架屏风，屏风两侧搁置鸡冠花、毛豆枝、芋头、花生、萝卜、鲜藕。屏风前设一张八仙桌，上置一个特大的月饼，四周缀满糕点和瓜果。祭月完毕，按皇家人口将月饼切作若干块，每人象征性地尝一口，名曰"吃团圆饼"。清宫月饼之大，令人难以想象。像末代皇帝溥仪赏给总管内务大臣绍英的一个月饼，便是"径约二尺许，重约二十斤"。清人袁枚《随园食单》介绍道："酥皮月饼，以松仁、核桃仁、瓜子仁和冰糖、猪油作馅，食之不觉甜而香松柔腻，迥异寻常"。北京的月饼则以前门致美斋所制为第一。《燕京岁时记》："中秋月饼以前门致美斋为京都第一，他处不足食也。呈供月饼到处借有。大者尺余，上绘月宫蟾兔之形。"清代荣陛的《帝京岁时纪胜》："十五祭月，香灯供品之外，则团圆月饼也，雕西瓜为莲瓣，摘萝卜叶做婆罗。"《帝京景物略》记载，中秋节祭月要有一个大号月饼，大的直径可至一尺多，分食这一月饼一定要人人有份。因而分切月饼前要把全家人数点算清楚，外出的、在家的都算在一起，有多少人切多少块，绝对不能少切或多切，而且要切得大小一样。如果家有孕妇，又得多切一份。也有的人家，把祭月的月饼保存到除夕晚上再拿出来分食，名称仍叫作"团圆饼"。围绕中秋拜月、赏月还产生了许多有地方特色的月饼吃法，如江南的"卜状元"：把月饼切成大中小三块，叠在一起，最大的放在下面，为"状元"；中等的放在中间，为"榜眼"；最小的在上面，为"探花"。而后全家人掷骰子，谁的数码最多，即为状元，吃大块；依次为榜眼、探花，游戏取乐。

到了现代，月饼在质量、品种上都有新发展。原料、调制方法、形状等的不同，使月饼更为丰富多彩。地区不同，月饼的形制也略有不同，大体来说，北方山西陕西一带，"月饼"没有馅料，体积硕大，中秋节时大家分切食用；南方江浙一带，"月饼"近似一种糕点，带有各种不同的馅料，形制小巧制作精美。现代月饼从种类上分有自来白月饼、自来红月饼、提浆月饼和酥皮月饼等四个品种。

自来白月饼，是指以小麦粉、绵白糖、猪油或食用植物油等制皮，冰糖、桃仁、瓜仁、桂花、青梅或山楂糕、青红丝等制馅，经包馅、成形、打戳、焙烤等工艺制成的皮松酥，馅绵软的月饼。

○蛋黄月饼

自来红月饼，是指以精制小麦粉、食用植物油、绵白糖、饴糖、小苏打等制皮，熟小麦粉、麻油、瓜仁、桃仁、冰糖、桂花、青红丝等制馅，经包馅、成形、打戳、焙烤等工艺制成的皮松酥，馅绵软的月饼。

提浆月饼，其皮面是冷却后的清糖浆调制面团制成的浆皮。以小麦粉、食用植物油、小苏打、糖浆制皮，经包馅、磕模成型、焙烤等工艺制成的饼面图案美观，口感艮酥不硬，香味浓郁的月饼。所谓提浆，是因为过去在熬制饼皮糖浆时，需用蛋白液提取糖浆中的杂质，提浆月饼由此得名。

酥皮月饼，又称翻毛月饼，指以精制小麦粉、食用植物油等制成松酥绵软的酥皮，经包馅、成形、打戳、焙烤等工艺制成的皮层次分明，松酥可口

○最经典的五仁月饼

的月饼。

按照口味分，目前已形成京、苏、潮、广等四种特色风味月饼品种。

（一）京式月饼

是北方地区汉族月饼类食品的代表品种之一，花样众多。起源于京津及周边地区，在北方有一定市场，其主要特点是甜度及皮馅比适中，一般皮馅比为 4 ∶ 6，重用麻油，口味清甜，口感脆松。

○京式月饼

（二）苏式月饼

为苏式糕点，原名酥式月饼，进而相传为苏式月饼，受到江浙地区人民的喜爱，皮层酥松，色泽美观，馅料肥而不腻，口感松酥。苏式月饼用小麦粉、饴糖、食用植物油或猪油、水等制皮，小麦粉、食用植物油或猪油制酥，经制酥皮、包馅、成型、焙烤工艺加工而成。

　　苏式月饼制作区域为江苏、浙江、上海等三地，传统的正宗技艺保留在苏州。此项技艺技的基本内容包括：选料、初加工、擦馅、制皮、制酥、包酥、包馅、成型、盖章、烘烤、包装等过程。制作过程中没有任何模具，使用器具也比较简单，有刮刀、油光纸、烤盘等。

　　苏式月饼的花色品种分甜、咸或烤、烙两类。甜月饼的制作工艺以烤为主，有玫瑰、百果、椒盐、豆沙等品种，咸月饼以烙为主，品种有火腿猪油、香葱猪油、鲜肉、虾仁等。其中清水玫瑰、精制百果、白麻椒盐、夹沙猪油是苏式月饼中的精品。苏式月饼选用原辅材料讲究，富有地方特色。月饼馅口味分为甜、咸两种。甜月饼馅料用玫瑰花、桂花、核桃仁、瓜子仁、松子仁、芝麻仁等配制而成；咸月饼馅料主要以火腿、猪腿肉、虾仁、猪油、青葱等配制而成。酥皮以小麦粉、绵白糖、饴糖、油脂调制而成。

（三）潮式月饼

　　潮式月饼又称朥饼，是广东省潮汕地区汉族糕类名点，属酥皮类饼食，是中国四大月饼流派之一。朥字，潮汕方言指猪油。用猪油掺面粉作皮包甜馅烤焙熟的饼便是朥饼。朥饼终年应市，以中秋节上市为最合时。常见的潮式月饼（圆形）的主要特点是皮酥馅细，油不肥舌，甜不腻口。其按内馅种类可分

○潮式酥皮月饼

绿豆、乌豆、水晶、紫芋等种类，馅心则包括蛋黄或海鲜等多种（可无馅心）。潮式月饼身较扁，饼皮洁白，以酥糖为馅，入口香酥。

（四）广式月饼

广式月饼是广东省汉族特色名点之一，在中国南方地区，特别是广东、广西、江西等地民间中秋节应节食品，是中秋月饼的一个形式，广式月饼闻名于世，最基本的还是在于它的选料和制作技艺无比精巧，其特点是皮薄松软、造型美观、图案精致、花纹清晰、不易破碎、包装讲究、携带方便，是人们在中秋节送礼的佳品，也是人们在中秋之夜，吃饼赏月不可缺少的佳品。

○广式月饼

广式月饼起源于1889年，当时城西有家糕酥馆，用莲子熬成莲蓉作酥饼的馅料，清香可口，大受顾客欢迎。光绪年间，这家糕酥馆改名为"连香楼"，莲蓉馅的饼点已定型为现时的月饼。宣统二年（1910），翰林学士陈太吉品尝该店月饼后大加赞赏，但觉"连香"二字不雅，建议改成"莲香"，并手书了"莲香楼"招牌，沿用至今。广州市由"莲香楼"始，各食肆、饼家纷纷仿效生产月饼，又形成"陶陶居""广州酒家""金口月饼""趣香""大三元"等月饼名牌，广式月饼逐渐闻名海外。

广式月饼原产广州，现广东、香港、江西、浙江、上海等地都有生产。以小麦粉、转化糖浆、植物油、碱水等制成饼皮，经包馅、成形、刷蛋等工艺加工而成的口感酥软的月饼。

广式月饼的主要特点是重油，皮薄、馅多。馅料多选用当地著名特产，如椰丝、橄榄仁、蜜橘饼、广式香肠、叉烧肉、咸蛋等。在工艺上，制皮、制馅均有独到之处，外皮棕红有光，并有清晰、凹凸的图案；馅心重在味道和质地。在风味上，善于利用各种呈味物质的互相作用构成特有风味，如用糖互减甜咸、用辛香料去肉类腥味，利用各种辅料所具有的不同分子结构而产生不同的色、香、味，形成蓉沙类馅细腻润滑、肉禽类和水产制品类口味甜中带咸的特点。

广式月饼品质繁多，传统广式月饼按其馅心不同可分果仁型、肉禽型、椰蓉型、蓉沙型等，20世纪90年代后又开发了水果型、果酱型、蔬菜型等。广式月饼配料讲究，皮薄馅多，美味可口，花色繁多，不易破碎，便地携带，也易于保藏，因此在国内和国际的食品市场上深受欢迎。它的品名，一般是以饼馅的主要成分而定，如五仁、金腿、莲蓉、豆沙、豆蓉、枣泥、椰蓉、冬蓉等。它的原料极为广泛，如蛋黄、皮蛋、香肠、叉烧、鸡丝、烧鸭、冬菇等。都可作为原料，并配制成众多的花色品种。

延伸知识

食用月饼注意事项

1. 先吃咸味的再吃甜味的。如有甜、咸两种月饼，应按先咸后甜的顺序来品尝，否则就吃不出味道来。

2. 品尝月饼需要伴有茶水。月饼吃多了易腻，若配饮一杯淡茶（以花茶为宜），边吃边饮，味道更是妙不可言。

3. 吃月饼要适量。月饼中含糖量和油脂较高，吃多了则会引起肠胃不适，尤其是老人、儿童或肠胃功能较弱者，吃时更要注意，一定要适量。

4. 要吃新鲜的月饼。过节时人们往往一次买许多月饼，而月饼放置时间过久，饼馅容易变质，吃后可能会发生食物中毒。因此，月饼最好随买随吃。一般家庭过节时，所买月饼大都能到节日过后，甚至更长时间，为了防止月饼的变质，对吃剩的月饼应妥善保存。

月饼的饼馅一般分为软硬两种．软馅中含水分较多，只能保存7到10天左右，而硬馅月饼则可保存1个月左右。月饼一般不宜存放在密封的容器内久藏，最好存放在竹篮里，在上面加盖一张干净纸，然后挂在通风阴凉的地方。盒装月饼，应将盒盖打开，使其通风；或者直接放在冰箱中冷藏。另外，因月饼中含脂肪较多，存放时还应注意避光，以防油脂氧化酸败。

中秋月饼是应时食品，最宜现产、现销和现买、现吃，不宜存放过久，才能保持月饼的色、香、味和应有的特殊风味。

除了月饼外，中秋节的餐桌上还有很多特色食品。

用桂花。传说月宫中有桂树，桂花成为中秋节的一种象征符号或者吉祥物。许多地方有在中秋节食用桂花的习俗。

○南京人爱吃的桂花鸭

南京人喜欢在中秋节吃"桂花鸭"。桂花鸭是当地特产，本是盐水鸭的一种。盐水鸭平时就有，但以秋季桂花飘香时节的桂花鸭为上品。桂花鸭取当年长成、肉嫩皮薄的仔鸭为原料，将净鸭用热盐抹过，下汤锅焖煮，做熟之后，浇以桂花浆，吃起来皮脆肉嫩味鲜。桂花浆用节前采摘的桂花，加糖和酸梅制成。

一些在秋季的时鲜也是中秋节餐桌上的必备食品，比如明代宫廷时兴吃螃蟹。螃蟹用蒲包蒸熟后，众人围坐品尝，佐以酒醋。食毕饮"苏叶汤"，并用之洗手。宴桌周围摆满鲜花、大石榴以及其他时鲜，演出中秋的神话戏曲。现代人们也会在餐桌上摆上应季的大闸蟹。

有些地方中秋节还有一些特色饮食，例如，在东南沿海过中秋节还一定要吃"糖芋艿"。

芋艿，古称"蹲鸱"，因为它的外形看起来很像一只鸥鸟下蹲的样子，由此而得名。又称为莒，民间称为"芋头"。属天南星科多年生草本植物的球茎，主要生长在东印度群岛和马来西亚半岛的热带雨林区，至今这些小岛上仍然种植

○糖芋艿

着。芋艿可以作为粮食，也可以作为蔬菜，还可以制作为点心食用。是一种天然的多糖类高分子植物胶体，营养丰富，是人们青睐的食物。

芋艿在中国种植的历史悠久，司马迁的《史记》当中就有记载说："岷山之下沃野千里，下有蹲鸱，至死不饥。"南宋著名的饮食烹饪著作《山溪清供》有诗称赞："深夜一炉火，浑家团围坐。芋头时正熟，天子不如我。"芋头，香糯美味，吃法多样。

中秋节吃芋艿的习俗，相传起源于明代。明代时，东南沿海有倭寇来入侵，百姓深受其苦。将军戚继光受命抗倭，取得很大胜利。中秋这一天，戚家军在营地里欢度中秋。半夜里倭寇偷袭，将戚家

军围困在山上，断其粮草。数天后，士兵们没有任何粮食了，只能以挖到的野芋艿充饥。没想到，煮后很好吃，但不知道这种东西叫什么名。戚继光说："为了纪念遇难的士兵，就叫它'遇难'吧。"一天夜晚，戚家军饱餐"遇难"后奋勇突围，将倭寇全歼在睡梦中。此后，东南沿海人民在过中秋节时，都要吃糖烧芋艿，以志不忘民族危难和戚继光的抗倭功绩。时间一长，"遇难"便渐渐变为了"芋艿"，而民间就留下了中秋节吃糖芋艿的风俗。

最后，农历八月是许多时令瓜果成熟的时期。诸如葡萄、石榴、枣、苹果、橘子、梨等水果，西瓜、南瓜、地瓜、甜瓜、脆瓜等各种瓜也很多，这些都成为中秋时节的美食。晚上，许多人家都摆出这些瓜果，连同月饼、瓜子等，在中秋赏月、拜月。

Chapter Three
The Customs of the Mid-Autumn Festival

While the Mid-Autumn festival was established at latest, most of its customs like moon worship, the temple fair, lantern fair and festivals' specific diet continue down, which is followed by the modern people.

1. Worshiping and Enjoying the Moon

The ancient emperors have the rituals of offering sacrifices to the sun in spring and the moon in autumn. People called the sun, East Mother and the moon West Mother in the Shang Dynasty, while people according to the period of the sun and the moon offered sacrifices to the sun in the daytime and the moon at night in the Zhou Dynasty. The Book of Rites records: "Do great things must be adapted to the time, for the day and night will imitate the example of the sun and the moon." According to the explanation of Kong Yingda in the Tang Dynasty, people offered sacrifices to the sun in the morning of vernal equinox outside the West Gate, while to the moon in the autumnal equinox in the evening outside the West Gate. Because the side of the sun in the autumnal equinox looks almost directly to the earth, the moon looks big and round. It is saying that, "Sacrificing to the moon should not be late, and the second months of spring and autumn just fit." The way of sacrifice in the Zhou Dynasty is: "Offering sacrifices to the sun in the Altar (prominent above the ground standing for brightness), and the moon in the Kan (under the ridge, and the earth's surface representing the quietness)." Altar and Kan symbolized of the sun and the moon.Sacrifice mainly served pigs, cattle, sheep and jade objects and silk fabrics. The worship of the sun and the moon was still the royal ritual sacrifice in the Qin and Han Dynasties. The Sun and Moon Temple stands in Qinyong (area of ancient Qin now refers to Xian, Shaanxi Province) while the Sun Temple and the Moon Temple stand in Shandong. People used the cattle to worship the sun, while the pigs, sheep and calves to show the respects to the moon in the period of Emperor Wu of the Han Dynasty. Since then, the rituals of worshiping the moon feature from the Northern Wei Dynasty, the Sui and Tang Dynasties to the Ming and Qing Dynasties. "The Temple of the Moon" in Beijing specially built for the Royal family to hold the ceremonies of worshiping the moon in the year of Jiajing, Ming Dynasty.

The royal sacrifice ritual evolved into the ceremony of worshiping the moon in the folk. The common people call the Moon God, "Yue Shen", "Yue Gu", "Moon Goddess", "Moonlight God", or "Chang'e", so there are a series of moon worshiping activities. There still remain many historic sites, such as "the Worship Altar," "the Worship Pavilion" and "Wang Yue Tower" throughout the country.

Annual Customs and Festivals in Peking recorded Beijing folk worship scene in the Mid-Autumn Festival in the Ming Dynasty:

"The portrait of the Buddha was regarded as 'the God Horses' in Beijing, which deserves respect. The picture of the Moonlight Horse is colorful, which the Moon God is painted at the top of the paper, like the image of a bodhisattva in Buddhism, and the palace of the Moon God are painted at the bottom of the paper where a rabbit just like a person standing here and making heavenly medicine next to it. The picture is colorful. The larger paper has seven or eight *chi* (a unit of length, =1/3metre), and the smaller one has two or three *chi*, and a red-green of yellow flag is at the top of it. The tribute is put in front of the incense burner for people to burn incense. Then people will burn the paper, the Oroxylum indicum (a kind of fragrant medicinal leaves) and the paper-making ingot together to send the Moon God away."

The paper painted with the statue of the god is called "the Horse of God" in Beijing and the origin of the name comes from a ceremony that the paper has to be burnt like the horse sends the God away. There is the God Horse specially used for the worship ceremony in the Mid-Autumn Festival, called "the Moonlight Horse", which the Moon God is painted at the top of the paper, like the image of a bodhisattva in Buddhism, and the palace of the Moon God are painted at the bottom of the paper where a rabbit just like a person standing here and making heavenly medicine is next to it. The picture is colorful. The size of the paper ranges from two or three *chi* (a unit of length, =1/3metre) to seven or eight *chi*, and a red-green or yellow flag has been on the top of the paper. When the round moon rises to the sky at the night of the Mid-Autumn Festival, people put the paper on the table toward the moon, placing fresh vegetables, fruits and moon cakes in front of the paper. The tribute is put in front of the incense burner for people to burn incense. After finishing it, people will burn the paper, the Oroxylum indicum (a kind of fragrant medicinal leaves) and the paper-mak-

Beijing Marco Polo Bridge is also a great place to admire the moon in the Mid-Autumn Festival

ing ingot together to send the Moon God away. Beijing's moon worship in the Qing Dynasty had a slight change, to which the picture of the Moonlight Horse was given from the Taoist temple, entitled "the Moon God".

There are many ways to worship the moon, such as offering sacrifices to the Moonlight Horse, kneeling before the moon, or using the wood to carve out the image of Yue Gu (the Moon God). People hang the statue of the Buddha towards the direction of the moon and put various offerings on the altar table. People will burn the paper that is painted the Moonlight Horse and withdraw the altar table after finishing it. And people who show respect to the moon can enjoy the food.

Offerings are different in different places, and most of them are fresh fruits and vegetables in autumn. Northerners offer sacrifices like pears, apples, grapes, soybeans, cockscomb and watermelon while southerners offer grapefruit, taros, bananas, persimmons, water chestnut, peanuts, and lotus root, etc.

Both men and women participated in the worship activities before the Song Dynasty. The residents went up stairs to the tower or burnt incense in the courtyard, praying to the Moon God in the capital of the Song Dynasty at the Mid-Autumn night, whether rich or poor, kids and young teenagers wearing the adult clothes. People went up stairs to the tower or burnt incense in the courtyard, praying to the Moon God: Boys are expected to pass the Imperial Examinations, winning posts in the imperial court, while girls are praying for a beautiful appearance and a happy marriage as is recorded in *New Tippler on the Record*. Sacrificial rites have greatly changed after the Ming and Qing Dynasties. The men worshiped less, while the women regarded the moon as the special worship object. There is a proverb in Beijing: "Men don't worship the moon, while women don't offer sacrifices to the Kitchen God." Generally speaking, men do not participate in the worship of the moon, but there are exceptions in some places where men can worship the moon. Worshiping the moon also has a certain order. When the moon rises, women burn incense first, then it is children's turn to do so. The elderly women in the worship of the moon often say: "The moon is round on August 15. Watermelons and cakes are used to respect the God to make him happy and ensure peace and security throughout the year."

Generally speaking, we can worship the moon without moon or even it's raining outside in the Mid-Autumn Festival. We can hold worship ceremonies where the places are illuminated by the moonlight. We can also put the altar towards the moon in cloudy days. These are what we need: ① The altar or Jiji (the table for sacrifice). It can be a small table. ② Some mats made of reeds or the ordinary straw mats. We can put a cushion on it for showing respect to the moon. ③ A censer or an ordinary small incense burner and some incense. ④ Some plates, dishes, bowls, small cups and other containers. ⑤ Two red candles for lighting, foiling the atmosphere and incensing. ⑥ An ordinary bottle of wine and three glasses. ⑦ Tributes: moon cakes, wild animals, round glutinous rice cakes, fruits, soybeans, cockscomb and other fresh food in season.

The worship rites can be implemented when the moon appears in the sky at night. There are people who officiate at sacrificial rites, a master of ceremonies, a number of deacons, and other subordinate participants. Generally speaking, the female elder or housewife officiates at sacrificial rites. The chief is also selected from the women when people worship the moon together. The style of the clothes for the ritual can be quite casual. The leisure clothes will do, instead of the formal clothes.

People need to take a bath and put on clean clothes to show respect to the Moon God before worshiping the moon. Then they should read the short and beautiful congratulatory message which is supposed to be transcribed with a brush in rice paper with traditional forms of poetry in four, five or seven words, in the occasion of worshiping the moon.

The Han's rituals are adopted in the worship of the moon. First, sit on the mat in the traditional "Jing Sitting" (a posture of sitting) way. The "Jing Sitting" demands people to sit on the heel with knees pinching, the instep snapping down onto the ground, hands on the knees, and eyes looking straight ahead. It has the same reason for the "Hu sitting" (non-Han sitting posture): legs may not be split with sitting still, while hands can be put on the knees or the abdomen, or make a fist forwards. Second, the way of worshiping the moon needs to be based on the formal Han "Baili" (the worship) without bow or hands clasped together: raise hands on forehead like "Zuoyi"(a traditional way to salute in China) which is like making a deep bow with hands folded in front, then stand upright with hands putting before the brow, and then kneel down the two knees at the same time to bow down slowly with the palm close to the ground, and the forehead should be close to the palm. This is called the "Baili". Then stand upright, which is called "Xing." Stand up after kowtowing, which means putting hands before the brow and standing upright and then putting hands down, or worship twice, which refers to worshipping two times continuously, namely "Worship–Xing–Worship–Xing–Standing up after kowtowing", according to the etiquette.

The specific ritual procedures for worshiping the moon are as follows:

• Take a shower and then put on clean and tidy clothes.

145

• Place the sacrificial table, and light the red candle, and set a mat towards the moon.

• The participants sit in the sacrificial area. The deacon and master of ceremony are in place.

• Master of ceremony sings: "Worshiping the moon." The person who officiates at a sacrificial service comes to the front seat, and kneels on the mat.

• Master of ceremony sings: "Offering incense to Buddha three times." Then the deacon passes three sticks of incense to the person who officiates at a sacrificial service, then she lights the candle, bowing to the Moon God, and then inserts the incense in the incense burner. So these people do this three times. Master of ceremony sings: "Offering liquor to Buddha three times." Then the deacon fills the glass and gives it to her to spill the liquor in front of the seats to the ground and then puts the goblet on the table. So these people also do this three times.

• Read congratulatory message. The deacon hands in the congratulatory message of worshiping the moon, and then the person who officiates at a sacrificial service reads aloud towards the moon under the moonlight and the candlelight.

• Burn the congratulatory message and the paper offerings: the congratulatory message and the paper offerings will be placed by the person who officiates at a sacrificial service before the small bowl to burn.

• Master of ceremony sings: "Worshiping the moon." Participants worship in accordance with "Worship–Xing –Worship–Xing–Standing up after kowtowing" in the order. The person who officiates at a sacrificial service and the participants worship twice continuously together.

• Master of ceremony sings: "Cong Xian (Refers to the ancient sacrifices or after the food and drink offerings) ."

The worship ceremony

The person who officiates at a sacrificial service leaves the seat, and then the attendants follow the order of the elder and the younger to the seat, kneeling and incensing (each of them take three sticks of incense or one), and praying in silence and then praying to the moon until all the worshipers complete.

• Master of ceremony sings: "The worship ritual is completed."

At this point, the Mid-Autumn Festival's worship ceremony is completed.

The custom of enjoying the moon has begun from the Han Dynasty. It's said that the Emperor Wu of the Han Dynasty had built the specific pavilion and a pool to admire the moon. The images of the dancing concubines could be reflected into the pool, when they enjoyed the moon in the pavilion. People have had more rational understanding of the moon, and have enhanced the delight in the moonlit night with the rich knowledge of astronomy and cultural progress of the times since the

Sui and Tang Dynasties. In particular, people in the Tang Dynasty were romantic, and loved to be close to nature, regarding the moon as a beautiful landscape. The Mid-Autumn Festival was formally established in the Song Dynasty, and there was a greater increase in the proportion of the content in the Mid-Autumn Festival's moon activities because of the prosperity of the city's secular life. From then on, the ceremony of worshiping the moon and the activities of admiring the moon were closely linked together.

Forgotten Tales of the Kaiyuan and Tianbao Periods recorded the story of the Emperor Xuanzong and Yang Yuhuan (the favorite concubine of the emperor Xuanzong of the Tang Dynasty) in the Mid-Autumn Festival: The Emperor Xuanzong and Yang Guifei were indulged in happiness, with the smell of sweet-scented osmanthus, For fear of the moon going down, the Emperor Xuanzong issued an order to build the "Platform for Enjoying the Moon" which was a hundred *chi* high (chi, a unit of length =1/3 meter) on the west bank of Taiye Pool. *YiShi* recorded that the Taoist Luo Gongyuan and Xuanzong enjoyed the moon in the palace at the Mid-Autumn Festival night in the early years of Tianbao in the Tang Dynasty. Luo Gongyuan said to the emperor: "would you like to follow me to the moon palace?" Then he took out his cane which could change into a silver bridge and threw it into the air, and then he invited the emperor to board the bridge. Xuanzong and Luo Gongyuan walked on the bridge about tens of miles away, and suddenly they found they came to a brilliant and chilly city. Luo Gongyuan said to the emperor, "This is the moon palace," and they saw hundreds of fairies with white silk clothing, dancing in the courtyard. Xuanzong asked Luo Gongyuan, "What's name of this beautiful music?" Luo Gongyuan replied, "This is called Melody of White Feathers Garment". The emperor bore the music score in mind secretly, and returned back with Luo Gongyuan. Xuanzong found the silver bridge gradually disappeared with the steps when he looked back on the way. The emperor asked the official professional musician to write down the song named Melody of White Feathers Garment when he returned to the world. Then the story of Emperor Xuanzong traveling the moon palace was widespread.

The custom of enjoying the moon prevailed in the palace of the Song Dynasty on the Mid-Autumn Festival. According to the *Miscellaneous Notes in Guixin Street* by Zhou Mi, "the Bridge for Enjoying the Moon"in the Deshou Palace was pure and crystal-clear, which was built from the stone that were offered as tribute by Wu Lin. The royal tea table, couch and liqueur sets were made of crystal in the early Southern Song. Maids in an imperial palace and musicians were separated standing on the north and south of water, and the number of pipers was over 200 with string and bamboo flute music in Mid-Autumn Festival. Admiring the full moon in folk in the Song Dynasty was also very lively. Each of the inns began to sellfresh brewed wines before the Mid-Autumn Festival for people to drink and to have a good time in Dongjing which was the capital of the Song Dynasty (the present Kaifeng City, Henan Province). *Dongjing Meng Hua Record* by Meng Yuanlao recorded that wealthy people would decorate their own pavilions again for watching the full moon in the upstairs. And the ordinary people would compete with other people for space on the high-rise tavern to enjoy the full moon on August 15. The royal family would hold "Mid-Autumn evening party" at that time, and the nearby residents could hear the music from the imperial haremat the middle of the night. The ordinary people would not rest early, and even the children were reluctant to sleep.

The Mid-Autumn Festival was more bustling in the Southern Song Dynasty's Hangzhou. *Meng Liang Record* by Wu Zimu recorded that the aristocrats and wealthy people mounted the pavilion for enjoying the full moon or built the stage for sipping wine as well as singing loudly, lingering music which was being played on the lute in order to have a wonderful time the whole night in this cool, sweet-scented osmanthus fragrance of the Mid-Autumn Festival night. The small or middle merchants of the Southern Song Dynasty also mounted the small pavilion for the family feast with sons and daughters for the Mid-Autumn Festival. Even the poor people would pawn their clothing to buy the wine to celebrate the Mid-Autumn Festival. People enjoyed the moon in an endless stream until the dawn because the night fair was open all night.

The Mongolian had no Mid-Autumn Festival. They accepted the Han customs after entering the Central Plains (comprising the middle and lower reaches of the Yellow River), so they celebrated the Mid-Autumn Festival as well from then on.

The Activities of moon appreciation get grander among people from the Song Dynasty to the Ming and Qing Dynasties. People sing and dance together at night just like in the day, especially on the Su causeway at the West Lake in Hangzhou.

The book depicts the scene of the Mid-Autumn Festival in the region of Huqiu. Many people like official scholar, young ladies from a rich family, singing and dancing performers, idlers, unemployed vagrants and so on all go out to admire the moon and play at the night of the 15th day of the 8th lunar month in Shenggong Platform, One-thousand Stone, Crane Stream, Sword Pool, Shenwending Shrine, Sword-power-test

Rock and so on. When the moon rises, people will play the music with a deafening sound of gongs and drums in many places in Huqiu, so that people can't hear what others say. Music played by drums and cymbals faded away when the orchestration and people's singing started at about eight o'clock in the evening. Many people come to the cruise ship to have a feast, appreciating music and playing at about ten o'clock at night. There will be a variety of vaudeville on the cruise ship and some people listen to music in gradually-faded moonlight until dawn.

According to the record, the custom "Walking in the Moon" at the Mid-Autumn Festival night prevails in Wuzhong District in Jiangsu. Many shops decorated their doors with hanging lanterns to celebrate the Mid-Autumn Festival under the moonlight. Therefore many young ladies in groups walk around on the street with noise and excitement. There is a small Fortune God in the shop and also in the tower, a few tables, musical instruments and some sundries used for decorations, which looks exquisite and interesting. That's why some walkers stop to have a look, which makes it extremely crowed. Women dress up for outings or a visit to nunnery with the crowing of cocks at the night of the Mid-Autumn Festival, which is called "Walking in the Moon".

For the literati, their poetic and artistic flavor can be triggered on the Mid-Autumn Festival. Many famous poems have chanted the moonlight since the Tang and Song Dynasties, of which the most famous poetry was "A Moonlit Night on the Spring River" by Zhang Ruoxu. It is known as "a poetic masterpiece through the ages" and there is no poem chanting and singing of the moonlight can compare with it:

A Moonlit Night on the Spring River
In spring the river rises as high as the sea,

And with the river's rise the moon upraises bright.
She follows the rolling waves for ten thousand li,
And where the river flows, there overflows her light.
The river winds around the fragrant islet where
The blooming flowers in her light all look like snow.
You cannot tell her beams from hoar frost in the air,
Nor from white sand upon Farewell Beach below.
No dust has stained the water blending with the skies;
A lonely wheel like moon shines brilliant far and wide.
Who by the riverside first saw the moon arise?
When did the moon first see a man by riverside?
Ah, generations have come and pasted away;
From year to year the moons look alike, old and new.
We do not know tonight for whom she sheds her ray,
But hear the river say to its water adieu.
Away, away is sailing a single cloud white;
On Farewell Beach pine away maples green.
Where is the wanderer sailing his boat tonight?
Who, pining away, on the moonlit rails would learn?
Alas! The moon is lingering over the tower;
It should have seen the dressing table of the fair.
She rolls the curtain up and light comes in her bower;
She washes but can't wash away the moonbeams there.
She sees the moon, but her beloved is out of sight;
She'd follow it to shine on her beloved one's face.
But message-bearing swans can't fly out of moonlight,

Nor can letter-sending fish leap out of their place.

Last night he dreamed that falling flowers would not stay.

Alas! He can't go home, although half spring has gone.

The running water bearing spring will pass away;

The moon declining over the pool will sink anon.

The moon declining sinks into a heavy mist;

It's a long way between southern rivers and eastern seas.

How many can go home by moonlight who are missed?

The sinking moon sheds yearning o'er riverside trees.

(Translated by Xu Yuanchong)

Nowadays, activities of enjoying the moon become richer with the bright moonlight on the Mid-Autumn Festival.

2. Inviting God to Divine

Mid-Autumn Festival is a time when gods come to the earthly world. Besides the God of the Moon, people also need to offer sacrifices to many other gods due to the tradition of "thanking offerings ritual".

The first is the Earth God that can be called "the Father of Earth" or "The God of She". It was recorded in the *Collection of Apocrypha's Revised Edition ·Spiritual Deed of the Piety Scripture* that the land was granted to the Earth God to express thanks, because the ground was too vast to visit. Offering sacrifices to the Earth God came from the nature worship. Taoists also believe the Earth God, which is called Tai She God, Tai Ji God, Tu Weng God and Earth Goddess. But the Earth

God is recognized in lower status in their belief of Taoism. The worship of the Earth God who is regarded as the local patron saint in the folk religion of the Han nationality prevails across the country. The Earth God was respected in the place where a flock of human lived in old days, which left the Earth Temple made of stones or woods everywhere in China.

The Earth God, approachable and amiable, is usually dressed plainly with white beard and hair. His spouse, called "the Mother of Earth" or "the Grandmother of Earth", is also worshipped besides the Earth God in Earth Temples without any special duty.

It is said that the Earth God was born on the second day of the second lunar month, while he became the god on the 15th day of the 8th lunar month, which made showing respects to the Earth God become one of the activities on the Mid-Autumn Festival. It has been recorded that people offered sacrifices to the local Earth God as they did on the second day of the second lunar month to express thanks to the god in *Zhuluo County Annals*. When the music and songs began on all sides, the village opera started.

The Earth God with lower status administrates many things in folk belief. He takes charge of weddings, funerals, disasters, and small tricks. People like to reveal their true feelings and pray to him due to his amiable look and kind personality. It was said that Earth Temples were everywhere, while the status are like old men with white hair and wrinkled skin, or red-faced valiants with long black beard, which can be totally called "the Mother of Earth" (the Earth God) in *Truths of Interpretations*. People offer sacrifices to them sincerely for good harvest or favorable weather, which makes the incense very busy in small temples. People in Han nationality believed that "the official in county cannot order people around like one right here", "the dog cannot bit the chicken without the permit of the Earth God", and "the Earth God makes crops flourish in normal harvest, and people safe in small land".

In addition, "Invoking the God of Basket" features the customs in Guangzhou. "The God of Basket", also called Aunt Basket, is one of the folk goddess who should be worshipped by women. People place a basket in a dark corner, attaching a rice spoon made of coconut shell when they worship "the God of Basket". It looks like a person with a body made of the basket, a head made of the shell, and a woman garment. A stool is put in front of the coconut shell which is the substitute of "the God of Basket" in the basket. Two women, sitting around and holding a basket, sing the song of invoking the God of Basket before burning incense: "God of Basket, God of Basket, you are the daughter of Foshan People, the mother of citizens, but you passed away due to your mother-in-law and husband". The trend of the basket determines whether the God of Basket is successfully invoked. If the god comes, the basket will make a kowtow to the stool, which means you can raise a question, while the God of Basket will answer through kowtow, too. If not, you fail.

Unmarried or underage silk reeling girls like to place Taiyin Table in Nanhai, Shunde District, especially in Xiqiao Town. Girls make pink tomatoes (a kind of traditional dessert with pork, mushrooms and bamboo shoots in it), placing them on the altar to make a pray. Meanwhile, girls compete with each other to decide which one is more unique and delicate, smelling good, tasting delicious.

People also regard Invoking the Lad, also called the Lad Coming Down, as an old custom, which has no relationship with the Mid-Autumn Festival besides that it is hold at the night of the day. A 12 or 13-year-old boy will be selected within several days of the festival who will be asked to sit properly and close eyes, while a person practises magic, and others stroke and draw a circle in front of him with a fistful of incenses. The boy will mutter in about 30 minutes, and then people around will shout, "Shifu(master worker) is coming!" they will also ask the boy, "The sword and the knife, which one do you prefer?" the boy will choose one and say it is to his liking. Then he should wave the weapon that is awarded by people in the clang. "Maichong" is another sorcery that is similar to "Invoking the Lad". Four people lie on the ground in different directions, while others walk around them, muttering incantations until they fall asleep. The one will be helped up and asked to perform martial arts like professional person. After that, another, who wakes up for unknown reasons, will do the same things in turn.

Inviting the God of Table can be hosted by both men and women. A four-legged table is put on a bowl filled of water in the opposite direction. People stand on each corner of the table, pressing table legs slightly with the left hand finger, circling table legs with incenses in right hand while they say, "The God of Table walks around, and four people walk around." Four people walk around fast after the table which turns around itself. They will be substituted when they fail to keep pace with the table.

Residents earn their living by the sea, believing the tide as god in southeast coast, for which they see and worship the tide. *The Chinese National Customs·Zhejiang* recorded, "It is the most popular period for people in Hangzhou to watch the tide from the 11th to the 18th day of the 8th lunar month. Men and women come to visit, which makes no more place there for another in ten-*li* length(a Chinese unit of length =1/2 kilometer). Some young people who do well in swimming go to the estuary to wait for the tide with green flags and umbrellas. They walk in wild waves and perform variously, which shows their good skills. Rich people will give tips, while artists play the ball on the horses for fun. In fact, people pursue pleasure in the name of watching the tide."

It is also a good chance to pray for children on the Mid-Autumn Festival. *Beautiful Dream to Dongjing·Vol.8* recorded, "The woman goes back to her mother's home late, presenting cucurbits and jujubes from grandfather, aunt and uncle." The cucurbit with many seeds is a mascot, standing for repeated pregnancy. Elders will give newly harvested cucurbits and jujubes to the married juniors for many children on the Mid-Autumn Festival.

Sending melons is more common to pray for children on the Mid-Autumn Festival, which you can find in Hunan. The *Chinese National Customs·Vol.6* said relatives and friends would present the melon to rich family without a child in Hengcheng at the night of the Mid-Autumn Festival. They would steal a melon without awareness of the garden owner. Then the melon would be made a colorful mask and changed into a person with cloths. A lucky elder would carry it to the family as firecrackers exploded. He should place the melon covered by the quilt on the bed, and say, "You must reap what you have sown." The receiver should treat them, while the wife should open and have the melon. It was said that it was the most effective way. So relatives and friends send melon to the family without kids for some years on the Mid-Autumn Festival.People often stick pater-cutting such as "Kylin (a mascot in ancient) sending a child" on the wall. *The Chinese National Customs·Anhui* recorded that women placed fruit and cakes in the yard to worship the moon, while children held the torch to pick fruit or beans together in the field at the night of the 15th day of 8th lunar month in Anhui, which was called "Momo". This custom is similar to "picking up melons" in other regions, which is also witchcraft to pray for children.

The Mid-Autumn Festival is also important for divination besides worship;

People can predict the weather of the night on the 15th day of first lunar month the next year through the moon at the night on the 15th day of the 8th lunar month. As the saying goes, if the moon is surrounded or covered by the thick cloud, it will snow or rain on the Lantern Festival (the 15th day of first lunar month) the next year. As the experience shows, the connection is right.

Oilmen often forecast the oil price by observing the rightness of the moon on Mid-Autumn Festival. Bright moon means enough oil, which would make the oil price decrease. On the contrary, the lack of oil leads to the increase of the price.

"Moonlight Book", a kind of divination, which was based on Wooden Fish Book, prevails in Guangzhou including suburbs. Wooden Fish Book that performed in Cantonese in Guangdong was popular after the middle period of the Qing Dynasty. The works were abundant, like *Song of the Exile*, *Prosperous of Family* and *Meng Zheng's Worship to Kitchen God*. "Moonlight Book" is to divine through selling popular Wooden Fish Book at the night of the Mid-Autumn Festival. "Those who sold the Wooden Fish Book came together to the street on the Mid-Autumn Festival, shouting, 'Win the moonlight, and win the moonlight.' People were afraid of 'failure' for 'failure' and 'book' sound the same in Chinese. Women and children bought The Wooden Fish Book to divine and they could only buy it in order and then check it. The *Song of the Exile* meant omen, while *Meng Zheng's Worship to Kitchen God* meant that all things were difficult before they were easy."

"Hitting the sayings" is also a kind of divination. Women in alleys worship the god in front of their houses at the night of the Mid-Autumn Festival, inquiring what they want. Then they go out alone to listen carefully to others' discussion, deciding whether it is good or bad

In addition, releasing Kongming Lanterns is also a popular way to divine in the Qing Dynasty.

"Kongming Lantern", which is also called "sky lantern", "wishing lamp" and "praying lamp", is an ancient handicraft of ethic Han (China's main nationality), often used for military purposes. It is said that the lantern was invented by Zhuge Liang who had been trapped in Pingyang, for which he could not send the army out of the city for help. He forecasted wind direction, making floating paper lantern with messages for help, which made them out of danger. So then the lantern became Kongming Lantern in the later generations. Another legend also prevails. Shen Qiniang, a woman in Five Dynasties period, fought with her husband in Fujian. She made square shelves, using bamboo sticks and paper, which formed the headlight. Burning resin was placed on the bottom, and then the lantern could fly driven by the hot air, which could be used as military signals. The lantern made of resin is called Kongming Lantern in Sichuan, because it looks like Zhuge Liang's hat.

People release Kongming Lanterns on the Lantern Festival, the Mid-Autumn Festival and other important days, forecasting the fortune through the height of the Kongming Lantern.

3. Parties and Flower Lanterns

The Mid-Autumn Festival is also called "Reunion Festival" when people on the ground get together like the full moon. According to the customs, wanderers should come home, while wives in parents' houses should go back to their husbands' houses. So the Mid-Autumn Festival is a day when people get together. They had enough time to hold parties when it became the official holiday in the Song Dynasty. The party is not only held in a family, but also a gathering in local areas.

Releasing Kongming lanterns

The Chinese national customs·Jiangsu said that big parties would be held in Lili county on the Mid-Autumn Festival

The big party which meant exorcising was started in the Tang Dynasty, recorded in *Li Records*. It was held every Mid-Autumn festival. It was ready when people beat the drums at the night of the 12th day of the 8th lunar month. The event was brought to climax on the 14th and 15th day, while the 16th was for women.

Drums and flags were put in front of the honor guard, followed by the statuses of gods which were led by similar guards in order- Jiancha God, Anle God,Guangyou God, which were called the God of City. It was said that his last name was Li who was the crown prince in the Tang Dynasty. Hundreds of devout notables including men and women were followed with incenses in hand. They worn red cloths with the sign of crime, or were in handcuffs, which was strange and inconceivable. What was the most surprising was that censers hung at the one's right arm, but he felt nothing at all. He should beat a pair of the gongs 13 times, walking with them which were more than 10 *jin* (a unit of weight=1/2 kilogram). The protector sprayed water to the contact area every time the one walked 10 more steps calmly, which was really miserable. Those who made a big wish deserved sympathy due to the poor sufferings. All the above was about the big event on the 14th day and the 15th day.

The Event of Madams which was similar to the former in arrangement was held at the night of the 16th day. The hostess was the madam of the god. People presented paper flowers to the madam everywhere she passed. And then the chaperon helped her wear them. The flower would be sent to people the next day to fight evil. There was the condition of the Event of Madams.

Stores were well-decorated, which sent a thriving sight at that time. Actors performed all the time from the 13th day to the 16th day in the City God Temple. All came to the temple to watch the performances cheerful. Stages were everywhere, which made no place to stand. Everyone was crazy for several days in the noisy atmosphere.

People on the ground light lamps to echo the big and

Huge moon lantern of porcupine

bright moon on the Mid-Autumn Festival, for which it is also one of the three largest festivals of lanterns in China.

Playing "Little Red" (a kind of lantern) in the water was ecorded in *Tales of the Old Capital* as a custom on the festival. People in water towns in southern Yangtze River play and enjoy the flower lanterns, which means to send blessings. Flower lanterns are various, like sesame lamp, shell lamp, shaving lamp, straw light, scale light, chaff light, melon seed lantern, bird and flower lanterns and so on, all of which are beautiful, delicate, and worthy of the praise.

The *Chinese National Customs·Vol.5* recorded the popular

162

Tile Lamp in the south. Children in Jiangxi Province picked up the tiles, putting them into a round-tower building with some holes. People burned it in the wood tower under the moonlight at dusk until tiles began to turn red. And then they poured kerosene to it, which would light up the surrounding area like the daytime. The lamp which was called Tile Lamp was put out when nobody enjoyed it at night.

"Holding the Mid-Autumn Festival" features the customs in Guangzhou. It was said that the first emperor Zhu Yuanzhang in the Ming Dynasty began to stage an uprising with Liu Bowen selling the hierogram, after people regarded the lights as signals. The custom of holding lights and flags formed in Guangzhou after that. Houses were often equipped with balconies in old times in Guangzhou. People placed white seven-star flags, edged with red god tooth, made of paper or cloths at the balcony or the roof. A rectangular flag was put under the seven-star flag with "Happy Mid-Autumn Festival" on it. In addition, the lantern would be tied to the flagpole or bamboo pole with burning candle in it at night. The rich hung hundreds of lanterns, forming the shape of "Celebrate the Mid-Autumn Festival". Candles were used in lanterns, while the bright lights were also put into the lanterns in the early Republic of China. Family members got together to enjoy delicious food on the balcony with a flagpole which was more than 10 meters high. A flagpole and two lanterns brought happiness to common families, but the poor did not have houses or lanterns. Therefore, a saying went in Guangdong that someone was happy while someone was distressed on the Mid-Autumn Festival. Somebody played the vertical flute upstairs, but somebody frowned on the ground. Exquisite and various lanterns are made of bamboo sticks and colored paper by every family, which will be sold on the street, including fruit lanterns, bird and beast lanterns, fish and insect lanterns. Citizens celebrate the festival, holding lanterns on the street that is filled with flower lamps at night. The light is like the star, which shines with the moon.

Simple grapefruit lanterns, pumpkin lanterns, orange lanterns are also popular, besides lanterns made of paper and bamboos for children in Guangxi and Nanning. Grapefruit lantern is made of the empty peel with simple patterns and a rope. A burning candle is put into it, which gives out gentle light. Pumpkin lanterns and orange lanterns can be made in similar ways. Although they are plain, the simple ways make them popular. Some children put grapefruit lanterns into the river for games. Huqiu lanterns are made of six bamboo circles with write paper outside and candles inside, which can hang on the table for worshiping the moon, or provide children with joy.

> ### Tips for Tourism
>
> ## Lantern fairs in Longtanhu Park in Beijing
>
> People are used to watching the large festival party held by television stations in China, eating mooncakes with family at the night of the Mid-Autumn Festival. Meanwhile, grand lantern fairs will be held in large and medium parks in every city.
>
> Abundant activities will be held at Tian'anmen Square, the Fragrant Hill, Happy Valley and many other places in Beijing, such as lantern party, enjoying flower lanterns, guessing lantern riddles and eating mooncakes. In addition, lantern party in Longtanhu Park is also very popular.
>
> Longtanhu Park is located in Dongcheng District inside the Left Tian'anmen in Beijing, forming from depression which used to bake wall bricks under the region of Jiajing in the Ming Dynasty. It constitutes 3 connected water areas with moat at the south and east, crossed by left

Tian'anmen Street. The whole park which focuses on the water landscape is 120 Square Meters with green waves and trees. The feature of dragon and lake is stressed. The lake is near the Dragon Mountain, the Forest of Dragon Steles, the Dragon Pavilion, classical architecture Longyin Pavilion, Dragon—Shaped Stone Caving, and Dragon Bridge. People enjoy them—selves with the full moon, water, and original flower lanterns decorated on the antique buildings.

Address: No.8 Longtan Road, Dongcheng District, Beijing

4. Recreational Activities

The children's recreational activity "playing the Grandpa Rabbit" is popular during the Mid-Autumn Festival.

Besides toad, it is said that the moon is also called rabbit, including jade rabbit, gold rabbit and toad rabbit. Therefore, the Chinese people also worship the rabbits while sacrificing the moon. Sometimes, they even pay respects to the rabbits only.

The Grandpa Rabbit is mostly made of mud, with multi-

Traditional Chinese folk handicrafts in Old Beijing —
Grandpa Rabbit puppet

ple models, ears, and colors and some even painting in gold. Grandpa Rabbit is generally moulded with plastic: First, mix up the clay and the paper pulp well and fill them in the mold which is divided into two parts of the front and back. Take out the 80% or 90% dry mud to stick the halves of statue together with two horns. Once the statue becomes full-dry, spread a layer of glue on its body and paint some patterns with colored pigments. The big statue can reach about one meter high while the small one only about ten centimeters. The image of the statue is represented by Jinao(a kind of turtle in Chinese myths) with white face, wearing a coat armor and holding a mortar in the left hand, and a pestle in the right hand and carrying a umbrella or flag on the back. The pedestal covers the design of tiger, deer, lion, camel and lotus. Once the Grandpa Rabbit occurred, it was rapidly favored by children. The exquisite Grandpa Rabbit made in Beijing is both the children's toy and the mascot of the Mid-Autumn Festival. Besides, there are also some plays about the Grandpa Rabbit and the Rabbit Car.

According to *the Rest Manuscript of Peony Pavilion* written by Ji Kun in the Ming Dynasty, the custom of playing Grandpa Rabbit started around the end of Ming Dynasty. It is said, "People in Beijing usually knead mud rabbit which sits well with clothes like a person to worship." The rabbit became more and more delicate and was treated as children's toy in the Mid-Autumn Festival instead of being the sacrifice offered by the Qing Dynasty. Some are dressed up as a general who wears a helmet and armour, or carrying a paper flag or a paper umbrella on the back, standing or sitting on a kylin(the Chinese unicorn), tiger or leopard. Some are dressed up as a barber, a cobbler, a merchant selling wonton and soup or a pedllar with human body and the head of the rabbit. "Some handy people sell some rabbit statue made with loess, which were called the Grandpa Rabbit." The area around the Dongsi memorial arch in Beijing was filled with stalls, dealing the Rabbit Gandpa for worshiping the moon on the Mid-Autumn Day exclusively. And we can also find the joss sticks and candles are sold in southern paper stores.

The Grandpa Rabbit with a man's body and a rabbit's head holds a jade pestle had been anthropomorphized after a bold creation by the folk artists. Modeled after the opera characters, the Granpa Rabbit became warriors in shining armour, some of which ride a beast like lion or elephant, some of which sit on the back of a bird like peacock or crane. Even though the scene of a rabbit riding on a tiger is super weird, it's still a creative transformation of image by folk artists. Besides, the Grandpa Rabbit with a movable elbow joint and jaw, known as "Gua Da Zui" seems more attractive. The lively stalls that sell the Grandpa Rabbit can be found in the Wu memorial arch in the Qianmen Street, the front of the drum-tower in Houmen Street, Xidan, Dongsi and almost everywhere after the August 15th in Chinese Lunar Calendar.

There is also the Grandma Rabbit with the clothes, air and hairstyle of women at that time, coupled with the Grandpa Rabbit. And a kind of the Grandpa Rabbit called "Gua Da Zui" with a movable upper lip and an empty mouth can move by the hanging strings inside the body. Or the strings attached to the arms, which makes it able to move with the strings like making heavenly medicine. Another type of the Grandpa Rabbit is represented by a group of the Grandpa Rabbits living in a specific scenes of life: Some little rabbits are inches in height dressed as the customers, waiter and manager under the grape trellis or teahouse made by a kind of toy with one *chi*(=1/3 metre) size. The waiter comes and fills the glass of the customers who are sitting near the table with water while the manager is calculating on abacus on the other side.

Tips for Tourism

Dongyue Temple in Beijing:

The relationship between the Mid−Autumn Festival and the Grandpa Rabbit are just the same as the relationship between the Spring Festival and dumplings in old Beijing. A high fake mountain filled with the Grandpa Rabbits will be put on the Dongyue Temple for people to pray for bless− ing on each Mid−Autumn Day in accordance with local customs in old Beijing. The Grandpa Rabbit mountain in the Dongyue Temple is also becoming a scene of the Mid−Autumn Festival in Beijing, and praying to the Grandpa Rabbit in the Dongyue Temple has gradually become a habit. The old natives of Beijing also have their own custom of inviting and sending the Grandpa Rabbit to their relatives and friends.

Dongyue temple is located at the north side of the street outside the Chaoyangmen in Chaoyang District in Beijing, which used to be the larg− est jungle of "Zhengyi Taoism" in North China. The grand, magnifi− cent, elegant−decorated, and crafty−designed temple exudes the spirits, qualities and romantic charm of Han nationality's traditional culture. Now, the temple has also established a Beijing Folk Custom Museum and keeping a large number of Taoist buildings and stone steles past dynasties with dif− ferent characteristics and are very useful for the research of historical origin and development of ancient Chinese Taoist and Xuanjiao.

Address: No. 141 Chaowai Street, Chaoyang District, Beijing

The weather during the Mid-Autumn Festival is usually sunny and cozy, which is perfect to hold some activities.

First, people like rowing and appreciating the moon and lotus, and women are used to planting and wearing flowers at the Mid-Autumn night, which represents "wishing the flowers are always in the season" and "wishing the moon is always full". The jujube trees fruit during that time and children tend to pick four green jujubes and peel them for playing game, known as "Zhupaimo".

Second, the Cricket Fighting is loved by the young and the old. The one called "the Cricket Fighting of Nine Kids" stands for praying for children. Raising crickets is also an important activity in autumn.

Besides, singing, dancing, and acrobatics are also indispensable. For instance, the Folk Songs Festival on the Mid-Autumn Day in Mei County in Guangdong is held to commemorate Liusanjie, the "Fairy Singer". And a kind of gathering called "the Gathering in the eighth lunar month" is prevailed in Hainan, in which people hold parties, sing and exchange mooncakes through all night.

The "Firecrackers of the Mid-Autumn Festival" in Jixi County in Anhui is described as, "Dozens of kids make an about-five-*chi* (=1/3 metre)-long firecracker with straws, which looks like a braid, submerging it in the water for a few minutes, and then strike it on a stone. For it sounds like the real firecrackers, it is called 'letting off the firecrackers of the Mid-Autumn Festival'."

5. Eating Customs

The "Mooncake" is the essential food of the Mid-Autumn Festival, and it's not really a Mid-Autumn Festival without mooncakes. Mooncakes, zongzi of the Dragon Boat Festival, Laba porridge of Laba Festival and the lanterns of the Lantern Festival are all the foods of one specific festival.

Mooncakes has been gradually evolved from a kind of sacrifice offering, which has a long history. The round "prime Minister cake" in the period of the Shang Dynasty, which is used to commemorate Wen Zhong (the prime minister in the Shang Dynasty), is the "ancestor" of the mooncakes, based on historical records.

Different flavors of mooncakes

The gingeli, walnuts were introduced when Zhang Qian was sent to the Western Region, as the accessories of the round cake preparation. Since then, the round cake with walnuts filling "Hu cake" has been prevailing.

It is said that the "Hu cake" renamed the "mooncake" owing to the talent of Yang Guifei (the favorite concubine of the Emperor Xuanzong of the Tang Dynasty). Xuanzong was upset for there's no such a best place to enjoy the moon with Yang in the Penglai poolside of the Daming Palace at the Mid-Autumn night in the early years of Tianbao period (742—756) of the Tang Dynasty according to the Forgotten Tales of the Kaiyuan and Tianbao Periods. And Xuanzong thought the moon appreciation was insipid while the servant happened to offer the "Hu cake" which sounds awful to him. Yang blurted out the name of "mooncake" wittily at the intense moment. That's how that name came from.

The "Palace cake", known as "little cake" or "moon dumpling" is favored by the royal household in the Northern Song Dynasty. Su Dongpo had a poem, "Eating the little cake just like chewing the moon, which tastes crispy and joyful." The name of "mooncake" first appeared officially in *Tales of the Old Capital* written by Zhou Mi in the Southern Song Dynasty, in which he first mentioned "mooncake"when describing the knowledge and information in Lin'an (the capital city of the Southern Song Dynasty). The mooncake is like the shape of the flower of the water caltrop, and exists in the same year with the chrysanthemum cake and the plum flower cake according to *Dream in Lin'an* written by Wu Zimu in the Southern Song Dynasty. It said, "The mooncake can be found in the whole year, and everyone can eat in anywhere at any time." This shows that the mooncake isn't a festival food at that time.

The festival custom of eating cakes in autumn originated from the Han Dynasty. The etiquette system of respecting and supporting the elder at the Mid-Autumn Festival or the Beginning of the Autumn can also be found in the Han Dynasty and the emperor will award the elders with the "Xiong Cu cake".

It is said that the custom of eating mooncakes at the Mid-Autumn Festival could date back to the Sui and Tang Dynasties (581—907). The emperor Xizong of Tang heard the Jinshies (the successful candidate in the highest imperial examinations) are having a party by the Qujiang Pool when he was eating the mooncake on a Mid-Autumn Festival, then he ordered the chefs who were serving in the imperial kitchen to offer them the mooncakes wrapped with red ribbons according to the *Information about Luozhong*.

171

The custom of eating mooncakes in the Mid-Autumn Festival is associated with the meaning of reunion owing to the local rebellion at the turning of the Yuan and Ming Dynasties. The Central Plains revolted against the ruling class because of the unbearable brutal reign at that time. Zhu Yuanzhang (founded the Ming Dynasty) brought parties together to prepare armed uprisings. However, the ruler searched them too strictly to pass the messages. Liu Bowen, the military counsellor camp up with an idea that ordered the subordinates to put a note saying "uprising at the night of August 15th" in the filling of the mooncakes, then transmitted them separately to the insurrectionary army everywhere, to instruct them to respond the uprising at the night of the lunar August 15th. Each insurrectionary army responsed concurrently which is like a single spark causing a big fire on the day of uprising. The rebellion had been successfully carried through as Xu Da occupied the capital of Yuan Dynasty in no time. Zhu Yuanzhang rejoiced at the news and decided to celebrate with soldiers and all the people together on the Mid-Autumn Day and awarded all the state ministers with the "mooncakes" that were used to pass massages secretly during the uprising. Since then, the "mooncakes" are made more sophisticated with different varieties, and the big one may look like a huge disc. It also becomes a good choice for gifting. The custom of eating mooncakes during the Mid-Autumn Festival began to spread among the people from then.

Not until the narrations about eating mooncakes during the Mid-Autumn Festival became more and more in the Ming Dynasty did the custom begin to spread among the common people. The ingenious baker pressed the pattern of the legend of "Chang'e Flying to the Moon" on the mooncakes, making the mooncake the basic food of the Mid-Autumn Festival favored by people. "People exchange mooncakes with each others, taking the meaning of reunion." said by Tian Rucheng in *the Records of Sightseeing in Xihu*. People baked round cakes as a gift to others and got together to celebrate the day. In the *Jiaxing Government Records* of Zhengjiang in the Ming Dynasty, it is said, "people make a big cake with all kinds of fruits on the day of August 15th , which is called 'mooncake'." It is recorded in *Wan Shu Notes* written by Shen Bang, "People make moon-shape cakes with different sizes, which are called mooncakes, and give them away to each other." And another words in *Zhuo Zhong Records*, "Imperial families usually admire begonias and the flowers of fragrant plantain lily while mooncakes seller can be seen everywhere on August. Mooncakes and fruits are offered by every household on the day of August 15th. And the left-over mooncakes, which are called reunion cakes, are put in a dry and ventilated place for sharing on the end of the year." Mooncakes, the essential offering for worship of the moon in the Mid-Autumn Festival were used to be homemade but sold on the market with a variety and more exquisite procedures now. "The mooncake made with the pattern of the Moon Palace and a pair of rabbits, reminds us the touching story of Chang'e Flying to the Moon. She stuck in the Moon Palace with regret and enduring youth." described in the *Local customs in Youzhou*, which is written by Peng Yunzhang in the late Ming Dynasty.

The custom of eating and gifting mooncakes on the Mid-Autumn Festival has been prevailing since the Yuan and Ming Dynasties with the symbolic meaning of "reunion".

Eating mooncakes in the Mid-Autumn Festival has become a popular custom in the Qing Dynasty with more proficient making skills. A screen was usually put in a yard of the palace in the Qing Dynasty, facing east. Cockscomb flowers, green soy beans, taros, peanuts, radishes and fresh lotus roots were set on both sides of the screen. And an outsize mooncake was put on the Baxian table (a kind of old-fashioned square table for eight people) with various pastries and fruits in front of the screen. "The crisp crust mooncakes which taste crunchy and gooey are made with pine nuts, walnuts, melon seeds, crystal sugar and lard for filling." described by Yuan Mei (a famous poet in the Qing Dynasty) in *Sui Yuan Menu*. The most delicious mooncakes in Beijing must be those made by Zhimei Room in the Qianmen Street. "The mooncakes for worshiping the moon can be brought everywhere, and the big ones can reach the diameter of more than one *chi* (=1/3 metre) with the pattern of the Moon Palace and rabbits. But you should go to Zhimei Room in the Qianmen Street if you want to eat the most amazing mooncakes in Peking." introduced in *Yanjing Chronicle* (*Annual Customs and Festivals in Peking*). It is said in *Dijing Chronicle* (a annal of customs in Beijing) written by Rongbi in the Qing Dynasty, "Besides the incense light offerings, the mooncakes which are decorated by the lotus petal shaped watermelon and laurel shaped radish leaf are necessary on the day of worshiping the moon." "A big mooncake, which can reach to the diameter of more than one *chi* (=1/3 metre) is indispensable for worshiping the moon and sharing with everyone on the Mid-Autumn Day. Therefore, figuring out the number of the family members before cutting the cake is important for it should be cut into exactly the same number of pieces as that of the family members, which requires that the people who stayed at home or went away from home should be counted together, and it should be cut one more piece if there is a pregnant woman at home. However, some families saved the mooncakes to the New Year's Eve and shared them with each other, which is also called the 'reunion cake'." recorded in *Dijing Sceneries*. The types of eating mooncakes with local characteristics have emerged around the worship and appreciation of the moon, like "Bu Zhuangyuan" in Jiangnan area. People cut a mooncake into three pieces of large size; medium size and small size, and pile them together. The biggest one which called "Zhuangyuan" is put underneath, the medium size one which called "Bangyan" was put in the middle and the smallest one which called "Tan-hua" was put on the top. And then the whole family rolls the dice to get the piece of the mooncake for fun. "Zhuangyuan" belongs to the winner with the largest point, while the "Bang-yan" and "Tanhua" belongs to the participants with the second largest point and smallest point in order.

Mooncakes

The quality of the mooncakes has been improved greatly while the varieties have been renovated constantly with different ingredients, making processes and shapes by modern times. The shapes of mooncakes vary from region to region. Generally, The "mooncake" in northern area like Shanxi and Shaanxi are very big without fillings. People there cut it into pieces to share with each other; The "mooncake" in southern areas like Jiangsu and Zhejiang almost are like a kind of small and delicate pastry with different fillings. The mooncakes in modern times can be grouped into four varieties, such as white mooncakes, red mooncakes, purifying syrup mooncakes and crisp crust mooncakes.

The white mooncakes with crisp crusts and soft fillings are made after the process of filling, forming, stamping and baking with the crusts made from wheatmeal, soft sugar, lard oil or edible vegetable oil and the fillings made from crystal sugar, walnuts, shelled melon seeds, osmanthus flowers, green plums or haw jelly and slices of the green and red pepper.

The red mooncakes with crisp crusts and soft fillings are made after the process of filling, forming, stamping and baking with the crusts made from refined wheatmeal, soft sugar, malt sugar, and baking soda and the fillings made from cooked wheatmeal, sesame oil, walnuts, shelled melon seeds, crystal

The combination of tradition and fashion——
chocolate mooncake

sugar, osmanthus flowers, and slices of the green and red pepper.

The crisp and fragrant purifying syrup mooncakes with exquisite patterns are made after the process of filling, molding and baking with the crusts made from wheatmeal, edible vegetable oil, baking soda and syrup. The crusts of the purifying syrup mooncakes are made from the dough concocted by the cooled pure syrup. The name of "purifying syrup" comes from the process of brewing syrup which requires extracting impurity of the syrup by protein fluid.

The crisp crust mooncakes, also known as suede mooncakes with the velvety and textured crusts and fillings with a delicate sweetness are made from refined wheatmeal, edible vegetable oil and other ingredients after the process of filling, forming, stamping and baking.

Currently, it has formed four distinctive flavors of mooncakes: Beijing style, Suzhou style, Chaoshan style, and Cantonese style.

5.1 Beijing-style Mooncakes

The mooncakes customized by Hermes and other
international fashion brands

177

The diverse Beijing-style mooncakes, which originated in Beijing, Tianjin and nearby areas, have a certain market in northern area and are one of the representative variety of the mooncakes of the Han nationality in northern area and characterized by the good proportion of the crust and filling (the crust mixes with the filling in proportion of 4 : 6) and a modest sweetness. And put more sesame oil relatively, which make it taste sweet, light, and crisp.

5.2 Suzhou-style Mooncakes

Formerly known as Crisp mooncakes, this kind of Suzhou-style pastry is renamed the Suzhou-style mooncakes since it is favored by the people in the areas of Jiangsu and Zhejiang. After the process of making crisp crusts, filling, forming, and baking, the mooncake tastes delicious and fluffy with the crisp crust and the fat but not greasy filling. The crust is made from wheatmeal, malt syrup, edible vegetable oil or lard oil, water and other ingredients while the crisp is made from wheatmeal, editable vegetable oil or lard oil.

The Suzhou-style mooncakes are usually made in Jiangsu,

Suzhou-style mooncake

Zhejiang and Shanghai, while the traditional and authentic skills are reserved in Suzhou. The basic process of this skill includes: sorting, preliminary processing, mixing filling, making crust, making crisp, wrapping crisp, wrapping filling, forming, stamping, baking, packing and so on. The moonmakes are made by relatively simple utensils without any mould during the making process, such as, spatula, slick paper, ovenware, etc.

The Suzhou-style mooncakes with a lot of local characteristics can be divided into two types: sweet and salty (or baked and fried), and the making materials of Suzhou-style mooncakes must be chosen fastidiously. Baking is usually the basic cooking method of sweet mooncakes, and the filling of it can be made from rose petals, all kinds of fruits, spiced salt, bean paste, osmanthus flowers, walnut, peanuts, pinenuts, sesame seeds, etc; Frying is usually the basic cooking method of salty mooncakes, and the filling of it can be made from ham, chives, lard, fresh meat, shrimp meat, etc. The crisp is made by wheatmeal, soft sugar, malt syrup, and grease. Among them, the flavors of rose petal, fruits, spiced salt and lard are the representatives of Suzhou-style mooncakes.

5.3 Chaoshan-style Mooncakes

The Chaoshan-style mooncake, one of the Four Major Varieties of Mooncakes in China is also known as Lao cake (the "Lao" character refers to lard in the dialects of Chaozhou and Shantou.) which is made after the process of mixing the lard and flour together, wrapping the sweet filling and baking it. It is a famous pastry of the Han nationality in Chaoshan Area (Chaozhou and Shantou area) of Guangdong Province. The Lao cakes are sold through the whole year, but the Mid-Autumn Festival is the perfect time to go on sale. The crisp crusts and the sweet but not greasy taste are the main features of the common Chaoshan-style mooncakes. They can be divided into varieties of mung beans, black beans, crystal, and purple taros according to the types of fillings. The kernels of the cakes can

Chaoshan-style mooncakes

be egg yolk, seafood, many other kinds or nothing. The mooncake with a comparatively flat body, pure white crusts and sweet filling, which is made of crunchy candies tastes really crisp and delicious.

Chaoshan-style crisp crust mooncakes

180

5.4 Cantonese-style Mooncakes

Cantonese-style mooncakes, which are a distinctive pastry of the Han nationality in Guangdong Province, a folk treat at the Mid-Autumn Festival in Guangdong, Guangxi, Jiangxi, and an important form of mooncakes. The high quality materials and the exquisite manufacture skills make the cantonese-style mooncake famous throughout the world. It's both the finest gift during the Mid-Autumn Festival and the indispensible food when enjoying the moon for its thin and crisp crust, delicate shape, exquisite and distinct pattern, unbreakable and elegant package and portability.

The Cantonese-style mooncakes originated in 1889 when there was a pastry store selling a kind of crisp cake with the filling made of lotus paste which tastes fresh and delicious and was favored by customers at the west of the city. The pastry store was renamed " Lian(means constantly in Chinese) Xiang House" during the Guangxu period of the Qing Dynasty(1875—1908), and the cake with the filling of lotus paste at that time is much the same as the mooncake nowadays. Chen Taiji, a Hanlin Academician (a member of the imperial academy), once tasted and sang the praises of the mooncakes from " Lian Xiang House" in 1910, but he thought "Lian Xiang" is somewhat inelegant and suggested to rename " Lian(lotus) Xiang House", and wrote the plague by himself which is still in use today. Following the example of "Lian Xiang House", many restaurants and pastry store in Guangzhou started to produce mooncakes, forming a lot of mooncake brand like "Taotao House", "Guangzhou Restaurant", "Jinkou mooncake", "Quxiang", "Da San Yuan". The cantonese-style mooncakes have been becoming famous overseas since then.

The cantonese-style mooncakes are native to Guangzhou,

but also are produced in Guangdong, Hong Kong, Jiangxi, Zhejiang, Shanghai, etc now. The mooncake with the crust made from wheatmeal, invert syrup, vegetable oil and lye tastes crisp and soft after the process of filling, forming, brushing egg wash and other steps.

Cantonese-style mooncake is characterized by oily taste, thin crust, and full filling. People mainly choose local well-known specialty products as fillings, such as coconuts, olive kernels, tangerine pies, Cantonese-style sausages, barbecued pork, salted eggs and so on. The process of making crusts and fillings is unique as the crusts with some clear and concave-convex patterns are brown and bright while the taste and texture of fillings are fabulous. People are adept at using the interaction between varied flavor matters to produce unique flavors then gift the special tastes to the mooncakes. For example, use the sugar to adjust the salinity, use spice foods to remove the smell of meats and use different molecular structures of all kinds of accessories to create different colors, aroma, and tastes, making the paste fillings taste smooth and soft and the fillings

The sticky, soft and sweet cantonese-style
yolk mooncake

of meats and sea foods taste salty and sweet.

Cantonese-style mooncakes have various qualities. The traditional Cantonese-style mooncakes can be divided into types of nuts, meats, shredded coconuts, pastes according to their different fillings and have developed some new types like fruits, jam, vegetables, and so on after the 1990s. The Cantonese-style mooncakes are famous around China and the world for the recherche ingredients, thin crusts and full fillings, delicious taste, multifarious patterns, firm body, and portability and they are also easy to preserve. Its name is generally based on the main ingredients of the fillings, such as wu ren (five nuts——almond, pistachio, pecan, cashew and macadamia), jin tui(cured ham) , lotus paste, red bean paste, bean paste, jujube, shredded coconuts, dong rong (shredded sweet white gourd), etc. Its raw materials are very extensive, such as egg yolks, preserved eggs, sausages, barbecued pork, shredded chicken, roast duck, mushrooms and so on. All of them can be used as raw materials to make various types.

Extension of Knowledge

Points for Attention:

• Mooncakes are offered a selection of sweet and salty. You should eat the salty mooncake first, then the sweet one if you want to enjoy a good taste.

• Prepare some tea (especially the scented tea) when eating the mooncake. That makes the heavy mooncake less greasy and taste wonderful.

• Don't eat too many mooncakes. Overeating mooncakes will lead to gastrointestinal discomfort for the high sugar content and fat. The elders, children or people who have the obstacle of function of intestines and stomach should pay more attention to that.

• Eat fresh mooncakes. People often buy a lot of mooncakes during the Mid−Autumn Festival, But the fillings of the mooncakes are easy to go bad and cause food poisoning if placed too long. Therefore, you should eat up the mooncakes as soon as you buy them. The leftover mooncakes should be properly preserved to prevent deterioration for many mooncakes can be left after the festival or even for a longer time.

The fillings of mooncakes are divided into two types: hard and soft. The mooncakes with soft fillings can only be preserved for 7 to 10 days for the high water content while the ones with hard fillings can be preserved for about 1 month. Generally, instead of being preserved in a sealed con−tainer for a long time, it's best to preserve the mooncakes in a basket with a piece of clean paper upon and then hung in a cool and ventilated place. The boxed mooncakes should be ventilated with the lid open or preserved in the refrigerator directly. Moreover, keep the mooncakes in a dark place to avoid oil oxidation for its high fat content.

The mooncake is a kind of seasonal food which should not be pre−served too long in order to keep its original color, aroma, taste and special flavor. The fresh−baked mooncakes taste best.

The mooncake is not the only food with the features of the Mid-Autumn Festival.

There is a legend about an osmanthus tree in the moon palace, so the sweet-scented osmanthus became a symbol or a mascot of the Mid-Autumn Festival. The habit of eating the sweet-scented osmanthus during the Mid-Autumn Festival has been prevailing since then.

People in Nanjing like to eat "Guihua Duck (Sweet Os-manthus Duck or Salted Duck)" in the Mid-Autumn Festival. Osmanthus duck is a local specialty, which was a kind of salted duck. The salted duck is very common while the one produced in the sweet-scented osmanthus season is regarded as high value. The Guihua Duck is made of the duck with thin skin and tender meat. The duck tastes delicious with the crisp skin and fresh and tender meat after the process of wiping the cleaned duck with hot salt, covered and simmered in the stockpot, and poured the sweet-scented osmanthus syrup which is made by mixing the sugar, sour plum and sweet-scented osmanthus picked before the festival on it after being boiled.

Some delicacies of season are the essential food of the Mid-Autumn Festival, such as the crab, which is favored by the royals in the Ming Dynasty. People sit around the table, tasting the steamed crabs with wine vinegar and drinking and washing hands with the "Perilla Leaf Decoction" after eating. People were performing the mythical opera of the Mid-Autumn Festival while the banquet table is filled with flowers, pomegranate, and other seasonal food. Now people also like to put some the seasonal crabs on the table.

Some special eating customs also prevailed in some places. For example, the "sugar taro" is the basic food with the feature of the Mid-Autumn Festival in the southeastern coastal areas.

Crabs in Autumn

Yu Nai (taro), originally known as "Dun Ou(squatting gull)" for it looks like a squatting gull, also known as Ju, and "Yu Tou" among the folks. Taro is a kind of herb of araceae, a natural nourished polysaccharide polymer colloid of plant, and a food favored by people, which is grown extensively in the tropical forests of the East Indies and Peninsular Malaysia until now. It can be treated as a kind of grain or vegetable, even can be made into snacks.

Taro tastes delicious and glutinous and has been planted in China for a long time. It is said in the *Records of the History*, "The region of Minshan Mountain boasts vast expanse of fertile land, which is filled with taros." "The whole family warms us up by the fire at night. It's the season of taro, which makes us happier than the emperor." It was praised by the poem in the *Delicacies on Mountains*, a famous recipe book in the Southern Song Dynasty.

The custom of eating taro during the Mid-Autumn Festival is said to be originated in the Ming Dynasty. People in the Southeast coastal area suffered the harassment of Janpanese Pirates (operating in Chinese coastal waters from the fourteenth to the sixteenth century) at that time. Qi Jiguang, the general was ordered to fight against them and won a great victory. The army, led by Qi Jiguang was celebrating the Mid-Autumn Festival at the camp when the Japanese Pirates attacked them at midnight, besieged and tried to starve them out. The soldiers had run out of food after a few days except the taros dug on the hill. Unexpectedly, the unknown food tasted delicious after being boiled, "We can call it 'Yu Nan (means died in an accident)' in memory of the soldiers who died in the fight." Qi Jiguang said. The Qi's army strived to break out of the encirclement after gorging themselves on "Yu Nan" at one night and annihilated all the Janpanese pirates who were still sleeping. The people in the Southeast coastal areas must eat the sugar taro during the Mid-Autumn Festival to honor the anti-pirate merits and achievements of Qi Jiguang and keep alive our sense of continuity with the nation's suffering of the past since then. The "Yu Nan" was gradually renamed "Yu Nai (taro)" over time and the custom of eating taro has been prevailing since then.

The lunar month of August is the time for many seasonal fruits to mature, such as grapes, pomegranates, jujube, apples, oranges, pears and other fruits, watermelon, pumpkin, sweet potatoes, sweet melons, crisp melons and other melons. All of them have become the food with the Mid-Autumn Festival feature. Families put these fruits, mooncakes, melon seeds, and other foods at night of the Mid-Autumn Day while enjoying and worshiping the moon.

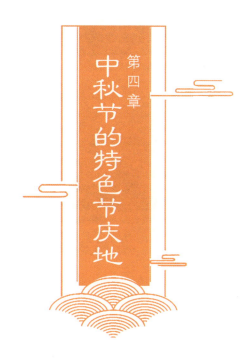

第四章

中秋节的特色节庆地

　　"姮娥药熟桂华新，满贮清光待出云。徐御冰轮行碧落，世间多少感秋人。"北宋诗人张耒的这首诗生动地刻画了人们在中秋之夜仰望夜空，思乡怀人的深切情感。中秋节不仅仅是中国汉族的传统节日，很多少数民族同胞也要在这一天欢庆节日。漫长的历史变迁当中，现在的中秋节已经与古代的节日有了一些不同，但各地的人们依然用自己的方式来欢度这一节日。

一、
少数民族的特色中秋节

除汉族外，中国许多的少数民族也过中秋节，但节俗各异。

壮族，旧称"僮"，是中国少数民族中人口最多的一个民族。国内主要分布在广西、云南、广东和贵州等地，国外主要分布在越南北部。壮族先人在中国古代曾先后称为"獠蛮""俚蛮""溪峒蛮""乌浒蛮"等。宋代始为"獠""撞""僮""仲"，明清又称为"僮人""良

○壮族中秋节习俗——放花灯

人""土人"。壮族与贵州的布依族，越南的岱依族、侬族、热依族的语言文化基本一致。

每年夏历八月中旬，或中秋夜，人们便在村头村尾露天处，设一供桌，供放祭品和香炉，桌子右边树一个高约一尺的树枝或竹枝，象征社树，亦作月神下凡及上天的梯子。活动分为：请月神下凡；神人对歌；月神卜卦算命；歌手唱送神咒歌，送月神回天等四个阶段。壮族习惯于在河中的竹排上用米饼拜月，少女在水面放花灯，以测一生的幸福，并演唱优美的《请月姑》民歌。

壮族人民能歌善唱，右江一带称为"欢"，左江一带称为"诗"，桂北一带称为"比"和"欢"，都是唱山歌的意思。定期举行的唱山歌会，称为歌圩。壮族的歌圩，一般在春秋两季最盛大，中秋节是举行歌圩的大日子。歌圩上所唱的歌，主要是以男女青年追求美好爱情理想为主题。其内容一般为见面歌、邀请歌、盘歌、新歌、爱慕歌、盟誓歌、送别歌等。歌圩，一般为期一天，也有连续两三天的。参加歌圩的除青年人外，也有中老年和少年。老人小孩主要是"观战"、欣赏、品评，有的老年歌手参与活动，但他们不唱歌，而是给青年人当参谋。歌圩非常热闹，除青年们对歌外，还有唱戏的、做买卖的。各种日用百货、绫罗布匹、饮食糕点、鸡鸭鱼肉、蔬菜等，应有尽有。实际上歌圩也带有几分交易会的性质。

除了要赏月和吃月饼外，还有一项重要的习俗活动就是"闹哥孩"，因为组织者和参与者都是女性，闹的对象是男性，所以叫"闹哥孩"，其实就是对歌，内容一般不涉及爱情，多是有关史实、社会一类的，尽兴方散。

畲族，主要生活在中国东南部崇山峻岭中一个古老纯朴的少数民族。人口约有70余万人，主要分布在福建、浙江、江西、广东、安徽等省。畲族使用畲语，属汉藏语系中的苗瑶语。99％的人使用接近于汉语客家方言的语言，但在语音上与客家话稍有差别，有少数语词跟客家语完全不同。无本民族文字，通用汉文。崇拜祖先和鬼神。畲族自称"山哈"，"哈"畲语意为"客"，"山哈"意即是从外地迁来居住在山里的客人。

　　每年的农历八月十五日，畲族把这天视为走亲访友的好日子，而陪客唱歌又是畲族的独特习俗。中秋歌节不但要陪客唱，还要集中到县城去对歌。对歌的时候，男女各站一边，女的还特别喜欢挤在一起，不参加唱歌的妇女，也要和歌者挤在一起，以壮声势。高明的歌手，可以随便转换曲调，除了对唱，他们最爱唱的一种叫"双条落"的双音，是一种属于重唱性质的歌唱形式，具有浓厚的畲族特色。

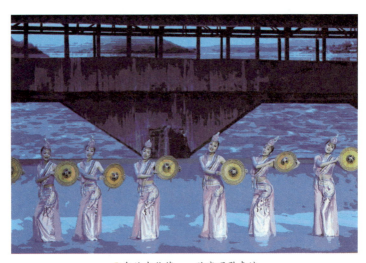

○畲族中秋节——陪客唱歌表演

　　仡佬族，中国少数民族之一，人口约 50 多万人，主要居住在贵州省。仡佬族历史悠久，商周至西汉时期称为"百濮"，东汉至南北朝时期称的"濮""僚"都与其先祖有渊源关系。"仡僚""葛僚""僚""仡佬"是隋唐以后，各个时期对他们的称谓，中华人民共和国成立以后，正式定名为仡佬族。

　　仡佬族最隆重的传统节日莫过于八月节，仡佬族的"八月节"
从农历八月十五日一直持续到八月二十日。节日的头天，即"虎日"，
全族老少都要穿上新装，齐集在寨子的地坪上。几个青年把一头头
戴大红花的黄牛牵来，寨中最长者——"族老"开始祷告，祈求五
谷丰登；乐队奏起"八仙"曲，同时要鸣放粉枪、放鞭炮。然后杀牛，
割下牛心，每户一份，表示全族团结一心。随后，"族老"还要率众
捧着小猪、老鸡、大鹅三牲，到菩提树下祭祀。礼毕，全族欢聚一
堂会餐，直到天黑。次日，各户举行家宴后，女性会偕儿带女回娘
家送礼；男人们串街会友，唱歌、谈天。青年男女的歌舞活动一直会
延续到节日的最后一天。

○仡佬族"八月节"场景

　　侗族，是中国的一个少数民族，居住区主要在贵州、湖南和广
西壮族自治区的交界处，湖北恩施也有部分的侗族居住。侗族人口
总数约 200 多万人。侗族的名称来自"溪洞"，这是当地人传统的行
政单位，今天当地还有许多地名叫"洞"。侗族自称 Gaeml（发音近

似于汉语的"干""仳"或"更"字），依据联合国倡导的"名从主人"原则，国际标准译名为"Kam""Kam People"。侗族的名称，最早见于宋代文献，记作"仡伶"。明、清两代曾出现"峒蛮""峒苗""峒人""洞家"等其他名称。新中国成立后统称为"侗族"，民间多称"侗家"。

中秋节侗族的青年人会举行郊游、欢会，第二天要举行对歌。小伙子都要化妆，向心上人表达情意。湖南侗乡中秋的"偷月"则别有风趣。传说古时候在中秋节的晚上，月宫里的仙女要降临凡间，她们也会把甘露洒向人间。在这一夜人们可以共享撒有甘露的瓜果蔬菜。中秋夜，侗家姑娘打着花伞，偷偷来到自己心上人的菜园，借着月光采摘瓜果，希望月宫仙女为他们牵上红线。倘若能摘到一个并蒂的瓜果，将预兆两人相亲相爱，白头偕老。

傣族，即"傣泰民族"，自称"dǎi"与"tài"之间的发音，是中国的少数民族之一，也是泰国和老挝的主体民族。"傣泰"在中国的史籍文献中，先后被称为"哀牢""掸""乌蛮""白蛮""白衣""金齿""黑齿""白夷""僰夷""摆夷"等。第二次世界大战前，在暹罗王国的推动下，国际社会开始把分布于各国的"傣泰"统称为"泰（Thai）"。第二次世界大战后，各国政府将分布在各自境内的"傣泰"分别命名：在泰国、柬埔寨、越南等国仍被称为"泰（Thai）"；在老挝被称为"佬（Lao）"；在缅甸被称为"掸（Shan）"；在印度被称为"阿萨姆（Assam）"；在中国被称为"傣（Dai）"。

中秋节举行支火雀是云南元江、新平一带花腰傣族的民间传统节日。在每年农历八月十五日举行。这时元江坝子正是谷物金黄的时候，成千上万的火雀将飞来啄食谷粒。为了保住庄稼，精明能干的傣家男子先从杉松木上用干树枝蘸取一些寄生物的黏液，再把这些枝条在头天的黄昏放在鸟雀最喜欢栖息的地方。清晨，不知情的火雀一落在枝上便被死死粘住，落到了人们的小布袋中，成为中秋佳节的美味佳肴。节日期间，妇女们则相约到河边、池塘里捞鱼摸虾，老阿妈忙着舂糯米粑粑。傍晚，各家都摆好一张小方桌子，四角均放一个圆饼，饼心插一炷香。待各种饭菜摆齐后，全家人同拜圆月，并朝天鸣放火枪。然后围坐饮酒，品尝汤锅、干巴、腌蛋和干黄鳝，谈笑望月。

黎族，是中国岭南的少数民族之一，人口有 100 多万。以农业为主，妇女精于纺织，"黎锦""黎单"闻名于世。汉晋时期，黎族先民被包括在"里""俚""蛮"等名称之中，隋唐时又有"俚"与"僚"并称。唐末，在汉文史籍文献中出现了"黎"的称呼，标志着黎族作为单一的民族共同体出现在历史舞台上。宋代，"黎"逐渐代替"俚"，成为黎族的普遍族称。黎族普遍自称"赛"，因分布地区、方言及服饰等差异，其内部又有"侾""杞""美孚""润""赛"等称呼。

黎族称中秋节为"八月会"或"调声节"。届时各集镇举行歌舞聚会，每村由一个"调声头"（即领队）率领男女青年参加。人员会齐后，大家互赠月饼、香糕、甜粑、花巾、彩扇，成群结队，川流不息。入夜便聚焦在火旁，烤食野味，痛饮米酒，开展盛大的调声对歌演唱，未婚青年趁机挑寻未来的伴侣。

阿昌族，是中国云南境内最早的世居民族之一。古代汉文史籍中的"峨昌""娥昌""莪昌"或"阿昌""萼昌"等，都是不同时期对阿昌族的称谓。新中国成立后，统称为阿昌族。他们聚居在高黎贡山余脉的丘陵山

○黎族八月会的歌舞聚会

地、峡谷平坝。这里土地肥沃，气候温和，雨量充沛，为阿昌族农业生产的发展提供了良好的条件。阿昌族自古即以擅种水稻而闻名。阿昌族主要从事农业。

对于阿昌族来说八月十五日是一个传统的农业祭祀节日，叫作"尝新节"。在这一天阿昌族人不拜月娘，而是祭祀老姑太。

关于老姑太的来历，阿昌族人传说：很久很久以前，有一个妇女善于种田和纺织，里里外外都是一把好手，人们尊称她为"老姑太"。老姑太有个独生儿子，儿子娶了媳妇后，媳妇对老姑太不好，经常对她打骂，渐渐儿子对她也不孝顺了。老姑太只好拄着竹棍离开了家，成了无家可归的人，沿路乞讨。后来遇到一对好心的兄弟，收留了她，认老姑太作娘，一起过日子。老姑太就把自己种地的本领传给了哥儿俩，日子过得很富足。她又教左邻右舍耕田、种菜，得到人们尊敬。两兄弟娶了媳妇，有了孩子。兄弟俩对老姑太很好，但是两个媳妇见老姑太年老不中用了，不愿意伺候她，还煮大蚂蟥给她吃，气得老姑太又一次离家出走了。而两兄弟到处找她。当他们在山下苞谷地的窝棚里找到老姑太的时候，老姑太已经奄奄一息了。兄弟俩把老姑太背回了家，老姑太在临终前留下话："我死后，每年三月播种的时候，你们给我上一次坟；每年八月十五，你们再给我上一次坟，在竹棍上捆一棵新苞谷，放在堂屋里，保管你们有吃有穿。"说完，老姑太就去世了，兄弟俩和乡亲们每年祭祀她两次，代代相传，就形成了祭拜老姑太的三月播种节和八月十五的尝新节。

到了这个日子，阿昌族家家户户都要把房子收拾干净，到地里拔一棵果实结得最多的芋头，砍一棵双穗的玉米，把它们捆在一根竹棍上，放在堂屋里，代表谷物神老姑太，再摆上各种刚收获的新粮食水果，举行祭祀老姑太的仪式。然后用刚舂好的新米做成丰盛的饭，全家聚餐。

瑶族，是中国一支古老的民族，是古代东方"九黎"中的一支，民风淳朴且彪悍。瑶族自称为"勉""金门""布努""炳多优""黑尤蒙""拉珈"等。

　　瑶族在中秋之日举行"舞火狗节"。南方民族大都崇拜火神，"舞火狗"意在驱邪避邪。当天，各村的未婚女青年上山采来藤条和黄姜叶，各家都准备好香火。晚上，全村寨的姑娘们在手臂、腰和腿上用藤条缠满姜汁，头戴斗笠。年长的妇女在姑娘们身体的这些部位点上香火，列队先向村中的峒主爷和祖先叩拜。姑娘们叩拜完祖先，然后舞蹈。拜毕，再穿街走巷到每一户人家向灶王爷行礼，如果途径菜园，还要绕园一周。最后到村外的河边，将身上的藤、姜叶和香火全扔进河里，姑娘们就到河里洗手洗脚，同时泼水嬉戏。如有邻村的姑娘，场面就更热闹了。青年男子则在一旁燃放鞭炮。待姑娘们玩够后，男女开始对歌。按照当地习俗，姑娘必须参加三次以上的"舞火狗"活动，才能结婚。

　　白族，是中国第15大少数民族，主要分布在云南、贵州、湖南等省，

○瑶族少女秋收忙

197

其中以云南省的白族人口最多，主要聚居在云南省大理白族自治州。此外四川省、重庆市等地也有分布。白族自称"白子""白尼""白伙"，汉语意为"白人"。居住在大理、昆明等地及湖南桑植一带的白族，汉语称为"民家"；居住在丽江、迪庆、怒江一带的白族，纳西语称之为"那马"，傈僳语称为"勒墨"，藏语称之为"勒波"，彝语称之为"娄哺""洛本""罗基颇"；贵州一带的白族有"七姓民""九姓族""罗苴""龙江人""南京人"等不同称呼；在贵州威宁一带的白族，因有七姓，被称为"七姓民"。

每年农历八月十五日，大理、洱源一带的白族都要到苍山洱海最北端的洱源沙坪去赶渔潭会。渔潭会是大理地区的秋季物资交流会，会期7~8天。会间除了农具、渔具以及大牲畜的交易外，置办嫁妆也是渔潭会的主要内容。白族的婚礼一般集中在腊月，而订婚则在农历八月以前。男方在订婚后要先送部分彩礼给女方。因此人们就在渔潭会上置办彩礼，如柜子、玉镯、服装、刺绣品等。久而久之，嫁妆交易成了渔潭会的主要内容，渔潭会也被称为"嫁妆会"。白族传说，观音菩萨吩咐人们在此交易渔具，以困住危害百姓的鱼精，慢慢发展成为"渔潭会"。因时逢中秋团圆节，又以置办嫁妆为主，渔潭会洋溢着"月圆人更圆"的浪漫。

中秋之夜，善于踏歌的白族还有"漂河灯"的习俗。人们把特制的各种形状的纸灯点上蜡烛或香火，沿河漂放，或将各种彩灯燃放于沿河两岸。此时还有划龙船和唱山歌、跳民族舞蹈等各项娱乐活动。

白族的河灯和汉族的河灯制作有所不同：有的是将南瓜剖开两半，将内部掏空，在罩上各种纸灯；有的是用玻璃制成的，如荷花灯；也有的以青蒿绑上数十的香，点燃后如星星一般，等等，独具匠心、别具一格。白族的中秋之夜是灯的长河，灯的夜晚。

台湾高山族，是中国台湾南岛语系各族群的统称，指台湾岛及其附属岛屿上汉族及其他大陆民族以外的"中华民族"人口，范围大概相当于历史上汉族所谓"生番"，日本殖民当局所谓"番人""高砂族"，或当前台湾当局法律上"山地原住民"和"平地原住民"的总和。

○ 台湾高山族的节日舞蹈

高山族同胞每到中秋之夜，都要穿起美丽的民族服饰，齐聚在日月潭边的月光下，男男女女玩起"托球舞"的游戏，集体观月。据说这种活动是为了纪念传说中的青年夫妇尖哥和水花姐。

相传古代，大清溪边住着一对青年夫妇，男的叫大尖哥，女的叫水花姐，他们靠捕鱼度日。一天，太阳和月亮突然都不见了，天昏地暗，禾苗枯萎，花果不长，虫鸟哭泣。大尖和水花决定要把太阳和月亮找回来。他俩在白发老婆婆指点下，用金斧砍死了深潭中吞食太阳的公龙，又用金剪刀杀死了吞食月亮的母龙。他们还拿到了大棕榈树枝，把太阳和月亮托上天空。为了征服恶龙，他们永远守在潭边，变成了大尖和水花两座大山。这个大潭，人们就称它为"日月潭"。于是，每逢中秋，高山族同胞想念大尖和水花夫妇的献身精神，都要到日月潭边玩模仿他们夫妇托太阳、月亮的彩球游戏，不让彩球落地，以求一年的日月昌明，风调雨顺，五谷丰登。

延伸知识

少数民族的礼俗禁忌

少数民族的礼俗禁忌代表着民族宗教文化和文明习惯。旅游者到了民族地区，如果对民族礼俗禁忌略知一二，就可以避免麻烦，减少误会，使你旅途更顺利。

1. 不能随意摸小孩、小和尚和少女的头和头饰。

2. 进傣族寺庙的大殿或上傣家竹楼须脱鞋。

3. 在傣家竹楼留宿，头的方向不能对着主人家房门，而要把脚向着主人房门，也不能从妇女的脚上跨过去。

4. 别人给你盛饭，应双手接；你给别人盛饭菜，不能盛满，也不能只添一勺。

5. 不能触摸和践踏民族宗教标志。

6. 不要向少女赠送装饰品。

7. 不要进入产妇和病人的房间。

8. 不能在屋子里吹口哨、戴草帽。

9. 不能用筷子敲碗、打猫狗。

10. 禁止在家中谈论性方面的话题。

11. 不许背靠神位而坐。

12. 不得跨越火塘上的三脚架，也不能用脚蹬或在上面放鞋袜、衣裤。

13. 对方给你敬酒，不能拒喝，多少都得喝一口或尝一下。

14. 如果你吃饱了，对方还给你盛饭时，不能说"不要了"，而要说"吃好了"。

15. 不能坐在门槛中间。

16. 不能往火塘里吐痰。

17. 白族女主人向你敬三道茶时，必须站起来双手去接。

18. 往火塘里加柴，柴根应往里，不准柴尖往里。

19. 清早不能谈梦见的事，傍晚不扫地。

20. 不能一进家门就抱婴儿。

二、
山东的拜月、唱月

山东在中国古代旧称为"鲁"，是中国儒家圣人孔子的故乡，历来是中国礼仪制度保留最完整的地方。山东的中秋节最有传统特色。

八月十五这一天，儿孙们要团聚到老人身边吃晚饭，在外乡的也都赶回家过节。中秋之夜赏月、吃月饼。中秋前后亲友间互相走动，送月饼。已出嫁的妇女在八月十六回娘家，所谓"十五的月亮十六圆"。月亮升起时，在院子里挂月光马儿，上面印有嫦娥奔月样的神像，称作太阴星君，下面有一个小兔。供品除月饼、水果外，还要供一

201

捆或一碗青豆，是给玉兔吃的。当地也有玩兔爷儿的习俗。

潍县的拜月，大人和小孩分开进行：大人在院子里，小孩在门外。孩子们在门外板凳上放个"月儿"，一个孩子手托"月鼓"——一种蒸制的面食，手臂绕着圆圈，边绕边唱："圆月了，圆月了，一斗麦子一个了！"另一个孩子手持着一棵点燃的麦蒿，叫作"蒿子灯"，手臂也绕着，火点晃动如流星，与手臂绕圆月者相应和。拜月之后，再吃月饼赏月。

潍坊有中秋唱月以祈求来年丰收的习俗。晚上，孩子们拿着买来的月饼或自制的圆饼，在门口、街巷里边走边唱："唱月来，唱月来，来年的日子好过来！唱月饼，念月饼，明年是个好光景！"

在济宁中秋节这天的晚饭要很丰盛。这里还有一个独特的习俗，青年男女恋爱，男方想向女方提亲，就在八月十五这一天提着一只大公鸡，还有月饼、水果等东西，去女方家里探望。如果姑娘的父母同意这门亲事，就收下那只大公鸡，如果不同意，就把那只大公鸡扔出去。

三、

江苏的烧斗香

苏州、无锡、常熟等地在中秋节晚上要点燃"斗香"，这是江浙一带很有特色的习俗。

傍晚，月亮出来时，人们开始在门前或院子里放置斗香。斗香的制作方法是：将许多根细香捆扎成圆柱形，作为底盘；再扎一个较小的圆柱，摞在地盘上，成为第二层；这样一层一层叠上去，一般有六七层多，越往上捆越细，整体上呈塔形，所以也叫"塔香"。两层中间的地方用彩色纸黏糊起来，可以起连接作用，同时每层黏糊的彩纸呈圆斗形，把香捆围住，这样每层香燃烧时，香灰都落在斗内。材质上往往绘有图案。斗香的上部两边插两个小彩旗。这是家庭自制的斗香，比较简单。店铺里出售的斗香更精致一些：一般外边用纱绢黏糊，上面有嫦娥、桂树、玉兔、月宫等图画。斗香高的有十六七层，甚至二十多层，将近一人高。层数越多，底盘越粗，需要用的香数越多；斗香搭的越高，显示越富有。

○无锡斗香。香斗四周糊有纱绢，绘有月宫中的景色

203

四、
安徽的舞香龙

　　安徽徽州中秋节有舞香龙的习俗。香龙是用稻草编扎而成的，龙身插满棒香，夜晚舞龙时，将香点燃，龙身一片星光，舞动起来，如同一条火龙，在夜空下耀眼夺目。香龙的体积很大，可长达三十丈，身围约两尺。中秋之夜，要表演"五龙闹中秋"，五条香龙一起舞动。五条香龙由五路锣鼓开路，互相配合，协调一致，队形和舞姿都有一定常规，依次摆出"五龙献月""五龙盘月""五谷丰登""金龙追月"

○中秋节舞香龙表演是传统节目，香龙由香和稻草扎成，场面蔚为壮观

等阵型，场面很壮观。

中秋节这天在安徽黟县，小孩子们早早起来，到田地里去捡拾稻草，扎成龙形，糊上彩纸，夜里在龙身上插香烛，在街巷里舞动。大的草龙要十多人舞动，小的可以一个人独舞。五龙的时候，锣鼓喧天，爆竹齐响。传说，没有孩子的人家可以将龙身上的蜡烛换下来，能够有利于子嗣的繁衍。

五、
浙江的钱塘江观潮

中秋节期间，杭州、绍兴、余杭、海宁等钱塘江附近的人们有到钱塘江观潮的习俗。

钱塘江的潮涌是世界上名列前茅的观潮胜地，其壮观的景观只有南美洲巴西的亚马孙河可以与之媲美。宋代著名诗人苏轼有“八月十八潮，壮观天下无”的诗句。

中秋节前后在浙江省海宁市盐官、新仓、黄湾等地的沿岸长堤上，汇聚了来自四面八方的游人。潮水来时，其势如万马奔腾，呼啸而至，潮头高达 2 米左右，最高接近 3 米，遇到河床阻力翻起的浪头可以达到 10 米以上。潮水推进的速度可以达到每秒 4 米到 6 米，涌潮推力达到每平方米 7 吨，可以轻易卷走几吨重的大石头。

钱塘江的潮涌与其入海的杭州湾地理形状有关。杭州湾呈喇叭状，海潮进入喇叭口时，开始并无障碍，但到瓶颈处，潮水在较狭窄的河道内遇到阻挡挤撞，而后边的潮水一波一波涌来，潮头升高，再往前行，遇到长达数里、横在江中的积沙带时，潮水遇到阻碍喧腾并层叠推高，激发成气势磅礴的大潮。观潮的最佳处在海宁盐官镇。

○钱塘江大潮

早在北宋时期，中秋节观潮就成为杭州一带风行的习俗。大诗人苏轼有《八月十五日看潮》："定知玉兔十分圆，已作霜风九月寒。寄语重门休上钥，夜潮流向月中看。"八月十五的月亮特别的圆，秋风吹来似乎带来了一些九月的寒意了。告诉杭州城的看门人，今夜不要锁城门，保持城门开放能够让人们去看半夜月光下的大潮。南宋吴自牧的《梦粱录》记载了当时观潮的盛况：

"临安风俗，四时奢侈，赏玩殆无虚日。西有湖光可爱，东有江潮堪观，皆绝景也。每岁八月内，潮怒胜于常时，都人自十一日起，便有观者，至十六、十八日倾城而出，车马纷纷，十八日最为繁盛，二十日则稍稀矣。十八日盖因帅座出郊，教习节制水军，自庙子头直至六和塔，家家楼屋，尽为贵戚内侍等雇赁作看位观潮……其杭人有一等无赖不惜性命之徒，以大彩旗，或小清凉伞、红绿小伞儿，

各系绣色缎子满竿，伺潮出海门，百十为群，执旗泅水上，以迓子
婿弄潮之戏，或有手脚执五小旗浮潮头而戏弄。"

　　大意是说，临安当地的风俗是一年四季都非常重视玩乐。此地
名胜风景众多，西面有美丽的湖光，东面有汹涌的潮汐，都是别处
看不到的绝佳景致。每年到了八月，钱塘江的潮涌要比平时壮观许多，
城里的居民从八月十一日就有人前来观潮，到了中秋节前后，特别是
八月十六至十八日，几乎全城的人都会从家里来到江边观潮，街上
车水马龙，热闹异常，一直到二十日人数才渐渐减少。在八月十八
日这一天驻扎在杭州的水军司令还会率领水军进行军事演习。而从
庙子头一直到六和塔，几乎每一家的楼屋都被有权势和有财富的人
租赁下来，用于观潮。而杭州的一些不惜性命的底层百姓，会手里
拿着大彩旗，或者小清凉伞、红绿小伞儿，在旗杆上系上色彩斑斓
的绸带，等待潮水涌出入海口，伺机入水，百十人一群，拿着旗在
水中表演，场面很是热闹。

　　直到现在，中秋节观潮仍然是江浙一带必不可少的节日习俗。

旅游小贴士

钱塘江观潮

　　每年的农历八月十八前后，著名的钱塘江将进入最佳观潮期。
然而，潮水汹涌，应安全观潮，增强自我保护。

　　观潮时须注意：1. 对钱塘江潮水的涨落规律、习性特别是潮水
的危险性要有充分的认识。钱江潮水并非只在农历八月十八有，而
是一年四季天天都有，要注意媒体发布的钱塘江潮汛信息。2. 观潮

与活动要选择安全区域和地段，注意警示标志，服从管理人员的管理。不要越过防护栏到河滩、丁字坝等上面去游玩、纳凉，更不要在江中游泳、洗澡。3.掌握自救的方法。在面临危险的情况下，不要惊慌失措，要迅速、有序地向安全地带撤退，并立即向周边的工作人员或其他人呼救。撤离时，不要为了抢救财物而失去宝贵的自救时机。在万一落水或被潮水击打的情况下，要尽量抓住身边的固定物，防止被潮水卷走。周边人员在看到有人落水的紧急情况下，要迅速采取救援措施并立即拨打110报警。

钱塘江有七个危险看潮点：大缺口、老盐仓、美女坝（此处有2个）、七格、三堡和九溪。这些危险点应当格外小心。

六、
中国十大赏月胜地

自古以来，中秋节赏月玩月是一项历史悠久的中国习俗，因此在中国有"十大赏月胜地"之说，分别是：江苏无锡惠山山麓的"二泉映月"，杭州西湖的"三潭印月"，扬州的"二十四桥明月"，四川宜宾的"三江映双月"，杭州西湖白堤西端的"平湖秋月"，江西庐山牯牛岭的"月照松林"，苏州西南湖的"石湖串月"，青岛崂山太清宫的"太清水月"，广西桂林象鼻山的"象鼻山夜月"，苏州网师园的"三月共赏"。下面简单介绍几个：

首先是苏州的"石湖串月"。石湖是太湖的支流，在苏州城西南十八里处，西邻上方山。石湖边上有座行春桥，是有九个环洞的桥。据说在农历八月十八日前后，夜晚能看到水面上有一串月亮，这就是"石湖串月"。清代顾禄《清嘉录》里对此景有这样的描述："八月十八日，月光初起，入桥洞中，其影如串。"八月十八日月圆之时，月亮刚升起来的时候，月光透过桥洞投射到水面上，形成一串月影。因为桥洞是圆形的，那透过桥洞投射到水面上的九个圆形的月光斑圈就像一串月亮一样。看串月的时刻有明月初起和夜半两种说法，地点在行春桥附近。每年八月十八日前后，石湖岸边、上方山上，聚满了赏月的人们，水面上也是游船如织。人们有赏月的，有上香的，有爬山的，有唱歌的，有吹箫的，非常热闹，是全苏州人的欢乐节日。石湖串月与北京的"卢沟晓月"、杭州的"三潭印月"、太湖的"石公秋月"并称为中国四大月景。

○石湖景色

其次是广西桂林的"象山水月"。象鼻山是桂林的象征，位于城南桃花江与漓江的交汇处，从远处望去，整座山像一头大象，鼻子垂入水中，好像一直正在喝水的大象。象鼻与象身之间有一个东西通透的圆形空洞，犹如水面上树立起一轮明月，因此被称作"水月洞"，

○象鼻山

○象山水月

210

是桂林山水的一大奇景。洞底有漓江水流贯其间，可以乘坐小船从洞中穿越而过。中秋月明之夜，在水月洞一带泛舟而行，空中的明月、水中的月影和象鼻山的如月山洞相映成趣，是赏月玩月的最佳去处。宋代诗人有"水底有明月，水上明月浮。水流月不去，月去水还留"的诗句，描写的正是这一浑然天成的月夜奇观。

再有就是杭州西湖的月景了。"西湖十景"中有三个是"月景"："平湖秋月""月岩望月"和"三潭印月"，可以看出中秋节西湖赏月是久负盛名的。

"平湖秋月"以景观广阔取胜。中秋之夜，明月朗照，微风送爽，万顷平湖像蒙上了一层银白的面纱，显出柔美旖旎的万种风情。漫步湖边、苏堤，或者乘船泛舟湖上，令人心旷神怡。

"月岩望月"的景观要在湖边的凤凰山上才能够观赏到。山上有一石壁名叫"月岩"，岩壁上有一个圆孔。中秋之夜，明亮的月光穿过圆孔，投射到湖面上，形成空中、岩上、水面各有一轮圆月的奇

○平湖秋月

特景观。

　　"三潭印月"更是一个专门以月景出名的地方。三潭印月是一个岛，又称为"小瀛洲"，是位于外西湖偏南湖面上的一个人工岛，面积约有 7 万平方米。岛的西南方不远处水面上，竖立着三个高约 2 米的白色石塔。石塔的结构可以分为四部分：最下面是底座，水面上露出一小部分雕有花纹的圆柱形底座；底座上是圆球形的塔身主体，球体中空，上面有 5 个洞孔；圆球之上是一个形似圆亭的部分；圆亭之上是塔尖，呈葫芦形。

　　三潭印月岛的前身是水心保宁寺遗址，北宋时期，苏轼在杭州为官，组织当地百姓疏浚西湖，建了这三座石塔。建塔的目的是为了树立一个标志，告诫众人，为防止西湖淤塞，不准在三塔之内的湖区种植菱藕。北宋时期建的三塔毁于元代，到了明代万历年间，钱塘县令聂心汤令人围绕原来湖心寺的遗址，用疏浚西湖的淤泥砌筑了环形堤坝，围成岛基，堤坝内圈有湖水，形成了"湖中有岛，岛

○三潭印月

中有湖"的格局，并且在塔基之上按原貌修复了三座石塔。后来人们在西湖泛舟赏月，发现石塔倒映水中，好像塔下有深潭，潭中有月亮，"三潭印月"的声名就此传开了。传说清代康熙皇帝到西湖赏月，将"三潭映月"改为"三潭印月"，既指岛名，也指石塔月景。清代雍正年间，在浙江巡抚李卫的主持下，人们在岛内沿着东西向修建柳堤，在南北向修建曲桥，堤和桥相交成十字，加上周围的堤坝，全岛呈现出"田"字形状。中秋月明之夜，在石塔的球体洞孔内放置灯烛，将洞口用薄纸蒙住，灯光外透，明亮的洞孔就像圆月一般，每个塔上就像有五个小月亮。如此，则空中月、塔中月、水中月，交相辉映，与宽阔的湖面、影影绰绰的小瀛洲岛，构成了一幅和谐柔美的画面，犹如人间仙境。

旅游小贴士

苏州

俗语说："上有天堂，下有苏杭。"除杭州外，苏州是不容错过的游览胜地。

苏州是中国首批 24 座国家历史文化名城之一，是吴文化的发祥地。苏州园林是中国私家园林的代表，被联合国教科文组织列为世界文化遗产。苏州素来以山水秀丽、园林典雅而闻名天下，有"江南园林甲天下，苏州园林甲江南"的美称，又因其小桥流水人家的水乡古城特色，有"东方水都"之称。苏州现有 2 个国家历史文化名城（苏州、常熟）、12 个中国历史文化名镇，保存较好的古镇（如吴江的黎里、盛泽、平望，太仓浏河等）、中国历史文化名村（吴中陆巷古村、明月湾），中国首批十大历史文化名街之二的平江路、山塘街。现有保存完好的古典园林73处，其中"拙政园"和"留园"位列中国四大名园。

　　苏州小吃是中国四大小吃之一。浇头品种很多、讲究汤水的苏式面条是广受欢迎的小吃。苏式招牌菜有松鼠鳜鱼、响油鳝糊、蟹粉蹄筋、清溜虾仁、叙糟、母油整鸡、太湖莼菜汤、雪花蟹斗、樱桃肉、酱汁肉、熏鱼、三件子、蜜汁火方、暖锅、枣泥拉糕等。苏式糖果有轻糖松子、粽子糖、浇切片、三色松子软糖、脆松糖、松子南枣糖等。苏式蜜饯以金丝蜜枣、奶油话梅、白糖杨梅、九制陈皮最为著名。

Chapter Four

The Places with Special Characteristic of the Mid-Autumn Festival

---

"Chang'e boils herbs when the cassia tree blossoms, The moon is going to shine after leaving the clouds. When the bright moon rises, the sky was lightened up. How many people will feel sad?" This poem, written by a poet Zhang Lei in the Northern Song Dynasty, vividly depicts the deep feelings of homesickness and yearning when they see the night sky in the Mid-Autumn Festival. The Mid-Autumn Festival is not only a traditional festival in ethnic Han, but an important day celebrated by minorities. The Mid-Autumn Festival is different from that day in ancient times with the long historical changes now, but people around the country still enjoy this festival in their own ways.

1. The Characteristics of the Mid-Autumn Festival in Minorities

Many ethnic minorities in China celebrate the Mid-Autumn Festival besides ethnic Han, but it has different customs.

Zhuang ethnic group, called "zhuang" (different words in Chinese) in past time and Bouxraeuz in Zhuang language, has the largest population in Chinese minorities. Zhuang people mainly live in Guangxi, Yunnan, Guangdong, Guizhou and other provinces in China and in the north of Vietnam abroad. The ancestor of Zhuang was successively named "Liaoman", "Liman", "Xidong Man", and "Wuhu Man"(the impolite name of minority in the south of China) and so on in ancient times. It was called "Liao", "Zhuang (撞)", "Zhuang (僮)", and "Zhong" in the Song Dynasty, and then called "Zhuangren", "Liangren", and "Turen" in the Ming and Qing Dynasties. The language culture of Zhuang nationality is basically consistent with those of Bouyei in Guizhou, Daiyei, Nung and Reyei in Vietnam.

People will place sacrifice offerings and censer on tables which will be set on the edge of the village in mid-August of lunar calendar or at the night of Mid-Autumn Festival every year. A branch or a bamboo stick about an inch high which can symbolize the Sheshu (ancient people call soil "She", and tree on the land was named "Sheshu".) stands on the right of table. It is taken as the ladder for Luna to come down to the earth and go back to heaven. There are four stages in this festival activity including the invitation of the goddess of the moon, singing with the goddess, making divination by the goddess, and singing a song to send the goddess of the moon to return. Zhuang people are accustomed to using rice cake to worship the moon on the bamboo raft in the river. Girls will place flower lanterns on the water to know who her Mr. Right is and sing the graceful folk song of *Invite the Yuegu.*

Zhuang people are good at singing and regularly hold a party of singing folk songs which is called Geyu (a festival of singing in Zhuang).Singing folk songs is named "huan" on the right side of Yangtze River, "shi" on the left side of Yangtze River and "bi" or "huan" in northern Guangxi. Geyu is usually held in spring and autumn, especially in the Mid-Autumn Festival. Songs in Geyu, based on the theme of young people pursuing true love, contain meeting, invitation, pan (singing in antiphonal style), new, admiration, trothing and farewell songs and so on. Geyu often lasts for one day, sometimes two or three days. Not only young people can take part in the Geyu, but middle-aged and elderly people and teenagers. Old men and children mainly focus on watching, admiring and evaluating. Some elderly singers also join this game, but they are advisers for young people instead of singing. Geyu is a very lively celebration activity in which besides antiphonal singing, the youth can also sing Chinese opera and do some businesses including daily necessities, cloth, cakes, meat and vegetables and other things. In a word, they have everything that you except to find. Actually, Geyu has some natures of trade fair.

Besides admiring the moon and eating mooncakes, there is another important custom that is antiphonal singing between women and men. This activity is dominated by women and includes historical facts and social except love and they can leave when it is enough to be happy.

She nationality, an old and pure minority, mainly exists in mountains of southeastern China. This minority has about 700 thousand people who mainly live in Fujian, Zhejiang, Jiangxi,

Guangdong, Anhui and other provinces. She nationality speaks She language which belongs to Miaoyao ethnic languages department of Sino-Tibetan. The language related to Chineses Hakka dialects is accepted by 99% She people, but the pronunciation is slightly different with Hakka and a few words are totally different with Hakka. She nationality uses Chinese as they don't have their own words and they worship ancestors and ghost. She lists itself as "Shanha" which refers to outsides guests who live in mountains, while "Ha" means "Ke" (visitors) in She language.

She minority takes August 15 in the annual Lunar New Year as a great day and a special custom to visit relatives and singing with them. Not only will She people sing with visitors, but they all need to s sing in antiphonal style in town. Men and women stand aside when they are singing and women like to crowd with other women. Some women who don't sing also want to stand next to singers in order to strengthen their courage. Clever singers can change tunes easily and they like diplophonia best which is called "Shuang Tiao Luo". It is a singing method that has the character of ensemble, which is full of She minority's characteristics.

Qilao minority has about over 500 thousand people and most of them live in Guizhou province. Qilao has a long history. It was called "Baipu" from the Shang and Zhou Dynasties to the Western Han Dynasty and called "Pu" and "Liao" from the Eastern Han Dynasty to the Northern and Southern Dynasties, which all has original relationship with its own ancestors. It was officially named Qilao after the founding of the People's Republic of China, before that, it was called "Qiliao", "Geliao", "Liao" and "Qilao" in different dynasties after the Sui and Tang Dynasties.

The most important traditional festival in Qilao minority is the Bayue festival (the Mid-Autumn Festival) which is from the 15th day to the 20th day of 8th lunar month. All people need to wear new clothes to gather together on the ground of the stockade. The eldest, called "Zulao", begin to pray for harvest after several youths bringing a cattle with a big red flower on its head, meanwhile, the band will play a song of "Baxian" (eight immortals in Chinese legend story) and some people need to set off powder guns and firecrackers. Then the cattle will be killed and its heart will be distributed to each family, which refers to unity. Next "Zulao" will lead other people to sacrifice under the linden with porket, old chicken and goose. All people will have dinner together until dark after finishing all festival activities. Women will return to mother's home with their children after having their own family feast the next day. Men will meet friends, singing and youths will sing and dance until the last day.

Dong nationality, one of the Chinese minorities, has about over 2 million people who mainly live on the border of Guizhou, Hunan and Guangxi Zhuang autonomous regions and some Dong people live in Enshi, Hubei province. The name of Dong comes from "Xidong" that is regarded as a traditional administrative unit by local people, while many names of places in Dong minority are still called "Dong" nowadays. Dong minority is named "Gaeml"(the pronunciation of it is similar to "Gan"(干), "Gan"(佄) or "Geng" in Chinese) by itself, while the international standard name of it is "Kam" or "Kam People" according to the principle of "complying with the original forms of expression" advocated by the United Nations. "Qiling", the name of Dong, was firstly found in the article of the Song Dynasty. Dong minority was called "Dong-man", "Dongmiao", "Dong people", "Dongjia" and others in the Ming and Qing Dynasties. It has had the official name, Dong minority, since the founding of the People's Republic of China, while it is called "Dongjia" in folk.

Young people of Dong will have a picnic and party on the Mid-Autumn Festival and will hold antiphonal singing the next day. All the boys should make up to show their affection to their sweethearts. "Touyue" (stealing the "moon") is a special activity on the Mid-Autumn Day in the country of Dong in Hunan. It is said that people could get manna from fairies that lived in the Moon Palace and would come to the world on the night of the Mid-Autumn Festival, which makes people share fruits and vegetables with manna together. Girls with beautiful umbrella pick fruits in their sweetheart's garden secretly on the night of Mid-Autumn Festival in order to pray the fairies to do match-making work. Girls and their sweethearts could have a happy life if girls get a double fruit.

The Mid-Autumn Festival in Dong ethnic group

Dai, "the nationality of Daitai", is one of the Chinese minorities and the main nation of Thailand and Laos and its pronunciation is between "dai" and "tai". "Daitai" was called "Ailao", "Shan", "Wuman", "Baiman", "Baiyi", "Jinchi", "Heichi", "Baiyi", "Boyi" and "Baiyi" and so on in Chinese historical articles. "Daitai" was officially named after "Thai" by international community with the help of the Kingdom of Siam before the Second World War. Each government named their "Daitai" respectively after the Second World War. It is still called "Thai" in Thailand, Cambodia, Vietnam and other countries, "Lao" in Laos, "Shan" in Myanmar, "Assam" in India and "Dai" in China.

Propping fire finch on branches, a traditional folk festival, is held by Huayao Dai in Yuanjiang and Xinping of Yunnan province on the fifteenth day of the eighth lunar month every year. It is the time of harvest in Yuanjiang dam, which attracts tens of thousands of fire finches to eat grain. Smart men cut some branches from Chinese fir and pine to dip some parasites' mucus and then they will put the branches on the favorite place of brids the day before dusk in order to protect crops. Fire finches would be stuck on the branches tightly once they stand on them the next morning, which enable Dai people to catch them with cloth bags to make delicious food on the Mid-Autumn Festival. Women go to the river and pond to get fish and shrimps together and old women pound Nuomici (glutinous rice cake) during the festival. Every family places a square table of which four corners all have a round cake with a stick of incense in the heart of it at night. All family members will worship the moon and set off fire guns towards the sky after all dishes are put on the table, and then they will drink and taste soup, Ganba (a special food in Yunnan province, it usually refer to the beef that is dried up), salted eggs and dried eels together when they admire the moon and chat happily.

The Li nationality, one of the Chinese minorities in Lingnan area of China, has about more than one million people. Li's economy was dominated by agriculture and women are skilled in textile, for which "Li Jin"and "Li Dan" (brocades and textiles of Li nationality) are famous throughout the world. The ancestors of Li was called "Li"(里), "Li"(俚),"Man" and other names in Han-Jin period, "Li" (俚) and "Liao" in the Sui and Tang Dynasties. It was found that "Li"(黎) was recorded in the Chinese historical documents in the end of Tang Dynasty, which marks the Li as a single ethnic community appeared on the history stage. "Li" (黎) became the common name of Li nationality, instead of the "Li" (俚) in the Song Dynasty. People of Li minority boast themselves as "Sai",while "Bo", "Qi", "Meifu", "Run", "Sai" and other names are also accepted inside the nationality as the result of different areas, dialects, clothes and so on.

The Mid-Autumn Festival is named "the August party" or "the Voicing festival" in Li minority. Young men and women led by "Tiaosheng Tou (leader)"will join in the singing and dancing party held by all towns on this festival. They come together in a steady stream. All participants will give mooncakes, cakes, sweet glutinous rice cakes, coloured kerchief and beautiful fans to each other. These people will toast wild food, drink rice wine and have a great activity of singing in antiphonal style. It is a great opportunity for unmarried youths to find their partners.

The Achang(阿昌) nationality is one of the earliest indigenous nations in Yunnan province in China. "Echang"(峨昌), "Echang" (娥昌), "Echang" (莪昌) or "Achang" (阿昌),

"Echang" (萼 昌) in the historical articles of China ancient times was the names of Achang(阿昌) in different periods. It has officially been called Achang(阿昌) since the the founding of the People's Republic of China. Achang(阿昌) people live in hills, mountains, valleys and flat areas of the ranges of Gaoligong Mountain where there are fertile land, mild climate and plentiful rainfall, which create good conditions for the development of agricultural products in Achang. Achang minority is mainly engaged in agricultural and famous for rice since ancient times.

The 15th day of the 8th lunar month every year, called "Changxin Festival", is a traditional festival of agricultural sacrifice for Achang minority whose people worship the Old Aunt instead of the Moon Mother on this day.

There was a story about the origin of the Old Aunt in Achang. A woman was addressed "the Old Aunt" respectfully by everyone because she was good at farming and textile and was a competent person inside and outside of family once upon a time. Her only son married a woman who treated her very badly and even often abuse her .The only son was also gradually not filial to her, for which the Old Aunt had to leave home with a bamboo stick and became homeless, begging along the way. A pair of kind brothers took her in as their mother and lived with her. The Old Aunt taught these two brothers farming and they had a rich and happy life. She also told neighbor how to plough and grow vegetables and receiving people's respect. The two brothers were still good to the Old Aunt after getting married and having children but their wives didn't want to serve her as she was too old to do something. The Old Aunt was very angry and left home again as the two wives cooked big leeches for her. She was dying when the two brothers found her at the shack in the land of corn at the foot of the hill .The two brothers took her back home. The Old Aunt said to these two brothers before death that they needed to visit her grave in March when was the sowing season every year and were asked to worship her and placed a bamboo stick with a new corn in the main room on the Lunar August 15 each year, which would bless them with foods and clothes. The two brothers and villagers sacrificed her twice a year after her death. This custom has been handed down from generation to generation and became "Ploughing Festival" in March and "Changxin festival" on the 15th day of 8th lunar month.

Every family of Achang minority will clean up their house and bundle a richest taro and a corn of double ears with a bamboo stick putting in the hall. The stick stands for the Goddess of grain, the Old Aunt. Achang people will also place all kinds of new grains and fruits to worship the Old Aunt, and then they have family dinner with pound new rice.

The Yao ethnic minority, with simple and rough folkway is

The Chanxin Festival in Achang ethnic group

an ancient nation of China, and one of the "Jiuli" (tribal alliances consist of nine clans) of ancient orient. People of Yao call themselves "Mian", "Jinmen", "Bunu", "Bingduoyou", "Heiyoumeng", "Lajia" and so on.

Yao has an activity named "dancing fire dog" on the Mid-Autumn festival. Most people in southern nations worship the god of fire and "dancing fire dog" aims to ward off evil spirits. Unmarried female youth in each village need to climb the hill to pick canes and turmeric leaves and all families prepare incense on the same day. All girls in the village will tie the cane bound with ginger on their arms, waists and legs, wearing a hat in the evening. The girls will march to worship the Lord of Cave and ancestors in the village after the elder women burn incense on these parts of the body of these girls and then they will dance .They salute the god of kitchen in each family through the streets and need to go around if they meet garden after sacrifice. The girls will throw the rattan, ginger leaves and incense into river when they get to the river outside the village. They go to the river to wash their hands and feet and then play the water at last, while young men set off firecrackers at the same time. It will be livelier if there is any girl from the villages nearby. Men and women begin to sing after girls play enough. A girl can get married only if she takes part in "dancing fire dog" more than three times according to the local customs.

Bai, the 15th largest ethnic minority in China, mainly distributes in Yunnan, Guizhou, and Hunan province. Bai has the largest population in Yunnan province and people mainly live in bai minority autonomous of Dalian in Yunnan province. In addition, they can also be found in Sichuan province, Chongqing and other places. People of Bai boast themselves as "Baizi", "Baini" and "Baihuo", which means "Bairen" in Chinese. People of Bai live in Dali, Kunming and Sangzhi area in Hunan Province and other places are called "local family". While those in Lijiang, Diqing, and Nujiang are named "Nama" (Naxi language) and "lemo" in Lisu language call it "le ink". They are also named "Lebo" in Tibetan, "Lou bu", "luo Ben"and "Luo-jipo" in Yi language. There are several names for Bai nationality in Guizhou, including "Qi Xingmin", "Jiu Xingzu", "Luoju", "Longjiang people", "Nanjing people" and so on. People of Bai minority in Weining, Guizhout are called "Qi Xingmin" as a result of seven surnames.

Bai minority in Dali and Eryuan area goes to the Eryuan Shaping located in the northernmost of the Cang Mountain and the Erhai Lake to take part in the Fishing Pond Party on August 15 in lunar calendar every year. The party, an autumn commodity fair in Dali area, lasts 7 to 8 days when people sell dowries besides farm tools, fishing gear and livestock on this fair. The reason why Bai people buy Bride Price such as cabinet, jade bracelet, clothing, embroidery, and so on on the fair is that Bai's wedding is generally in the twelfth month of the lunar year, while engagement is before August in the lunar calendar and the man need to give the woman part of the dowry after engagement. Dowry is the main content of this commodity fair which has another name "the dowry fair" over time. It is said that Guanyin Bodhisattva tell people to trade fishing gears in order to trap the harmful fish monster, which gradually evolves into a "the fishing pond fair". The fair will be permeated with romantic feeling of "one more round full moon" because it is held in the Mid-Autumn Festival and mainly trade dowries.

People of Bai minority are good at Tage (an ancient artistic form of dancing and singing) and have a custom of "Piao Hedeng" (float lights in the river) at the Mid-Autumn Festival night. People make special paper lanterns of various shapes with incense or candles float along the river, or set off the various lights along the river banks. There are various entertainment activities such as rowing dragon boat, singing folk songs and performing folk dances at the same time.

How to make a river lantern is different between Bai and Han. Some lanterns are made of pumpkins which are cut into halves, emptied and then covered with various papers. Some are made of glass such as lotus lanterns. Some are tied dozens of incenses up with sweet wormwood herb, which makes them like stars after lighting. All of these are unique in styles. The night of the Mid –Autumn Festival in Bai minority is the long river of lamps and the night of lanterns.

Gaoshan nationality(in Taiwan, China), a collective name of each group who speak the language of south island in Taiwan, China, refers to the "Chinese nation" populations except Han nationality and other mainland nations in the Taiwan Island and its affiliated islands. The range of the populations is roughly equal to the sum of the "savage" in the history of Han nationality, "Fanren" and "Gaosha minority" named by Japanese colonial authorities or "mountain aborigines" and "ground aborigines" on the current laws of the Taiwan authorities.

Gaoshan people all wear beautiful folk clothes to play the game called " the dance of holding the ball" and watch the moon under the moonlight of Riyuetan Pool at the night of the Mid –Autumn Festival. It is said that this activity is to commemorate a youth couple, Jian brother and Shuihua sister.

There were young married couples by the Daqing stream and they lived on fishing, the man was called Dajian brother and the woman was called Shuihua sister according to legend. The sun and the moon suddenly disappeared, which made the sky dark, the crops wither, flowers and fruits dead and pests and birds cry one day. Dajian and Shuihua decided to get the sun and the moon back. They killed the dragon with gold ax that swallowed the sun in the deep pool and the dragoness with gold scissors that swallowed the moon, and then they brought the sun and the moon to the sky with the big palm trees' branches with the help of the white-haired old woman. They became two mountains, and Dajian and Shuihua guard the pool in order to conquer the dragon and the pool is called "Ri-yuetan". Gaoshan people all come to the Riyuetan Pool to imitate the couple to hold the festival ball of the sun and the moon and not to let the ball to fall down when they miss the devotion of Dajian and Shuihua every Mid-Autumn Festival, which can pray for favourable weather and good harvest.

Festival Dance in Gaoshan Minority

Extension of Knowledge

The Customs and Taboos of Ethnic Minorities

Customs and taboos of ethnic minorities represent national religious culture and civilization. If tourists know something about the folk custom and taboo when they arrive in the area of ethnic minorities, they can avoid troubles and misunderstandings, making the journey smoother.

• Can't touch the head and the headdress of the children, the young monk and the young girls.

• Take off shoes when visitors enter the hall of the temple of Dai or bamboo homes.

• Don't turn your head towards the door, while visitors ' feet can do it and can't stride over the women's feet when stay in the bamboo house.

• You should receive with your both hands if someone gives you a bowl of rice. The bowl can't be full or added one scoop of food when you give others food.

• Don't touch or trample national religious symbols.

• Don't present decorations to girls.

• Don't come into the maternal or the patient's room.

• Don't whistle or wear straw in the room.

• Don't knock the bowl with chopsticks or beat dogs and cats.

• Forbidden talking about sex in the house.

• Don't sit back to the god.

• Don't cross the tripod on the fireplace and also cannot push it with feet or put shoes and socks, underwear on it.

• You can't refuse to drink when someone propose a toast to you.

• You should say "I have eaten well" instead of "That's enough" when someone gives you another bowl of rice if you feel enough.

• Can't sit among the threshold.

• Don't spit into the fireplace.

• You must stand up to receive the cup of tea with your both hands when the hostess serves tea to you three times.

• The root of firewood should be placed inside not outside when the woods are added to the fireplace.

• Don't talk about dreams in the early morning and don't sweep the floor in the evening.

• Don't hold the baby as soon as you enter the room.

2. Moon-worshiping and Song in Shandong

Shandong, which is called "Lu" in ancient times, is the hometown of china's sage Confucius, and also the place where Chinese ritual system are retained fully. The Mid-Autumn Festival in Shangdong has the most traditional features.

Children should come back home to have dinner with the elderly, including those who are away from their hometowns on the 15th day of 8th lunar month. They enjoy the moon and eat mooncakes at the night of the Mid-Autumn Festival. Relatives and friends visit each other, sending mooncakes around the festival, while married women come to her parents' houses on the 16th day of 8th lunar month, which is called "the moon on the 15th will be round on the 16th day." The moonlight horse, imprinted with the statue of the goddess Chang'e flying to the moon, hangs at the yard with the moon in the sky. It is called Deity of Moon, and there is a rabbit under it. People provide the rabbit with a bundle of or a bowl of green beans besides mooncakes and fruits. Playing the grandpa rabbit is also popular there.

Adults and children worship the moon separately in Wei County. Adults are in the yard, while children are out the yard. Children place "Yue Er" on the stool outside. One holds "Yue Gu (a kind of steamed flour food)" on hand with an arm cir-

230

cling, and sings, "the full moon, the full moon, exchanging a bushel of wheat for one! " Another child holds burning wheat with an arm circling, which is called "Wheat Lantern". The fire shakes like meteor, echoing with the person who is swing their arms around. They enjoy the moon, eating mooncakes after worshiping the moon.

People in Weifang sing the moon, praying for good harvest on the Mid-Autumn Festival. Children carry the mooncakes which are brought or round cakes made by them at the gate or in the alley, and sing "Sing the coming moon, sing the coming moon, for the good day! Sing the mooncakes, read the mooncakes, for the auspicious time the next year!"

A big dinner should be prepared on the Mid-Autumn Festival in Jining. It is a special custom for men to visit his spouse with a big cock, mooncakes, fruits and other things on the 15th day of 8th lunar month if he wants to be engaged to her. If parents of the woman agree to the match, they will receive the cock. If not, they will throw it out.

3. Burning Tall Incenses in Jiangsu

People burn tall incenses at the night of the Mid-Autumn Festival in Suzhou, Wuxi, Changshu, and it is a special custom in Jiangsu and Zhejiang area.

People place tall incenses at the gate or in the yard when the moon rises in the evening. How to make the tall incense: the cylindrical bottom is made of many joss-sticks, and another cylinder is placed on the bottom as the second floor. It has about 6 or 7 floors made like this. The higher the floor is, the thinner the joss-stick will be. It is also called "tower incense" due to the shape. There are colored papers which are used to connect the 2 parts between the 2 floors. Meanwhile, joss-sticks

Tall incenses

are tied up by the conical colored paper, which can make incense ashes fall inside when the incense burns. Texture is often filled with patterns, and 2 colored flags are placed on the upper part, which forms the simple home-made tall incense. That in shops is more delicate: It is covered by silk and decorated with patterns of Chang'e, cassia tree, the Rabbit, the Moon Palace and so on. The tall incense can reach 16, 17, or even more than 20 floors like the height of a person. The higher the floor is, the thicker the bottom is , and the more incenses the maker needs, also, the richer the holder will be.

4. Incense Dragon Dance in Anhui

Incense Dragon Dance features on the Mid-Autumn Festival in Huizhou, Anhui Province. The dragon, made of straws with incenses on the body, is dazzling when the incenses burn. It is like a fire dragon in the night sky when the Incense Dragon Dance begins. The huge incense dragon can reach 30 *zhang* (a unit of length = 3 1/3 meters) long and 2 *chi* (a unit of length =1/3 meter) around the middle. "Five Dragons Celebrate the Mid-Autumn Festival" will start with five dragons waving together. Five drums open the way for them, and they cooperate with each other.Formation and dancing posture has a

Incense Dragon Dance

certain routine. They form "Five Dragons worship the moon", "Five Dragons Round the Moon", "Bumper Harvest", and "Golden dragon chases the moon", which is really splendid.

Children get up early, picking up the straw in the field in Yi County, Anhui Province. They make the dragon with straws and colored papers, and dance with them when dragons are decorated with incenses at night. More than 10 people are needed for big Straw Dragon Dance, while one person is needed for small Straw Dragon Dance. People start the dance in the deafening sound of gongs, drums, and firecrackers. It is said if families with no kid hold the candle on the body of the dragon, it will be good for progeny multiplication.

5. Watching the Tides by the Qiantang River in Zhejiang

People go to the area near the Qiantang River to watch the tides on the Mid-Autumn Festival in Hangzhou, Shaoxing, Yuhang, Haining and many other places.

Chaoyong of the Qiantang River is the top place where people can enjoy the scene of tides. Only that in Amazon River in Brazil, South America can be comparable. The famous poet Su Shi in the Song Dynasty said that "the most splendid tide is on the August 18th of lunar calendar".

Tourists come to the causeway in Yanguan, Xincang, Huangwan in Haining, Zhejiang Province around the Mid-Autumn Festival. The tides, which can reach 2 or 3 meters, are like the tramps of horses with the whistle. The wave can be over 10 meters high due to the bed resistance. The speed of tides can be 4m/s to 6m/s, while the thrust that can wash away the stone weighing several tons can reach $7t/m^2$.

The tides in Qiantang River are related to the topography of the trumpet-shaped Hangzhou Bay where it flows into the sea. When the tides flow into the trumpet, it is not blocked. But when it comes to the neck of the bottle, the tides will encounter obstacles of the narrow channel. The later tides come one after another, rising one by one. When the tides meet the sand deposition which is several miles in the river, splendid tide will appear with the tides folding together. The best place to watch it is Yanguan Town in Haining.

Watching tides on the Mid-Autumn Festival has been popular in Hangzhou since the Song Dynasty. Su Shi said in *Watch Tides on the 15th Day of 8th Lunar Month* that the autumn wind blew, bringing a chill of September in the air with the full moon on the 15th day of 8th lunar month in the sky. Please tell the porter to open the door of Hangzhou City at this night, letting people watch the tides under the moonlight. The spectacular event of watching tides was recorded in *Dream in Lin'an* written by Wu Zimu in the Southern Song Dynasty.

People had fun during the festival according to the custom

of Lin'an. Lakes in the west and river tides in the east were both superb sceneries. Tides of Qiantang River were much more splendid in every August. People come here to watch tides on the 11th day of 8th lunar month, during the Mid-Autumn Festival, especially from the 16th day to the 18th day, nearly people in the whole city will go to the riverside, watching the tides, for which the streets bustle with people until the 20th day. Navies will be led by the commander who is stationed in Hangzhou to carry out the military exercise on the 18th day of the 8th lunar month. Almost all the storeyed buildings are rented by powerful and wealthy figures to watch tides from Miaozitou to Liuhe Pagoda. People on the ground in Hangzhou who dare to lay down their lives will find the chance to swim with big colored flags, sunshades, and red or green umbrellas that are tied with colorful ribbons in hand when tides pure out from the estuary. A group of about one hundred people performs with flags in the water, which is really lively.

Watching tides is still a necessary custom in the Mid-Autumn Festival until now.

Tips for Tourism

Watching Qiantang River Tides

The best period of watching tides along the Qiantang River is near the 18th day of the 8th lunar month every year. However, self–protection should be improved to guarantee the safety of watching tides because of the strong tides.

Please pay attention to the following when watching tides: (a) Have good understanding of the rules, habit and especially the danger of tides. Qiantang River tide is not only on 18th day of the 8th lunar month, but also every day in a year. So pay attention to the message of tides released by the media. (b) Watch tides and do activities in the safe area, heeding warn—ing signs. And follow the supervision of managers. Please do not vault the barriers to the beach or the T—shaped dam to visit, enjoy the cool and even swim or take a bath in the river. (c) Master the self—help methods. Do not be confounded, and withdrew to the safe area quickly and in order, call—ing to the staff or other people for help in danger. Do not lose the valuable time of self—help when withdrawing. Catching the fixed objects can pre—vent you from being swept away with tides when falling into the water or being hit by tides. Seeing people falling into the water, others around them should take rescue measures rapidly and dial 110.

There are 7 dangerous places for watching tides, for which you should be especially careful. they are Daquekou, Laoyancang, the Beauty Dam（2 places here）, Qige, Sanbao, Jiuxi.

6. Top Ten Resorts of Enjoying the Moon in China

Watching and enjoying the glorious full moon is one of the many practices to celebrate the Mid-Autumn Festival in China, which has a long history. Therefore, the "Top Ten Re-sorts of Enjoying the Moon in China" is familiar to Chinese people, which are famous for the scenes respectively as follow: " the Moon Over a Fountain" on Huishan hill of Wuxi, Jiangsu province; "Three Pools Mirroring the Moon" on the west lake of Hangzhou; "Twenty-four Bridge Moon" in Yangzhou; "Three Rivers Mirroring the Twin-moon" in Yibin, Sichuan province; "Autumn Moon on Calm Lake" at the western end of the Bai Causeway in the west lake of Hangzhou; "Moon over the Pine Forest" on the Bull Ridge in the Mount Lu of Jiangxi province; "A string of Moons over the Stone Lake" on the Xinan Lake in Suzhou; " Water Moon" at the Taiqing Palace on the Mount Lao of Qingdao; "Night Moon on the Elephant Trunk Hill" in Guilin, Guangxi province; " Sharing the three-moon" in the Wangshi Garden of Suzhou. Here's a brief introduction of some scenes:

First, let's introduce the "a String of Moons over the Stone Lake" in Suzhou. Stone Lake is a tributary of the Lake Tai, which is bordered by Shangfang Mountain on the west and 18 miles away the southwest of Suzhou City. The Xingchun Bridge with nine arches stands by the side of Stone Lake. It is said that a string of moons can be seen on the surface of the water before and after the 18th day of the 8th lunar month, which is called the "a String of Moons over the Stone Lake". "The moonlight shines into the arches of the bridge on August 18th which makes the shadow looks like a string of moons." described in *Qing Jia Records* which is written by Gu Lu in the Qing Dynasty. The spot circle of the moonlight looks like a string of moons which is reflected by the the round arches. The perfect

A String of Moons over the Stone Lake

time to enjoy the string of moons can be either midnight or the beginning of the moonlight and the perfect site is the place near by the Xingchun Bridge. The Mid-Autumn Festival is a joyous and lively day to the people in the whole Suzhou. The shoreside of the Stone Lake, the Shangfang Mountain and the lake are filled with the people who come to enjoy the moon, to go to the temple to pray, to sing, and to pipe before and after the 18th day of the 8th lunar month. The "a String of Moons over the Stone Lake", the "Morning Moon over Lugou Bridge" in Beijing, the "Three Pools Mirroring the Moon" in Hangzhou, and the " Autumn Moon on the Shigong Mountain" at Lake Tai were known as the four great scenes of moon.

Second, it is the "Water Moon on the Elephant Trunk

The Water Moon in the Elephant Trunk Hill

Hill". The Elephant Trunk Hill is a symbol of Guilin, which is located at the junction of the Taohua River and the Lijiang River. Looking from a distance, the entire mountain looks like an elephant who is drinking water with the trunk dipped into the water. A circular hole which can see things through from the west to the east exists between the trunk and body and it is called "Water Moon Cave" for its shape of a bright moon which is hanging above the water. It is a great wonder of the landscape of Guilin. The Lijiang River flows through the hole and people can also take a boat through over it. When boating around the area of the "Water Moon Cave" at the night of the Mid-Autumn Festival, the bright moon in the sky and the moon shadow in the water contrast finely with the moonish cave, which makes it the best place to enjoy the moon. "A bright moon hides in the water, and then floats on the surface. The moon won't go even if the water flows while the water still

The dreamy effect of the "Water Moon in the Elephant Trunk Hill"

stays even if the moon fades away." A moonlit wonder is described in the poem of Song Dynasty.

Another is the fascinating scene of the moon in the West Lake in Hangzhou. Three out of "Ten Scenes of West Lake" are the scenes of moon: "Autumn Moon on Calm Lake" , " Full moon over the lunar rock" and "Three Pools Mirroring the Moon". We could see that admiring the moon at the West Lake in the Mid-Autumn Festival has long enjoyed a good reputation.

The "Autumn Moon on Calm Lake" is famous for its vast landscape. The moon is bright and the breeze brings cool weather, fogging up the Calm Lake a layer of silvery veil, showing various soft and charming styles when the night of the Mid-Autumn Festival comes. Nothing is more relaxing and invigorating than strolling along the lake and Su Causeway or boating on the lake.

The landscape of "Full moon over the lunar rock" only can be seen on the Phoenix Mountain by the lake. There is a stone wall with a round hole called "lunar rock", through which the bright moonlight casts onto the lake, forming an exotic landscape of a full moon hanging over the sky, rock and the water surface.

"Three Pools Mirroring the Moon", also called "Small Yingzhou", is a special man-made island which is located at the southward lake surface of the outer West Lake with an area of about 70,000 square meters and is known to the scenes of the moon. Three white stone towers with two-meter high stands on the nearby water surface of the southwest of the island. The structure of the stone tower can be divided into four parts: at the bottom is a cylindrical base with some patterns, part of which breaks the surface of the water; Above the base is the spherical and hollow main body of the tower with five holes; Over the body is the part which looks like a garden house and a gourd-shaped tips stands above the garden house.

"Three Pools Mirroring the Moon", used to be the site of the Shuixin Baoning Temple. As an officer of Hangzhou in the

Northern Song Dynasty, Su Shi organized local people to dredge the West Lake and built the three stone towers in order to warn people not to plant lotus roots within the area of the three towers to prevent the West Lake from silting up. However, the three towers which were built in the Northern Song Dynasty were destroyed in the Yuan Dynasty, Nie Xintang, the county magistrate of Qiantang ordered people to build a circular dam around the site of Mid-lake Temple by the silt which was used to dredge the West Lake, enclosing the foundation of the island. A structure of "the island in the lake and the lake in the island" was formed for the lake water encircled in the dam and the three towers were repaired without changing its original appearance. The fame of the "Three Pools Mirroring the Moon" started to spread since people found the stone towers were reflected in the water which seemed like a deep pool under the tower while a moon is under the pool when rafting on the West Lake to enjoy the moon. It is said that the emperor Kangxi of Qing Dynasty changed the name "Three Pools Re-

Three Pools Mirroring the Moon

241

flecting the Moon" into "Three Pools Mirroring the Moon"when enjoying the moon at the West Lake. The name refers both to the island and the scenes of the moon in the stone tower. People constructed the Willow Causeway along east-west direction and built the curved bridge along south-north direction under the auspices of Li Wei, the provincial governor of Zhejiang in Yongzheng ruling years of the Qing Dynasty. The causeway and the bridge intersected into the shape of a cross with surrounding dams, forming the shape of "Tian"character（田）. Putting a candle in the spherical holes of the stone tower covering the holes with a piece of thin paper and then the light shining out through the paper, the bright hole looks like the round moon so that there are five little moons above each tower. Therefore, the moon in the sky, tower and water are merged into a harmonious and mellow picture with the vast lake and the shadowy island of "small Yingzhou", such as into the paradise on earth.

Tips for Tourism

Suzhou

As the saying goes, "Up above there is Paradise, down here there are Suzhou and Hangzhou." Besides Hangzhou, you absolutely cannot miss to visit Suzhou.

Suzhou is one of the first 24 Famous Chinese Historical and Cultural Cities and the birthplace of the Wu culture, which is also called "Oriental Water City" for its feature of old water town. It is famous for the splendid landscape and the elegant gardens and has always enjoyed the reputation of " the gardens in Jiangnan area（regions south of the Yangtze River) is the Best under heaven while the gardens in Suzhou is the Best in Jiang—nan area." Suzhou garden is a representative of Chinese private gardens and has been listed by UNESCO into the World heritage sites. Suzhou is home to two Famous Chinese Historical and Cultural Cities — Suzhou, Changshu(county-level city), 12 Chinese Historical and Cultural Towns, and some preserved ancient towns (such as Lili, Shengze, Pingwang towns of Wujiang District and Liuhe town of Taicang County, etc.), Chinese History and Cultural Villages (Luxiang ancient village in Wuzhong District and the Moon Bay), the two of the first top ten Chinese Historical and Cultural streets, Pingjiang Road and Shantang Street and existing 73 well-preserved classical gardens, which includes "Zhuozheng Garden" and "Liu Garden", the two of the China's four famous gardens.

Suzhou snacks is one of Chinese Four Famous snacks, among which Su-style noodles with a huge variety of toppings and the particular soup is the most popular one. Su-style specialties includes squirrel-shaped mandarin fish, eel paste, crab meat fried hamstrings, shrimp meat, tunzao, Muyou chicken, Taihu Water Shield Soup, snow crab, cherry pulp, Braised Soy Sauce Pork, smoked fish, San Jian Zi(cooked with chicken, duck, and trotters), Steamed Ham in Honey Sauce, Su-style hot pot, jujube paste cake, etc. Su-style candies includes pine nut candy, Zongzi sugar, sesame flake, three-colored pinenut fudge, Cuisong sugar, pinenut jujube sugar, etc. And the most famous Su-style preserved fruits are golden silk jujube, cream plum, sugared arbutus, and preserved mandarin peel.

结　语

中秋节是中国仅次于春节的第二大传统节日,农历八月十五日的月亮被人们认为是一年之中最大最远的月亮。对应着天上明亮圆润的朗月,地上的人们不管身在何方都要回家团圆,在清澈的月光下,拜祭月亮,玩赏月亮,分享月饼、瓜果和新鲜美味的食物。人们会走出家门,在月夜之下舞蹈歌唱,观赏花灯,猜谜、荡秋千、舞火龙……做各种各样的娱乐游戏。上至老人下至儿童,从塞北到江南,从大陆到港台乃至世界华人聚集地,中秋对于人们来说意味团圆、幸福。

中秋节的历史发展悠久,集合了对月亮的自然崇拜,对神灵的信仰,秋季的祭祀以及对祖先的追忆,起源复杂而多样。一说起源于古代帝王的祭祀活动。《礼记》上记载:"天子春朝日,秋夕月",夕月就是祭月亮,说明早在春秋时代,帝王就已开始祭月、拜月了。后来贵族官吏和文人学士也相继仿效,逐步传到民间。一说中秋节的起源和农业生产有关。秋天是收获的季节。"秋"字的解释是:"庄稼成熟曰秋"。八月中秋,农作物和各种果品陆续成熟,农民为了庆祝丰收,表达喜悦的心情,就以"中秋"这天作为节日。"中秋"就是秋天中间的意思,农历的八月是秋季中间的一个月,十五日又是这个月中间的一天,所以中秋节可能是古人"秋报"遗传下来的习俗。再加上嫦娥奔月、吴刚伐桂以及月兔捣药等神话传说,中秋节的含义丰富多彩。

优美的月色曾让多少文人墨客留下动人的诗篇,又让多少漂泊的游子心怀怅惘。尽管随着经济的发展,一些传统的节庆内容在现代人看来不甚科学,有些甚至完全是迷信,但那轮高悬的明月,那夜的精灵,仍然用她不变的温柔清辉照耀了大地,抚慰着海内外华人的思念与孤寂。2006年5月20日,中秋节被国务院列入第一批国家级非物质文化遗产名录,2008年起成为中国的国家法定节假日。中秋节在现代社会中依然发挥着重要的社会功能和情感纽带作用。

借此次编写本书的机会,笔者又一次温习和梳理了诸多与中秋节有关的文化知识。中秋节,不仅是人们欢聚团圆、畅游月夜的节日,也是继承传统、传承中华精神品格的重要日子。随着亘古不变的中秋之月,年青一代将继续传承中华悠久的历史与文明。

结

语

Conclusion

The Mid-Autumn Festival when the moon is considered to be one of the largest moons of the year is China's second-largest traditional festival after the Spring Festival. No matter where people are, they have to go home for reunion, worshiping the moon and sharing mooncakes, fruits and delicious food in the moonlight. People will come out of the house and do a variety of entertainment games, like dancing and singing in the moonlight, watching festive lanterns, guessing lantern riddles, playing on the swings and performing fire dragon dance and so on. The Mid-Autumn Festival means reunion and happiness for the people from the elderly to the children, from the northern frontier of China to the south of the Yangtze River, from the mainland China to Hong Kong, Taiwan and the Chinese gathering places in the world.

The Mid-Autumn Festival has a long history with a collection of the moon's worship, faith in the gods, sacrifice to autumn and recall for ancestors, which originated complexly and diversely. A saying goes that it originated from the ancient imperial sacrificial activities. *Book of Rites* recorded: "The ancient emperors worshiped the sun in the spring and the moon in the autumn". Xi Yue is to worship the moon, which shows that the emperor had already started worshiping the moon in the Spring and Autumn Period. Later, aristocratic officials and literati also followed it, which made it gradually spread to the folk. Another saying goes that the origin of the Mid-Autumn

Festival is related to agricultural production. Autumn is the harvest season, the explanation of the word "autumn" is: "the maturity of crops". The Mid-Autumn Festival is in August when crops and a variety of fruits gradually mature. Farmers regarded "Zhong Qiu (the Mid-Autumn)" as a holiday to celebrate the harvest and express the joyousness. "Zhong Qiu" has the meaning of the middle of autumn, while the lunar month in August is the middle of autumn, and the fifteenth day is the middle of the month. Therefore, the Mid-Autumn Festival may be handed down from the customs of the ancients' thanking offerings. The meaning of the Mid-Autumn Festival is rich and colorful combined with the legends of the Goddess Chang'e flying to the moon, Wu Gang Chopping the Cassia Tree in the Moon Palace and Jade Rabbit making herbal medicine and so on.

A number of poets left moving poems in the beautiful moonlight, making men traveling in a place far away from home with dismay. Although people think some traditional festivals are not scientific, and some are even completely superstitious with the development of economy. The moon still shines on the earth to comfort the Chinese in thoughts and loneliness at home and abroad. The Mid-Autumn Festival was included in the first batch of state - level intangible cultural heritage list by the State Council on May 20, 2006, which makes it China's national statutory holiday in 2008 and still plays an important social function and emotional bond in the modern society.

The author reviews and sorts out a lot of cultural knowledge related to the Mid-Autumn Festival by taking this opportunity to write this book. The Mid-Autumn Festival is not only a reunion festival when people can have fun in the moonlight, but also an important day of the inheritance of tradition and the Chinese spirit of the important character. The younger generation will continue to pass on the long history and civilization of China with the immortal moon of the Mid-Autumn Festival.

附　录 Appendix

冰皮月饼的制作方法
The Production Method of the Ice Skin Moon Cake

　　原料：糯米粉100克，粘米粉60克，小麦淀粉20克，牛奶350克，豆沙馅540克，紫薯35克，手粉30克，白糖50克，油30克，模具一个

Ingredients: glutinous rice flour 100 grams, sticky rice flour 60 grams, semolina starch 20 grams, milk 350 grams, bean curd filling 540 grams, purple potato 35 grams, hand powder 30 grams, sugar 50 grams, oil 30 grams and a mold

制作步骤 /Procedures

1.将糯米粉，粘米粉，小麦淀粉混合放入盆内。
1.Mix the glutinous rice flour, sticky rice flour, semolina starch into the basin.

2. 称量牛奶和糖，将糖倒入牛奶中，搅拌至无颗粒。
2.Weigh milk and sugar, and pour sugar into milk. Stir until no granules.

3. 把干粉筛入牛奶中，搅拌成糊，过筛。
3.Sift the dry powder into the milk then stir into a paste, and sift again.

4. 加入油，搅拌均匀，上锅蒸 25-30 分钟，期间搅拌两次。
4.Add oil and stir well, then steam it for 25-30 minutes. Please stir it twice during the time.

5. 紫薯蒸熟，压成泥，过筛。

5.Steam purple potatoes well and press it into a mud, then sift it.

6. 蒸熟的粉皮其中一半加入紫薯，揉团，盖保鲜膜冷藏 1 小时。

6.Add half of steamed flour to purple potatoes, rubbing them into a group, and then cover it with the plastic wrap for 1 hour.

7. 准备好馅料和手粉，并粉皮和馅料都捏成 25 克一个。

7.Knead the fill and powder .Each of them is 25 grams.

8. 紫薯面团压在白色面团下方，压平，在白色面皮一面放入馅料，旋转虎口收紧。

8.Put the purple potato dough under the white dough, flattening it, and place the filling to the white dough, rotating to tighten.

9. 将模具里抹入干粉，将多余的份磕出，放入包好的面团，紫薯一面朝下。

9.Put the dry powder into the mold, and pour out the excess that puts into the dough and the purple potato upside down.

10. 压实后去除表面干粉，即完成。完成后需要冷藏保存。

10.It is completed after the compaction to remove dry powder on the surface. Refrigerate after completion.

丛书后记

上下五千年的悠久历史孕育了灿烂辉煌的中华文化。我国地域辽阔,民族众多,节庆活动丰富多彩,而如此众多的节庆活动就是一座座珍贵丰富的旅游资源宝藏。在中华民族漫长的历史长河中,春节、清明、端午、中秋等传统节日和少数民族节日,是中华民族优秀传统文化的历史积淀,是中华民族精神和情感传承的重要载体,是维系祖国统一、民族团结、文化认同、社会和谐的精神纽带,是中华民族生生不息的不竭动力。

春节以正月为岁首,贴门神、朝贺礼;元宵节张灯、观灯;清明节扫墓、踏青、郊游、赏牡丹;端午节赛龙舟、包粽子;上巳节祓禊;七夕节乞巧,牛郎会织女;中秋节赏月、食月饼;节日间的皮影戏、长安鼓乐;少数民族的节日赶圩、歌舞美食……这一桩桩有趣的节日习俗,是联络华人、华侨亲情、乡情、民族情的纽带,是中国非物质文化遗产的"活化石"。

为了传播中华民族优秀传统文化,推进中外文化交流,中国人类学民族学研究会民族节庆专业委员会与安徽人民出版社合作,继成功出版《中国节庆文化》丛书之后,再次推出《多彩中国节》丛书。为此,民族节庆专委会专门成立了编纂委员会,邀请了国际节庆协会(IFEA)主席兼首席执行官史蒂文·施迈德先生、中国文联原执行副主席冯骥才先生、第十一届全国政协民族和宗教委员会副主任周明甫先生等担任顾问,由《中外节庆网》总编辑彭新良博士担任主编,16 位知名学者组成编委会,负责丛书的组织策划、选题确定、体例拟定和作者的甄选。

出版《多彩中国节》丛书，是民族节庆专业委员会和安徽人民出版社合作的结晶。安徽人民出版社是安徽省最早的出版社，有60余年的建社历史，在对外传播方面走在全国出版社的前列；民族节庆专业委员会是我国节庆研究领域唯一的国家级社团，拥有丰富的专家资源和地方节庆资源。这套丛书的出版，实现了双方优势资源的整合。丛书的面世，若能对推动中国文化的对外传播、促进传统民族文化的传承与保护、展示中华民族的文化魅力、塑造节庆的品牌与形象有所裨益，我们将甚感欣慰。

掩卷沉思，这套丛书凝聚着诸位作者的智慧，倾注着编纂者的心血，也诠释着中华民族文化的灿烂与辉煌。在此，真诚感谢各位编委会成员、丛书作者、译者以及出版社工作人员付出的辛劳，以及各界朋友对丛书编纂工作的鼎力支持！希望各位读者对丛书多提宝贵意见，以便我们进一步完善后续作品，将更加璀璨的节庆文化呈现在世界面前。

为了向中外读者更加形象地展示各民族的节庆文化，本丛书选用了大量图片。这些图片，既有来自于丛书作者的亲自拍摄，也有的来自于民族节庆专委会图片库（由各地方节庆组织、节庆主办单位报送并授权使用），还有部分图片是由编委会从专业图片库购买，或从新闻媒体中转载。由于时间关系，无法与原作者一一取得联系，请有关作者与本书编委会联系（邮箱：pxl@jieqing365.com），我们将按相关规定支付稿酬。特此致谢。

《多彩中国节》丛书编委会

2018年3月

Series Postscript

China has developed its splendid and profound culture during its long history of 5000 years. It has a vast territory, numerous nationalities as well as the colorful festivals. The rich festival activities have become the invaluable tourism resources. The traditional festivals, such as the Spring Festival, the Tomb-Sweeping Festival, the Dragon Boat Festival, the Mid-Autumn Festival as well as the festivals of ethnic minorities, represent the excellent traditional culture of China and have become an important carrier bearing the spirits and emotions of Chinese people, a spirit tie for the national reunification, national unity, cultural identity and social harmony, and an inexhaustible motive force for the development of Chinese nation.

The Spring Festival starts with Chinese lunar January, when people post pictures of the Door Gods and exchange gifts and wishes cheerfully. At the Lantern Festival a splendid light show is to be held and enjoyed. On the Tomb-Sweeping Festival, men and women will worship their ancestors by sweeping the tombs, going for a walk in the country and watching the peony. And then the Dragon Boat Festival witnesses a wonderful boat race and the making of zongzi. Equally interesting is the needling celebration on the Double Seventh Festival related to a touching love story of a cowboy and his fairy bride. While the Mid-Autumn Festival is characterized by moon-cake eating and moon watching. Besides all these, people can also enjoy shadow puppet shows, Chang'an drum performance, along with celebration fairs, songs and dances and delicious snacks for ethic groups. A variety of festival entertainment and celebrations have formed a bond among all Chinese, at home or abroad, and they are regarded as the "living fossil" of Chinese intangible cultural heritage.

In order to spread the excellent traditional culture of China, and promote the folk festival brand for our country, the Folk Festival Commission of the China Union of Anthropological and Ethnological Science (CUAES) has worked with the Anhui People's Publishing House to publish *The Colorful Chinese Festivals Series*. For this purpose, the Folk Festival Commission has established the editorial board of *The Colorful Chinese Festivals Series*, by inviting Mr. Steven Wood Schmader, president and CEO of the International Festival And Events Association (IFEA); Mr. Feng Jicai, former executive vice-president of China Federation of Literary and Art Circles(CFLAC); Mr. Zhou Mingfu, deputy director of the Eleventh National and Religious Committee of the CPPCC as consultants; Dr. Peng Xinliang, editor-in-chief of the Chinese and foreign Festival Website as the chief editor; and 16 famous scholars as the members to organize, plan, select and determine the topics and the authors.

This series is the product of the cooperation between the Folk Festival Commission and Anhui People's Publishing House. Anhui People's Publishing House is the first publishing house in Anhui Province, which has a history of over 60 years, and has been in the leading position in terms of foreign transmission. The Folk Festival Commission is the only organization of national level in the field of research of the Chinese festivals, which has experts and rich local festival resources. The series has integrated the advantageous resources of both parties. We will be delighted and gratified to see that the series could promote the foreign transmission of the Chinese culture, promote the inheritance and preservation of the traditional and folk cultures, express the cultural charms of China and build the festival brand and image of China.

The Colorful Chinese Festivals Series is bearing the wisdoms and knowledge of all of its authors and the great efforts of the editors, and explaining the splendid cultures of the Chinese nation. We hereby sincerely express our gratitude to the members of the board, the authors, the translators and the personnel in the publishing house for their great efforts and to all friends from all walks of the society for their supports. We hope you can provide your invaluable opinions for us to further promote the following works so as to show the world our excellent festival culture.

This series uses a large number of pictures in order to unfold the festive cultures in a vivid way to readers at home and abroad. Some of them are shot by the authors themselves, some of them come from the picture database of the Folk Festival Commission (contributed and authorized by the local folk festival organizations or organizers of local festival celebrations), and some of them are bought from Saitu Website or taken from the news media. Because of the limit of time, we can't contact the contributors one by one. Please don't hesitate about contacting the editorial board of this series (e-mail: pxl@ jieqing365.com) if you're the contributor. We'll pay you by conforming to the state stipulations.

Editorial Committee of *The Colorful Chinese Festivals Series*

March, 2018

《中秋节》英文翻译人员及分工

汪世蓉：负责全书统稿、译校。

潘　洁：负责第 1 章英文翻译。

彭子颖：负责第 2 章英文翻译。

章聿林：负责第 3 章英文翻译。

谭　笑：负责第 4 章英文翻译。